Janny de Moor
Nico de Rooij
Albert Tielemans

DUTCH
CULINARY ART
400 years of festive cooking

Veel Kook-kijk en leesplezier!

Enjoy Dutch Cooking.

Nico

3-12-09

Dutch Culinary Art is a production of the Dutch Culinary Art Foundation

© Dutch Culinary Art Foundation, Heemstede, 2009

Text © 2009 Dutch Culinary Art Foundation

Enlarged edition of Dutch Cookery, published by Kosmos-Z&K: Utrecht, 2001

Translation p. 27-178 Con van Eenschoten

Design and production: VaDéHa Communicatie bv – www.vadeha.nl

ISBN 978-90-9024426-6

Dutch Culinary Art Foundation / Heemstede

Contents

Johannes Vermeer, 'The milkmaid' (around 1660).

The Dutch settlers transported cows to New Netherland. Cow's milk was (and still is) an important ingredient in the Dutch daily diet. So essential, that it inspired Vermeer to this now world-famous painting of a devoted kitchen maid pouring milk into a bowl. Courtesy Rijksmuseum, Amsterdam.

Foreword by the Mayor of Amsterdam

Dutch Culinary Art, 400 years of festive cooking

Homesickness comes in many shapes. Most common is the need for contact with your family, nowadays often living quite far away. And this feeling does not only affect young people. Take for example Dutch adults working abroad. If you ask them what you can bring them from Holland, most will reply: "Cheese!". Cheese in its many varieties – Gouda, Edam, Frisian clove cheese, Leiden cumin cheese, all at different stages of ageing: young, mature, ripe. If you would let them have their way, you are certain to incur excess baggage fees!

This longing for food from your native country is a universal phenomenon. Early in life you learn to appreciate the tastes your parents apparently enjoy. This creates common ground for a national culinary tradition. You do not give up such ingrained preferences easily.

On the other hand, all gastronomic innovation would stop if everybody would hold on to his or her own cuisine. As with all cultural exchange, sampling the unfamiliar is the beginning of creative modification. Here it is that Amsterdam has a lot to offer. It is one of the most exciting melting pots of culinary art in the world. Strolling along the Albert Cuyp market you will encounter foods from all 174 nationalities Amsterdam harbours. More than 85 countries are represented among Amsterdam's restaurants. So you can always feel at home here!

Amsterdam also profits from its long history of international contacts. The extensive archives of the *Verenigde Oost-Indische Compagnie* (United East-Indian Company) show that many exotic products were imported which influenced Dutch cuisine deeply. Conversely, Dutch victuals were exported to its Asian establishments: Frisian butter, pickled meat, 'jenever' (Dutch gin), etcetera. Food to feel more or less at home abroad. This was also true when *Nieuw Amsterdam* (now: New York) and other early Dutch settlements along the Hudson River were founded (*Nieuw Nederlandt*, New Netherland). The phenomenon recurred when in the 19th and 20th centuries many Dutch emigrated to America. The newcomers recognized the necessity to adapt to their surroundings, but part of their inherited cultural identity, including their favoured dishes, survived. The authors describe this process in the first chapter of this book, that sketches Dutch culinary history from the seventeenth century onwards. It is abundantly illustrated with paintings from the Amsterdam *Rijksmuseum* and the *Amsterdams Historisch Museum*.

However, the rapidity of culinary development in the Netherlands increased enormously in the 20th century. As ever more inhabitants could afford eating out, restaurants cropped up everywhere and good chefs became celebrities. Therefore the greater part of this book is devoted to the past hundred years. May I invite you to a voyage of discovery in Dutch culinary art?

Job Cohen
Mayor of Amsterdam

Floris Claesz. van Dijck, Still life with cheeses (ca.1615).
The typical shape of Gouda was already there.
Courtesy Rijksmuseum, Amsterdam.

Introduction

The end of the millenium was a good reason for us to resurrect a century of culinary delights in the Netherlands. We decided to map out the 20th century, as devastating as it was creative, not in the least in cookery that is always able to adapt to the most dire circumstances. The century when girls forgot how to cook due to famine and poverty and had to be re-educated in domestic science schools. A century in which eating out became a common occurrence and in which *chefs de cuisine* were made national heroes. In which a steady stream of immigrants opened up the Netherlands to exotic tastes, which the Dutch then shared with America and Canada. The century that saw electric kitchen equipment become standard and the healthiness of food a public concern. The 20th century – a century like no other. And even though some of the bills of that century are still to be paid, it has given all of us goals to pursue.

Of course cookery in the Netherlands started much earlier. The first cookbook in the Dutch language was published about 1514. From then onwards follows a large number of culinary works. In addition, the gorgeous food paintings of the Golden Age prove that Dutch cuisine has a long history worth to be explored. This is why we decided to add a chapter about our culinary history before 1900 in the new edition on the occasion of the celebration of New York's birthday in 2009.

Why this connection? New York was founded by pioneers 400 years ago. They were Dutch and called the place *Nieuw Amsterdam*. Just like the immigrants all over the world they stuck to their own names, religion and cuisine. So the Dutch were not only the founding fathers of the province of *Nieuw Nederlandt* (New Netherland) but they brought what now is the State of New York its first outlandish cuisine. Which means that Holland and the United States share a culinary past of 400 years, consolidated by the second wave of Dutch immigrants in the 19th and 20th century. Testimony to that continuing love for Dutch food are the numerous webshops that sell Dutch specialties and products all over the USA.

Culinary history, although the mirror of civilisation, is a neglected subject, deemed too trivial to record. It took the Dutch several ages before they saw the relevance. Fortunately a number of reliable studies has been published recently which we warmly recommend for further reading and cooking. But first we suggest you to follow us on a trip along the tables of yonder in the 'land of milk and honey', as the country was called in the Bible-imbued Netherlands of the 17th century on the basis of old cookbooks and illustrated by paintings, selected from the famous collection of Amsterdam Rijksmuseum and Amsterdam Historical Museum.

Janny de Moor, Nico de Rooij, Albert Tielemans

Adriaen van Utrecht, detail from 'Still life'(1644). Delicacies of the 17th century.
Courtesy Rijksmuseum, Amsterdam.

Dutch Culinary Art: beginning and dissemination

From the 16th century onwards the Calvinistic faith dominated the life of people in the Netherlands. The joyous public parties of the Roman Catholic Middle Ages, depicted so lively in the paintings of the time, came to an end. Calvinistic austerity reigned. Outwardly! Because even the Calvinists themselves continued their wining and dining, be it behind closed doors or in private gardens. This was deemed permitted, as long as one did not irritate the neighbours by showing off. As late as 1907 a Dutch Reformed prime minister presided over a dinner of 14 courses accompanied by 8 select wines. But at the time he thought it wise to keep it private. So the Dutch have a secret culinary history and it is your privilege to be among the first to hear about it.

Anonymus, 'Family portrait' (1627). Calvinistic austerity at table. Courtesy Rijksmuseum, Amsterdam.

The very beginnings

The low countries, now The Netherlands and Belgium, were discovered by the Romans in the year 57 BC. This is was the end of Dutch culinary prehistory. By then the Romans were well aware of the importance of cookery, because Titus Livius writes in 187 BC that their cooking slaves had become very expensive and in high esteem. According to travel writer Tacitus (AD 98) the savage Batavians and Cananefates ('Leek masters') lived on wild fruit, fresh venison, or coagulated milk, and could easily be conquered when given enough beer. The Romans taught these primitives how to prepare food the Roman way. The Dutch verb 'koken', like its English equivalent 'to cook', is derived from Latin *coquere*.

One of the first coherent sentences in the Dutch language was found in the margin of an English manuscript dated around 1100: *Hebban olla vogala nestas hagunnan, hinase hic enda thu. Wat unbidan we nu* ('All birds have found nests, except you and me. What are we waiting for?'). A poetical start. But alas, no culinary vocabulary ... In the scarce source material, mostly administrative lists, no less than 13 Dutch words for pig are found, showing that our predelection for its meat started early. No recipes in the Dutch language have been preserved from this time, with the exception of a 13th century tale about how a bear cooked a cook ... However, manuscripts from aristocratic families, cloisters and city archives indicate that the wealthy were served a lot of game and poultry, for example braised swans, peacocks and herons, dished up in their own feathers on golden or silver dishes, a way of serving still fashionable in the 17th century.

Pieter Claesz., 'Still life with turkey pie', covered by its own feathers (1627). By then the American turkey had found its way to the Dutch tables. Courtesy Rijksmuseum, Amsterdam.

At the same time common people ate their simple stews, if they did not suffer hunger from wars or poor harvests, as in the disastrous years 1315-17. Then poor souls took refuge in dreams about the land of Cockayne (*Luilekkerland*), where the roofs were made of pancakes, the streets paved with ginger and nutmeg, and braised geese flew around freely.

Exotic tastes

Fairly soon after the invention of printing the first Dutch cookbook was published: *Een Notabel Boecxken van Cokeryen* (A Notable Booklet of Cookery), Brussels, about 1514. It was meant for weddings and parties. The recipes are very spicy, with Arabic aroma's. Small wonder, since part of the book is a literal translation of the French cookbook *Le Viandier* ('The Butcher/ cook', 1490), which in turn shows a remarkable resemblance to the *Kitāb al-Tabīkh* (Cookbook), an Arabic work written by a certain *al- Baghdādī* (Baghdad, about 1300). The Caliphs of Baghdad – where a 'green revolution' had led to an increased

Joachim Bueckelaer, 'The well-stocked kitchen' (1566) of the wealthy. Courtesy Rijksmuseum, Amsterdam.

consumption of vegetables around 1300 – and later on the Sultans of Istanbul embroidered on the ancient Middle Eastern cuisine. This cuisine was spread all over their immense Empire. Europeans could not but admire their exquisite cooking, but took it over reluctantly, as is demonstrated by names like 'Heathen cake' (a spice cake). All the same they followed the dietetics of the school of Salerno: the doctrine of the four humors, according to which the whole food circle was 'cooked', from the seed in the soil to the food in man. And so fruit and vegetables were seen by doctors as unhealthy.

In 1560 Doctor Gheeraert Vorselman from Antwerp published *Eenen Nyeuwen Coockboeck* ('A New Cookbook') which leans heavily on a book of Bartolomeo Sacchi (Platina), first librarian of the Vatican Library. Vorselman describes delicious and highly interesting salads. The green revolution of the Caliphs was taking root in The Low Countries. Of course salads were consumed at the beginning of a meal, because the stomac still had to 'cook' the raw leaves.

In 1588 doctor Carolus Battus, who had to give up his job in Antwerp because of his protestantism, became the town doctor of Dordrecht (South Holland). In the same year his 1000 pages *Medecyn-boec* ('Medicine book') was published. In the second edition (1593) Battus added a cookbook. He had a fabulous success with this book; it was reprinted no less than seven times. No wonder, because it was quite a sensation to be informed about getting rid of lice, repressing the stench of armpits and feet, and

David Vinckboons, 'The garden feast' (around 1610). Romantic cavorting in a private garden. On the table a peacock pie under its own feathers. Courtesy Rijksmuseum, Amsterdam.

preparing an apple pie to boot. The cuisine of the wealthy was extraordinary exotic at the time. Oranges, lemons, grapes were imported from southern Europe. Outlandish spices and daring combinations such as carp with gingerbread sauce were all the rage.

Golden Age cookery

The 17th century is called the Golden Age of the Netherlands. The enormous expansion of the United Seven Provinces overseas brought new ingredients from all over the world. The rich merchants of Amsterdam enjoyed their food so much that their Calvinistic pastor, the reverend Otto Belcampius, lamented in a stern sermon (in: *Hora Novissima, dat is laatste uyre*, Amsterdam 1661):

Sweetness and excess is today grown so greatly that were they not ashamed to do so, men would found an Academy to which they would send all cooks and pastry bakers to teach them how to excel in the preparation of sauces, spices, cakes and confections, so that they should taste delicious…[1]

Jan Victors, 'The feeding of the orphans' (1659-60). The diet of the poor was porridge with rye bread and thin beer – fresh water was still undrinkable. Courtesy Amsterdams Historisch Museum.

---

1 Translation Simon Schama, The Embarrasment of Riches,
   London: Fontana Press, 1991 p. 165

How horrified the good Belcampius would have been had he lived today! The Guild of Master chefs (*Meesterkoks*) founded some 70 years ago, who strive after the highest grade of their profession, counts 99 active members. All of them have had a demanding education behind them and had to pass rigorous exams. With 90 Michelin stars, the Netherlands can boast of the highest mean number outside France.

Or would Belcampius be horrified? If you hear him raving in great detail about dainty cakes, sauces, spices and pastries, you begin to suspect that in actual fact he may have been dreaming about a future he did not dare to advocate openly. He was a prophet in disguise. That's typically Dutch. They do know about good food, but prefer to keep it to themselves.

In the second half of the Golden Age we see a break with the past. Culinary historians have connected this with the arrival of the cooking stove, build in brick in the posh houses of rich merchants, especially those of the East (e.g. Indonesia) and West (a.o. Caribbean Islands and New York State) Indian Company. For those families one-pot cookery was over now, because more dishes could be prepared separately at the same time. Suddenly vegetables, salads and fresh fruit became even more *en vogue*. Whoever could afford it bought a country estate and laid out a phenomenal garden with flowers and all kinds of indigenous and foreign edible plants. This is ascribed to the revival of the Classic Civilisation which valued country life.

But that cannot be all. In a pioneering article Dr Rachel Laudan maintains that the old dietetics were criticized and had to make place for a new idea: the digestive system based on fermentation and no longer on 'cooking' inside the body. Although this presumption about fermentation is totally obsolete now, Europeans continue to feed themselves with the diet then created, in which sugar was banned to the dessert, and fresh herbs and vegetables were preferred over dried spices and pulses. Moreover the long sea voyages of that period, during which scurvy broke out often, must have been a prominent reason why some doctors grew suspicious of banning fruit and vegetables. And so in the only Dutch cookbook of the time *De verstandige Kock of sorghvuldige huyshoudster* (The Sensible Cook and Careful Housekeeper, Amsterdam 1667), wich was a supplement to the first Dutch book on gardening *The Pleasurable Country Life*, we find simple, light dishes: for instance the wonderful salads of Doctor Gheeraert Vorselman with blue borage flowers, recipes for at least 25 vegetables, which the affluent merchants grew in their

gardens, but also *hutspot* (hotchpotch), venison, oysters, crab, a heartshaped meatball, pancakes, several tarts and apple pies. Old-fashioned dishes composed of dried pulses, to this very day national fare (see p. 24-26) were left out, everybody knew how to prepare them. At the same time – and this is often forgotten but recorded by Dr. L Burema (1953) – some poor people had to eat raw broad beans, carrots, tree leaves and even grass ...

Picture from the title page of The Sensible Cook and Careful Housekeeper, Amsterdam 1667

Food at sea and in New Netherland

At the end of the 16th century the colony Dutch East Indies, now Indonesia, was founded. A voyage to the East took many months, and so the ships of the United East India Company (*VOC*) had to be loaded with victuals, more or less the traditional food of the lower classes such as white, green and grey peas (which were soaked in sea water), rye bread, wheaten bread, hard tack, cheese, stock-fish, ham, smoked meat and tongue (the last three only for officers), bacon, salted beef, salted pork, pickled herring, whale blubber, oil, brandy, wine, beer and water. After some time the water had to be drunk through the teeth because it contained too many small living creatures. When the meat supply was finished, rats were eaten. The supplies 'to mess the crew' (from Dutch 'mesten' = fatten) were most of the time scarce and meager. No picnic. So when Henry Hudson, under the authority of The United East Indian Company looking for a shorter way to the Indies, sailed the *Halve Maen* into what is now called the Hudson river in 1609, log keeper Robert Juet wrote happily that there were many salmons and mullets and rays, 'very great'. The people of the country were extremely hospitable and offered Juet some dried currants, which he found very sweet and good. They appeared to have a considerable store of 'Indian wheat' (corn), whereof they made good bread. And they brought fine oysters, grapes and pumpkins, 'which we bought for trifles'.. The captain was offered pelts and a great platter full of venison. In Juets own words after the first inspection:

"The Lands trhey told vs were as pleasant with Grasse and Flowers, and goodly Trees, as euer they had seene, and very sweet smells came from them" (transcription New Netherland Museum).

In a sense Hudson's mission was a failure, because he found no waterway to the East Indies. Yet it was the very beginning of the most famous town in the world and the end of the region's prehistory. The description of the land – especially of the beaver pelts bought by the captain – made it look worthwile to return. And so the Dutch did and established a city 'New Amsterdam' (1624) at the place called 'Manahatta' (Indian language for 'Island of the hills'), which they bought from the Indians for the sum of 60 guilders. A shameful transaction, we would say today, but they knew very well that the Indians saw this as a confirmation of their alliance. Furthermore they established the colony New Netherland consisting of what now constitutes most of Eastern New York State and parts of New Jersey, Pennsylvania, Connecticut, Delaware and Maryland (to be given away to the English by Peter Stuyvesant in 1664). Pioneer Van der Donck, who tried to persuade people from the Netherlands to settle over there, said of the region that it beared crops with less labour than in his home country and the Dutch poet Jacob Steendam depicted it as the 'land of milk and honey'. But this milk they had to bring themselves, by transporting cows to New Netherland.

And not only cows, but also sheep and horses they brought over in ships bearing meaningful names like 'The cow', 'The sheep', 'The horse'. The Dutch also planted apple and pear trees, even peaches, sowed vegetables such as lettuce, cabbage, parsnips, carrots and beets, and garden herbs. And what is more, wheat. A beautiful example of what is called in food history 'the Columbian exchange' between the Old and the New World. In return the Old World received corn, squashes, pumpkins, many beans, potato, tomato, capsicum peppers, plus the turkey, to name a few.

The Dutch settlers stayed after their colony had been handed over to the English, and retained their own culinary heritage. The fact that some leading families even owned the one and only Dutch cookbook of the 17th century, *The Sensible Cook*, fascinated Peter Rose, a Utrecht-born American culinary historian, so much that she undertook the task to translate it and to investigate the development of Dutch-American cuisine in later centuries (Syracuse, N.Y., 1989). The Dutch themselves had to wait until 2004 before a splendid translation into modern Dutch was produced by Marleen Willebrands. From handwritten notebooks Rose concludes that housewives really cooked the recipes, especially the traditional sweet dishes such as pancakes, waffles, donuts with cranberries instead of the traditional currants (*oliebollen*), apple pies, cookies (word derived from Dutch *koeckjens*) and coleslaw (from Dutch *koolsla*). Archeological research has established that the early Dutch settlers also ate herons or other big birds from the region.

When Albany (formerly Dutch 'Beverwijck') celebrated its 350th birthday in 2002, an exhibition was organized called *Matters of Taste* with 60 Dutch paintings from the 17th century, all connected with food and all collected from America. Again testifying to the close relations between the Dutch and American culture. Peter Rose, who wrote the catalogue in collaboration with Professor Donna Barnes, estimates that whether they know it or not, most Americans eat dishes from this Dutch heritage everyday.

Godfried Schalcken, 'Woman selling herring' (1675-1680). Salt herring was (and is) very popular in the Netherlands. It is said that Amsterdam is built on its bones. Courtesy Rijksmuseum, Amsterdam.

The age of the kitchen maids

The colourful Golden Age cookery was further developed and slightly modernized in the 18th century, when most provinces published their own cookbook, called: 'The Perfect Kitchen maid' in Guelders and Holland, whereas the 'Utrecht Kitchen maid' was merely 'clever' (*schrander*) and the Frisian a 'Sensible House Keeper' (*Verstandige Huishoudster*). Books meant for the well-to-do middle class, mostly written – or copied from older books like the 'The Sensible Cook' – by ladies who read them out aloud to their illiterate maids. A friend of 'The Perfect Holland Kitchen Maid' (*Volmaakte Hollandse Keuken Meid*, Amsterdam 1761) states in the preface: 'One should not think that since we already have books on this subject this work is uncalled for. Those books mainly describe how food is prepared in France, Italy and Germany, totally contrary to the Dutch way of cooking, which is much healthier and tastier, as well as less expensive ...'. The 'Perfect Guelders Kitchen maid' was a male professional cook writing at the request of some distinguished Nimeguen ladies. He describes a lot of delicious game dishes because Guelders, situated in the middle of the Netherlands, was and is a wooded area. The 'kitchen maids' themselves must have liked their food a lot, because they often add the specification *is puik* ('is excellent'). Rightly so. During restaurant campaigns of the Dutch Culinary Art Foundation in 1996 and 1997 which were dedicated to Dutch regional cooking we dished up several of their very interesting recipes such as 'Guelders lentil soup' and *Olipodrigo*, an artistic potpourri of game and vegetables, the name of which goes back to the Spanish occupation of the Netherlands in the late 16th and early 17th century. Or 'Holland leg of lamb with parsley' and 'Mrs. Binks lemon pie', with her comment: 'is extraordinary tasty'. It was.

From 1750 onwards the country saw a period of malaise in which a lot of people suffered poverty. This situation grew worse when, after France, the Dutch were the second nation to brave the wrath of the British by recognizing US independence (1782). The disabled Dutch fleet lost the Fourth Anglo-Dutch war (1780-1784) and the peace treaty with England forced the republic to cede its possessions in India. Hereafter the economy collapsed.

Alice and the soup kitchens

After having been a French vassal state for 18 years, The United Kingdom of the Netherlands was founded in 1815. William I assumed government in a period of distress. Several disasters such as floods, very wet years and cattle plagues hit the Netherlands. Soup was distributed by public kitchens since the fare at home was often insufficient. This was when Van Gogh painted his sombre potato eaters.

The well-to-do adhered to the French cuisine. Most of them spoke French and ordered their maids to cook from books written by French chefs. But the most popular cookbook was *Aaltje, de Volmaakte en Zuinige Keukenmeid* (Alice the Perfect and Thrifty Kitchen maid), first published in 1803. She – the real author is unknown – claims to have worked for 40 years in one of the wealthy canalside houses in Amsterdam. The publisher called it 'thrifty', but it is mainly a continuation of the rich and cheerful cuisine of the 18th century, with lots of eggs, butter and wine. New were the mashes and the combination of potatoes, vegetables and meat, still the pillars of daily Dutch meals.

At the end of the 19th century this cheerful book was rewritten by Odilia Corver, entitled *Aaltje, Nieuw Nederlands Kookboek* (Alice, a New Dutch Cookbook). She transformed it into a lot of dull prescriptions. About giving dinners she calls out to us: 'Long live simplicity and common sense – and true friendship which does not need a dinner for sustenance.' The same Mrs. Corver, a Domestic Science teacher educated in Germany, had given a public cooking course during the World Exhibition in Amsterdam (1887) to find out if the Dutch would be interested in cooking schools, such as already existed in England. Her success inspired the foundation of several Domestic Science schools, each with their own course book full of nutritious recipes. This is the way of cooking which Stephen Mennell, the well-known English sociologist, pronounced 'not highly sophisticated or pretentious, but simply good of its kind'. Apparently it was not disclosed to him during his stay in the Netherlands that the tradition of true Dutch culinary art which can be traced back to the 17th century, was continued surreptitiously at home where mothers dictated their daughters at the kitchen table how to make their favourite, often lavish dishes. The hidden cuisine of The Netherlands ...

Willem Joseph Laquy, 'The kitchen' (1760-1771). The lady of the house plucks a partridge, her maid shows her a plate with fresh fish. Courtesy Rijksmuseum, Amsterdam.

Jan de Ruyter, 'The kitchen maid' (1820). She shows a remarkably big slice of salmon. The story goes that kitchen maids had to eat (wild!) salmon so often that they took the job only if the employer promised to offer it not more than once a week. Courtesy Rijksmuseum, Amsterdam.

Adriaen Coorte, 'Still life with Asparagus' (1697). Courtesy Rijksmuseum, Amsterdam.

Dutch culinary heritage in America today

The culture of *New Netherland* is kept alive by the 'New Netherland Institute', located in Albany. Director of the project Dr. Charles Gehring dedicated years of his life to the translation of early Dutch documents preserved in America. Very important work, because the always tidy Dutch just 'cleaned up' nearly all documents they themselves had of this period. A great loss of precious history.

Two hundred years after the 'Old Dutch', new immigrants from the Netherlands settled in Grand Rapids and Holland (Michigan) as well as parts of Iowa and Wisconsin and in Canada. The 'New Dutch' were particularly interested in agriculture. Nearly every house had a garden where they grew 'Dutch' vegetables and planted for instance white asparagus beds 'as good as in Holland'.

Most of them were Protestants – with the exeption of a small group of Roman Catholics in Wisconsin. Calvinists, as we have seen, did not boast about their 'cuisine'. This is also true of the immigrants in the 20th century after the Second World War. But they did not abandon the cooking of their mother country. In 1949 a book was published in Grand Rapids entitled *The Real Dutch Treat* by Rie Ykema-Steenbergen. But even when the titles of American cookbooks do not reveal it clearly the intimate relations between American and Dutch cooking are evident. When leafing through *The Fifty States Cookbook* (Chicago: 1977), for example, you find in the chapter Connecticut *Ole koeks* (Oliebollen), and in Mohawk Valley *Buckwheat cakes*. Buckwheat is a loan word from the Dutch *Boekweit*. All over the USA we see *Waffles*, Dutch heritage and a Dutch word; in Upstate New York Split pea soup is eaten; and New York remembers 'Dawn's hutspot', a perfectly Dutch recipe. Michigan has Green pea soup 'Groene erwtensoep' and 'fat balls' (again *oliebollen*, hence the all American donuts). And is the expression 'as American as apple pie' really true? The 'Old Dutch' were the first to plant apple trees in 'New Netherland' and with their 17th century cookbook brought 6 recipes for applepie to the new continent.

Food from 'home' evokes feelings of nostalgia. Even today one can order *speculaas* cookies, *stroopwafels*, Gouda & Farmers cheese, as well as chocolate sprinkles (on bread) and smoked sausage (*rookworst*) all over the USA. Even *poffertjesplaten* (for puffy mini-pancakes from buckwheat) and *koekepannen* (pancake pans). Just like the 'Old Dutch' used. No wonder: the number of Dutch Americans is some 8 million by now. The good old taste is also kept alive by organizing asparagus feasts and herring parties, and by writing Dutch recipe booklets for charity sales in churches and schools. Jaarsma Bakery in Pella (Iowa) – a place where you can order an authentic Dutch meal in the Strawtown Inn – sells cookies called Goat legs (*bokkepootjes*) and Dutch Letters (*banketletters*). An aquaintance from Grand Rapids told us that several third and fourth generations Dutch Americans still prepare *hutspot*, sauerkraut mixed with mashed potatoes (*zuurkoolstamppot*) and pig in the blanket (*worstebroodjes*) as well as *nasi goreng*, an Indonesian dish the Dutch have come to recognize as their own. A representative from Vander Veen's Dutch Store confirmed this and pointed out that they have several Dutch cookery books in stock such as: *Eet smakelijk* (Enjoy your meal), Lets go Dutch, Dutch style recipes, Dandy Dutch recipes.

Savouring the 20th century and beyond

Our aim was to introduce the reader to the last century of culinary delights in the Netherlands. It proved no simple task. The first difficulty concerned the choice of chefs and their recipes. A fact is that from the first seventy years we know fewer names of top chefs than from the next thirty years, when the social respect for culinary artists improved radically. Every choice is somewhat subjective and even though we tried to make a selection that may be called characteristic for every decade, this does not mean we do not hold other professionals from that period in equally high esteem.

The second difficulty is inherent in all historiography. One tries to relive the past in a totally different time, under totally different circumstances. As a result, all historiography is inevitably coloured by the time and place of its authors. In the 20th century, a time of so much change, it would be unwise to reproduce every recipe to the original letter. That is why every now and then, whenever we deemed it necessary, we have taken the liberty to somewhat modernize a recipe. However, most often we cite the original source, so that those who want to pursue strict authenticity can do so.

Our third difficulty came from the fundamental impossibility to exactly record what goes on in the kitchen. Everyone who has seen a top chef at work will have been surprised by the speed and elegance with which he/she practises her/his profession in the most efficient way. And still the inimitable personal 'touch' of the master remains. Some time ago we asked a friend and top chef from the United States: 'How do you manage to get this saddle of lamb so tender?' His reply, 'Oh we kiss it before putting it in the oven. But do not tell anybody, please.'

So here we offer recipes from the 20th century to be reproduced at home, conscious of the fact that every recipe has an open end: it begs to be personalized. You will find ten from each decade, out of which a complete menu can be composed according to personal taste, with two starters, two soups, two intermediate courses, two main courses and two desserts. All meant for four persons. From these one can also compose a meatless menu.

Meanwhile the first decade of the 21st century is well underway and at the moment of writing this we are on the brink of celebrating 400 years of friendship between the Americans and the Dutch. The best way to remain friends is to enjoy a good meal together. We hope this will happen as often in the future as in the past. We have found two of our most outstanding chefs of the moment Margo Reuten and Jonnie Boer willing to give you an impression of what modern Dutch cuisine is capable of nowadays.

Jan Havickz. Steen, 'The feast of St. Nicholas' (1665-1668). Lots of traditional bakery connected with this typically Dutch family feast on the 5th of December. Courtesy Rijksmuseum, Amsterdam.

Captain's dinner / Kapucijnertafel

Word has it that the captian of a Groningen coaster invented 'Captain's dinner'. He was the owner of the ship, but didn't have two pennies to rub against each other. Dried marrowfats were healthy and cheap. To give his crew a good example he joined them for the meal occasionally, but adorned it with several titbits to his own taste. Hence the name. However, we do have much earlier references to this sailor's food. Grey peas – *pisum sativum convar. speciosum*, akin to marrowfats – featured on the menu of the East and West Indiamen in the 17th century. "At Sunday lunch time each man gets half a pound of smoked bacon, or one pound of beef or mutton and grey peas as many as everyone desires". Three drams a day and "light ale to their liking". But wine for the captain.
This is one of the dishes Dutch expatriates like to serve when they feel a bit homesick. But not only there. As you can read on p. 169 in the nineties of last century the humble pea was served with champagne and even a vegetarian version was created. But of course we present the true tar's original here: 'with all the trimmings'.

1. Marrowfats
2. Boiled potatoes sprinkled with parsley, recent addition
3. Crisply fried smoked bacon and 'Blind finches' (Blinde vinken: seasoned minced veal wrapped in thin slices of veal)
4. Piccalilli
5. Crisply fried suckling pork chops or slices of pork fillet
6. Amsterdam onions, spiced with kurkuma and mustard seeds
7. Sweet and sour pearl onions
8. Gherkins
9. Raw chopped onions
10. Mustard
11. Apple compote

• Rinse peas. Discard pebbles. Soak peas overnight in the cold water.
• Boil peas in soaking water for 1 ½ hour. Add salt after 1 hour. Keep warm.
• Fry bacon (beef) in butter, add vegetables and sauté for 5 minutes. Add drained peas.

☛ Serve with the photographed garnishes and/or:
   Golden fried onion rings
   Crisply fried rashers of pork belly
   Thin slices of pickled beef (pekelvlees)
   Cucumber slices
   A green salad

400 g (1 lb 2 oz) dried marrowfat peas
1 ½ l (6 ½ cup) water
1 teaspoon salt
100 g (3 ½ oz) smoked bacon or pickled beef in thin strips
15 g (½ oz) butter
150 g finely cut leek, onion, carrot and white cabbage
1 teaspoon salt

Pea soup / Erwtensoep

The porridge-like Dutch pea soup has a long history. In the first Dutch cookbook (1514) it is a sieved pea porridge, thickened with bread crumbs and seasoned with cumin, saffron and fried onions or other spices. Food, meat included, was cooked in one pot and therefore it was always a more or less thick soup.

As dried peas were fare for the common man, later books do not record recipes. But we know that orphans and students were often served green peas, with or without meat. Pulses were an important part of the victuals on ships and pea soup stayed popular during the 18th and 19th century, as it was the only dish cooks at sea could brew reasonably well. Today it is the signature winter dish of the Netherlands, connected with skating fun on the frozen lakes and canals, where it is sold in stalls. But that does not prevent people in the warm Netherlands Antilles to serve their own version to which they add a piece of hot pepper. Just as in Surinam it is ladled over a pudding of baked bananas.

Here we present a slightly adapted version from *The Perfect Holland Kitchenmaid* (1791). She served it with bread sippets. Today it is accompanied by black rye bread.

500 g (1 lb 2 oz) green split peas
2,5 litres (10 cups) water
500 g (1 lb 2 oz) fresh arm picnic / knuckle
250 g sirloin chops / spare rib chops
250 salt meager pork in one piece
1 teaspoon salt
100 g (3 ½ oz) onion, peeled
200 g (7 oz) leek (white only)
300 g (10 ½ oz) peeled celeriac
250 g (9 oz) smoked sausage
pepper
40 g (1 ½ oz) celery leaves
8 slices of black rye bread
mustard

• Wash peas in a colander. Cover with the cold water in a large pan. Add meats, chopped onion and salt. Bring to the boil slowly. Skim off scum several times. Simmer over a low heat for 3 hours, stirring now and then. Then discard the meat, leave to cool.

• Wash leek, cut into thick slices. Dice celeriac. Add to the soup with the sausage. Simmer for half an hour.

• Take the meat from the bones, dice it. Cut the salt pork into 8 slices with a sharp knife.

• Take the sausage from the pan, cut into slices, return with the meat to the soup. Stir in the finely chopped celery. Adjust the taste with salt an pepper and serve with ryebread, on which mustard and slices of the salt pork. If a thicker soup is desired, in which "the spoon stands upright", it is made the day before.

1900–1909
Oysters no bigger than a cent

Culinary facts

The time of truffles, oysters and goose liver.
Around 1850, when the first restaurants without hotel accommodation were opened, it was considered unusual to dine for pleasure anywhere else but home. People had to have an important reason. Or else had to be travelling – which, before the arrival of train, tram and car, was rather unusual as well. However, for the gentry, around the turn of the century, it slowly becomes fashionable to eat outside the home. Since French was spoken at home, French becomes the language on the menu. The restaurant business is booming.

Ten famous Dutch chefs write a thorough cookery book from which we have gratefully borrowed for this chapter. They deserve to be mentioned: J. Chiron, chef de cuisine of the Amstel Hotel; L. Kemper chef de cuisine of Brack's Doelen Hotel; L. Klein, chef de cuisine of Hotel des Pays-Bas; H.A. Kooper, chef de cuisine of the American Hotel; P. de Leeuw, chef de cuisine of the Kroon; G.E. Leefelaar, ex-chef de cuisine of Café Neuf; A. Stork, chef de cuisine of Krasnapolsky; O.V. De Vires, chef de cuisine of Restaurant Riche. Nutritional advice by dr. J. Schrijver, specialized in stomach disease (truly!).
This is what they write in their foreword:
'When the publisher asked us (...) to write the major part of Het Kook- en Huishoudboek (...) it did not take us long to agree, since we realized that Dutch Cuisine may bask in an excellent reputation, but so far not one single work of importance on the subject has been published in this country.'

This is also the time when cookery teachers (or home economists, a new occupational group) are making a fist against restaurant chefs, who in their eyes know nothing about modern nutrition. Both camps enlisted scientists to back up their ideas.

Dr. Schrijver – in what the chefs derisively call 'the lesser part of Het Kook- en Huishoudboek' - has this to say about taste: 'Anyone who overdevelops their taste buds will be punished and ruled by them. Gastronomy and gourmandise are very bad travelling companions on our route to a long and happy life

---

1900 · Opening night of Heijermans' play *Op hoop van Zegen*: the price of fish is dearly paid!
· Felix Ortt writes *Bekroond Propagandaschrift voor het Vegetarisme*
· First fair for the restaurant industry, held in the Velox building in Amsterdam
1901 · Princess Wilhelmina marries Prince Hendrik of Mecklenburg-Schwerin
· Promenade Pier of Scheveningen is built
· Abraham Kuyper forms his cabinet
· Martine Wittop Koning writes *Eenvoudige berekende recepten* (Simple recipes with pricing), which was to see 62 editions
1902 · Because of the illustrations of Johan Braakensiek *Het leven van Dik Trom* suddenly becomes very popular
1903 · Opening of the New American Hotel. There no longer remain menus of that year, but its chef, H.A. Kooper, was co-author of *Het Kook- en Huishoudboek* (Cookery and household book)
1905 · Louis Davids's star is shining in the first Dutch variety show 'Koning Kziezowat' ('King Iseethisandthat')
1907 · Pomona, first vegetarian restaurant, opens in Amsterdam
1908 · Kamerlingh Onnes calculates absolute zero: -269°C, and will receive the Nobel Prize for this
· A spectacular cookery book in three parts, written by ten of the best contemporary chefs is published: *Het Kook- en Huishoudboek*
1909 · Princess Juliana is born
· Completely revised fifth edition of *Nationaal Kookboek* by A.L.G. Westenberg
· Opening of the café and restaurant Electrique, the first with completely electric service

---

(...). Occasionally everyone will have experienced the benevolence, the happiness and the vitality a meal can provoke (...).' It is obvious that people had come to a crossroads in the first decade of the century. Culinary enjoyment was a happy occasion, but still slightly suspect.

At the same time, housewives are told in cookery books never to be as uninformed as the French, who start a meal with raw radishes: too heavy on the stomach! A fact is green salads are always served after the main course. Chef Westenberg gives this warning in reaction to the upcoming vegetarianism: 'limited nutrition with vegetarian food can result in green-sickness'. A fact lots of people were only too well aware of at the time! The poor, who in wintertime were often forced to beg, had to be content with potatoes and cabbage. The rich, however, ate with relish. Their meals were often of a profusion we now find hard to comprehend.
Therefore, Miss Manden of the Cooking School in The Hague introduces what she calls a 'hygienic menu' of 'only' twelve courses instead of the normal menu with seventeen courses, eight of which were meat dishes.

Drinks
Very trendy are what *Het Kook- en Huishoudboek* calls 'American drinks', such as Badminton Claret Cup (claret with port, Curacao, icing sugar, soda water, lemon juice, borage en cucumber peel) and Bosom Caresser (crushed ice with raspberry syrup, brandy, milk and beaten egg).

The table
Chef Westenberg: 'The laying of the table follows fashion. Even the seating is affected. Recently in Paris during a meeting of the Stewards Society it was decided to place the hostess on a slightly higher chair at the table. Even though the hostess thus has a better overall view, it cannot have encouraged conversation between her and the people next to her! The former French way of serving has been replaced with the Russian way of carving in the kitchen. The modern way is to quickly clean the table since we no longer are prepared to sit at the table for five or six hours.' On the table: low flower arrangements, fruit and desserts, no more temples of nougat or sculptures of fat. The best table lightning is with small electric light bulbs (a novelty!) placed in between the flowers, but candelabras with wax candles are all right too.

1909 Restaurant Electrique at Scheveningen, the first restaurant with completely electric service. Note the construction at the ceiling along which the trays would glide to the tables

Kitchen design
In these times, according to chef Westenberg, people often slept in the kitchen, which even held the lavatory. He holds a plea for light and space, electric or gas lightning (better than paraffin) and a circulation cooker. Because, as the saying goes: 'A quick fire makes for a quick cook.' And the cooker is the most important element. Often still with a 'stove' to keep the dishes warm. Those who can afford do well to buy a gas cooker because of 'tidiness and convenience'. Such a stove did not yet have open burners, but a plate with rings, just like the wood burning stoves. And then there is the 'ice chest', cooled with thick bars of ice put in isolated compartments. It had to be cleaned every eight days with hot water and soda – the only cleaning agent available. When it developed a stale smell one had to burn 'a couple of sulphur threads' in it. Pots were made of clay, copper, iron, sometimes enamelled, or of aluminium, at that time very expensive.

Mackerel of the Pier / Makreel van de Pier

(Maqueraux marinés)

For the Dutch the Scheveningen Pier symbolizes the beginning and end of an era:
a bridge to the distance built at the beginning of the century, at the end of which one
stares insatiably over the seemingly endless space of the new millennium.
According to a chronicler of the Kurhaus, that saw its clientele soar because of the Pier,
this 'new promenade' reflected the development of Scheveningen into a seaside resort for
one and all. Hence the recipe with simple mackerel instead of lobster, prepared, however,
according to the rules of the art of those times.

Recipe source: *Het Kook- en Huishoudboek*, Amsterdam: Hartog & Bos, 1908

600 g (1 lb 6 oz) mackerel (without head)
5 tablespoons tarragon vinegar
1 tablespoon crushed black
peppercorns
1 large onion, sliced
1 bay leaf
2 sprigs of thyme
½ tablespoon coriander seeds
salt
reduced fish stock

·

100 g (3½ oz) mixed green salad leaves
1 lemon
100 ml (½ cup) mayonnaise
1 tablespoon finely chopped chives

• Clean out the inside of the mackerels or ask the fishmonger
to do so. Wash the fish and put it side by side in a fitting pan.
Add herbs and vinegar with enough reduced fish stock to
cover. Bring to the boil and keep 12-15 minutes just below
boiling. Cool the mackerels in the poaching liquid. Remove
skin and bones and break the meat in large chunks.
• Divide the washed salad leaves on to 4 plates. Place the
mackerel in the middle. Garnish with lemon slices. Serve
with a sauce of mayonnaise, chives and a drop of lemon juice.

♟ Sauvignon Touraine. Refreshing white wine from the Loire Valley.

Pigeon with peas / Duif met doppers

In 1909 A.L.G. Westenberg, chef in Hilversum, held a plea for extended cooking lessons: 'They would replace the large dose of semi-wisdom the young boarding school girls carry as useless ballast.' Obviously emancipation had not yet reached the kitchen. In our times firm pigeon no longer is fashionable, we only use the breast. However, in those times Queen Wilhelmina was not above chewing the bones with relish, according to one delighted eyewitness who shared the table with her as a child. A salad with a bone, so to speak.

Recipe source: A.L.G. Westenberg, Nationaal Kookboek, Leiden: A.W. Sijthoff's Uitg. Mij., 1909

2 pigeons, legs and breasts separated
salt and pepper
50 g (1¾ oz) butter
1 bay leaf
sprigs of thyme and rosemary
150 ml (⅔ cup) red wine

·

3 slices of white bread
olive oil

·

1 tablespoon butter
50 g (1¾ oz) lean bacon, diced
50 g (1¾ oz) shallots, peeled
100 g (3½ oz) white mushrooms
200 g (7 oz) green peas (frozen)
salt and pepper

100 g (3½ oz) mixed green salad leaves
3 tablespoons olive oil
1 tablespoon vinegar
1 tablespoon finely chopped leek
½ teaspoon soy sauce
salt and pepper

• Season the meat with salt and pepper. Melt the butter in a heavy pan and brown the meat on all sides. Add the herbs and pour over the wine. After five minutes, remove the breasts from the pan, cook the legs for about 40 minutes until tender. Strain the cooking liquid through a moist cloth. Leave to cool.

• From the bread, cut circles of 7 cm (2¾ in). In hot oil fry until golden on both sides.

• Brown the bacon, shallots and mushrooms in the tablespoon of butter, add salt and pepper as well as the peas. Cool.

• Divide the salad leaves onto 4 plates. Place a bread crouton in the middle and top with a sliced pigeon breast and a leg. Scatter the vegetables around and pour over a sauce made of the oil, vinegar, leek, soy sauce and cooking liquid.

☞ Chef Westenberg makes little mounds of salad leaves on the plate, so we copied his method. The pigeon is prepared the modern way since it becomes rather tough when stewed the way it was done in those days.

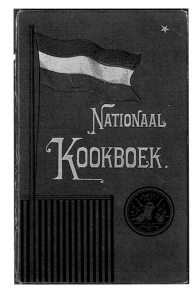

Sunday's leek soup from Brabant / Zondagse Prol

So as to give you an impression of the diet of 'ordinary people' every now and then we will share a recipe for a homely dish. This is a recipe for a one-pan meal without much ado, for it took a long time before country people and working class people could have circulation stoves installed, let alone gas cookers, that came into fashion around 1900. Everybody did have a paraffin oil cooker, though, after the discovery of oilfields in America half a century earlier. Ideal for simmering Sunday's soup! It differed from the everyday version in the use of meat.

200 g (7 oz) stewing beef
50 g (1¾ oz) corned beef (salted beef)
1½ litre (6 cups) water
nutmeg
salt

·

100 g (3½ oz) cleaned leek, sliced
50 g (1¾ oz) waxy potatoes, diced
25 g (1½ heaped tablespoon) long-grain rice
1 tablespoon finely chopped parsley

·

2 slices rye bread from Brabant (fine)
butter, chives

· Cook the meat with the herbs and salt for 2 hours on low heat (45 minutes in a pressure cooker).
· Add the leek, potatoes, and rice and cook for another 20 minutes. Dice the meat and return to the soup. Stir in the parsley.
· Serve with triangles of rye bread, spread with butter and sprinkled with chives.

☛ Enough for a first course. As a main course twice the amount of vegetables for filling is needed and more broth. A traditional, but nowadays very daring, way of garnishing is with crisply fried cubes of beef fat (in Dutch called 'kaantjes').

Vegetarian cream soup / Crème Pomona

In 1899 the first vegetarian restaurant Pomona opened in The Hague, followed by one in Amsterdam. The first of a chain of vegetarian restaurants in which rich vegetarians held shares. Sadly the chain did not have a long life, which reflects the attitude of the Dutch public rather than the quality of the cooking.

Mrs Valk, on the board of directors of the first Pomona, excused herself for serving a smooth soup which requires no chewing, since chewing is much more beneficial to the digestion. However, she did include this green cream soup in her published collection.

Recipe source: *Kookboek van den Nederlandschen Vegetariërsbond*, Amsterdam: S.L. van Looy, 1896

1899, 1909 Restaurant Pomona at the opening (below) and its 10th anniversary

½ litre (6 cups) water (or vegetable stock
made with a vegetarian cube)

300 g (10½ oz) flageolets, soaked

40 g (1½ oz) onion, chopped

1 tablespoon butter

2 tablespoons olive oil

drop of soy sauce

salt

·

cornflour

2 tablespoons finely chopped chervil

· Cook the flageolets in the water until very soft. Push them through a sieve and add the cooking liquid. Soften the onion in the butter and stir it into the soup. Simmer on low heat for about 15 minutes. If wanted the soup can be thickened with a thin paste of cornflour and water. Season with soy sauce and salt. Just before serving sprinkle with chervil (a modern addition).

 Non-vegetarians can add crisped bacon, mussels or shrimps. It is easier to use a 1 litre (1 quart) tin of flageolets.

Oysters for Abraham the Great / Oesters voor Abraham de Geweldige

(potatoes prepared in the oven and stuffed with scrambled eggs and oysters)

'Calvinistic' has the connotation of possessing a narrow view on life. That certainly did not apply to the reformed theologian and politician Abraham Kuyper, who was Prime Minister from 1901 to 1905. Political cartoons exaggerated his rotund posture, but the fact remains he exuberantly partook in the good of the earth. The Historical Documentation Centre for Dutch Protestantism in Amsterdam sent us some interesting menus of 'Abraham the Great', for example the one from 1907 in Restaurant Les Deux Villes: fourteen courses, eight wines, starting with Charles Heidsieck demi sec. Had they known, his followers, who proudly called themselves 'the humble people', would have frowned on this, since Abraham recommended sober family meals. In addition, few will have known he was fussy enough about his oysters to once, on a trip to America, send them back to the kitchen because they were too big: he liked his oysters 'no bigger than a cent'.

Recipe source: Het Kook- en Huishoudboek, Amsterdam: Hartog & Bos, 1908

---

4 jacket potatoes
3 eggs
20 g (¾ oz) butter
4 tablespoons double cream
4 oysters
4 sprigs of parsley

• Preheat the oven to 120 °C/250 °F/Gas Mark 2. Scrub the potatoes under running water. Sprinkle a thin layer of salt on a baking tray. Place the potatoes on the salt and bake until soft. The cooking time depends on the type and size of the potatoes, prick to see if they are done.

• Open the oysters. Remove the flesh and strain the liquid. When the potatoes are done, beat the eggs, butter, cream and oyster liquid in a bowl. Put the mixture into a saucepan and cook on low heat. Keep whisking. Chop the oysters and add to the scrambled eggs, but from the heat.

• Remove the salt from the potatoes, slice of the top with a sharp knife. Remove some of the flesh and fill with scrambled eggs. Put the tops back on, '... in such a way that it appears as if they are still whole'. Garnish with a sprig of parsley. Serve the potatoes on a plate covered with a folded napkin.

 Instead of oysters use smoked eel or salmon, shrimps, mussels or green herbs.

1901–1905 Abraham Kuyper Prime Minister

Braised haddock / Kniertje's schellevis

(Eglefin étuvé Hollandaise)

It is highly unlikely that on opening night of *Op hoop van zegen (in good hope)*, Christmas Eve, 1900, playwright Heijermans and his troupe would have dined in one of Amsterdam's top restaurants. Without a doubt they preferred the fish cart considering the social criticism of Heijermans's play that even at the end of the twentieth century still remained in production.

Recipe source: Het Kook- en Huishoudboek, Amsterdam: Hartog & Bos, 1908

4 fillets of haddock (about 600 g / 1 lb 5 oz)
50 g (1¾ oz) butter
salt
1 lemon
breadcrumbs
nutmeg

- Preheat the oven to 180 °C/350 °F/Gas mark 4. Check to see all bones have been removed from the fish. Put the fillets in an attractive buttered dish, sprinkled with salt. Add 4 tablespoons of water and 1 tablespoon of lemon juice. Place a slice of lemon, peel removed, on each fillet. Sprinkle with breadcrumbs and a little grated nutmeg. To finish put some lumps of butter on the fish. Bake for about 20 minutes in the preheated oven for a golden crust.
- Serve with boiled potatoes, a sauce boat with cooking liquid and a dressed green salad.

☞ If the sauce is too simple for your taste, beat over hot water a sauce of lemon and/or tarragon (see hollandaise sauce, 1950s).

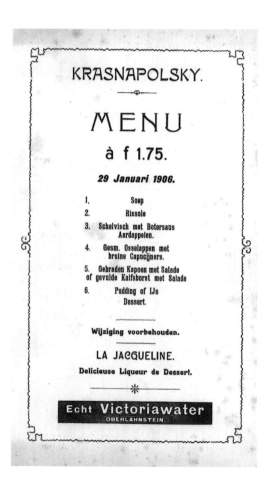

KRASNAPOLSKY.

MENU
à f 1.75.

29 Januari 1906.

1.   Soep
2.   Rissole
3.   Schelvisch met Botersaus
       Aardappelen.
4.   Gesm. Osselappen met
       bruine Capucijnen.
5.   Gebraden Kapoen met Salade
of gevulde Kalfsborst met Salade
6.   Pudding of IJs
       Dessert.

Wijziging voorbehouden.

LA JACQUELINE.
Delicieuse Liqueur de Dessert.

Echt Victoriawater
OBERLAHNSTEIN.

Royal chicken / Koninklijke kip

One of the dishes on the menu for the festive luncheon in honour of the wedding of Princess Wilhelmina and Prince Hendrik was *capon*. Too simple, such a capon? Definitely not! We have in our possession a 'day card' of those years from Krasnapolsky in Amsterdam, complete with prices. Strikingly enough, next to duck, chicken is the most expensive: *f* 3,50. Chicken dishes most often had 'royal' or 'imperial' attached to their name, in the French way. And imperial they looked! Prepared with the cockscomb and kidneys as big as pigeon eggs, which also tells a lot about the size of the fowl. Legendary nowadays! That's why we settled on *a poulet*, small but aristocratic, *à la châtelaine* – from the lady of the castle.

Recipe source: *Het Kook- en Huishoudboek*, Amsterdam: Hartog & Bos, 1908

1901 Queen Wilhelmina and Prince Hendrik, soon after the marriage

2 roasting chickens of about 800 g (1 lb 12 oz)
pinch of saffron powder
salt and pepper
2 large onions
parsley
50 g (1¾ oz) butter
a little arrowroot or potato starch

·

25 g (1 oz) butter
30 g (1 oz) wheat flour
300 ml (1¼ cup) reduced veal stock (jar)
salt and pepper
1 glass of Madeira

12 artichoke bottoms (tin)
12 whole, cooked chestnuts (tin)
1 tablespoon finely chopped parsley
butter
300 g (¾ lb) haricots verts
200 g (½ lb) carrots, in small balls

·

500 g (1 lb 2 oz) peeled potatoes

🍷 Côtes de Provence rosé. Spicy elegant dry rosé.

• Preheat the oven to 225 °C/425 °F/Gas Mark 7. Rub the chickens with saffron powder and sprinkle with salt and pepper (the inside as well). Put a lump of butter, a peeled onion and a sprig of parsley into the cavities. Put the birds breasts down in a roasting tray and spoon over melted butter. Roast for 45 minutes in the preheated oven. Turn after 20 minutes, add a dash of water and regularly baste with cooking liquid.

• Melt the butter in a saucepan, and brown the flour. Add the stock and keep stirring. Whisk until the sauce has thickened. Cook, covered, on low heat for about 10 minutes.

• Cook the haricots verts until tender, but crisp. Cook the carrots until tender. Heat the artichoke bottoms and chestnuts in a little butter. Remove the onions from the chicken, mash them and thicken the puree with a paste of a little arrowroot and water. Stir in the finely chopped parsley. Stuff the artichoke bottoms with this and stick in a few haricots. Garnish with a chestnut.

• Split the chicken (or do so at the table), put the halves on a plate surrounded by artichoke bottoms. Arrange a layer of thick French fries (pommes Pontneuf) around it. Stir the chicken cooking liquid into the brown sauce and season with Madeira and salt. Serve in a sauce boat.

Saddle of venison with cream sauce / Reerug in roomsaus

(selle de chevreuil à la crème)

If you ask non-vegetarians of almost one hundred years old: what did you enjoy the most?, without a doubt the answer will be 'saddle of venison'. It remained the most popular dish until the fifties. True, reindeer with mushrooms and morels also appeared on the menu, but considering the popularity of loin of pork with cream sauce it shows people's fondness for venison. One kept looking for an affordable substitute.

Recipe source: Het Kook- en Huishoudboek, Amsterdam: Hartog & Bos, 1908

50 g (1¾ oz) onion
40 g (1½ oz) carrot
60 g (1¾ oz) celeriac
400 ml (1½ cup) red wine
100 ml (½ cup) water
½ bay leaf
5 juniper berries
1 sprig of thyme
½ teaspoon sugar
600 g (1 lb 5 oz) loin of venison

·

50 g (1¾ oz) butter
50 g (1¾ oz) fatty bacon, diced
salt and pepper
200 ml (¾ cup) double cream

- Clean and dice the vegetables. Add the wine, water, spices and sugar and bring to the boil. Simmer this marinade for 10 minutes and leave to cool. Marinate the venison for at least two hours. Drain the vegetables and save the liquid. Preheat the oven to 220 °C/425 °F/Gas Mark 7.
- Pat dry the venison. In a casserole on medium heat melt the butter and cook the bacon for a few minutes. Turn the heat up and brown the meat on all sides. Add the vegetables and place the casserole in the preheated oven. Turn the meat after 5 minutes. After another 5 minutes take the meat from the casserole (or longer if the fillet is thick). Season with salt and pepper and keep warm.
- Strain the cooking liquid and return 3 tablespoons to the casserole. Add 100 ml (½ cup) of the marinade. Boil to reduce a little, add the cream and reduce again to a smooth sauce.
- Thinly slice the venison and put the slices on a plate. Preferably served with Brussels sprouts, mashed potatoes and compote of peach or cranberry.

☞ For larger parties the venison can be cooked with the bone and carved at the table. In that case adjust the amount of marinade and the cooking time. The recipe also works well with haunch of venison, saddle of hare and leg of hare.

Bombe Kamerlingh Onnes

(Bombe glace nouveau siècle)

Of course we dedicate an ice cream dish to the 'Man of the Chill'. Research into the behaviour of matter under duress of extreme cold (such as superconductivity) was still very much in vogue at the end of the twentieth century. This shows Kamerlingh Onnes's visionary spirit. Most probably he did not know a thing about the extremely cold *bombe* the chefs in his time created for their new century.

Recipe source: Het Kook- en Huishoudboek, Amsterdam: Hartog & Bos, 1908

For a bombe mould of 2½ litres (2 quarts),
or 8 individual small bombes

·

Filling:
250 ml (1 cup) double cream
100 g (3½ oz) crystallized red cherries
80 ml (⅓ cup) pasteurized egg yolk (= 4 egg yolks)
60 ml (¼ cup) pasteurized egg white (= 2 egg whites)
75 g (2½ oz) sugar
2 sheets of gelatine (4 g / ⅛ oz)
2 tablespoons kirsch

·

Lining: 1 litre (4 cups) ready-bought vanilla ice cream

·

Garnish:
300 ml (1¼ cup) double cream
30 g (1 oz) sugar
100 g (3½ oz) pineapple
20 crystallized red cherries

- Place the mould in the freezer. For the filling whisk the cream until stiff. Finely chop the crystallized cherries. Over a pan of quite hot water whisk egg yolk, egg white and sugar until thick and foamy. Into it dissolve the well squeezed gelatine. Whisk the mixture cold and light. Gradually add the kirsch. Fold in the cream and cherries.
- Line the frozen mould with a layer of not too solidly frozen vanilla ice cream. Spoon in the filling. Place in the freezer for a few hours. Also cover the top with vanilla ice cream. Cover with parchment paper and place in the freezer for about 6 hours.
- Unmould the *bombe* and put it back in the freezer for 30 minutes. In the meantime whisk the double cream until stiff. Cut the pineapple in cubes, the cherries in halves. Place a few pieces of pineapple in the middle of the *bombe*, arrange the cherries around it and pipe a decoration of cream.

- A bombe is an ice-cream pudding made in a spherical mould. First a layer of plain vanilla ice cream is put in. The ice cream must not contain too much alcohol, otherwise it will not harden. This in contrary to the cream filling, which should not be too hard.
- Turning out the bombe is made easier by first lining the mould with plastic foil.
- In a bombe often different layers of different coloured ice cream are used.

Prince Hendrik cake / Prins Hendrik-taart

This cake from the book of the ten chefs is called Gâteau Prince Henri, obviously on the occasion of the marriage of Queen Wilhelmina to Prince Hendrik. Such is the feature of chefs de cuisine: they react in their way to the times in which they live and immortalize famous people in the names of their creations. This cake is delicious, regardless of what in hindsight can be said of Prince Hendrik.

Recipe source: *Het Kook- en Huishoudboek*, Amsterdam: Hartog & Bos, 1908

For a springform pan of 24 cm (9 in)

Top:
500 g (1 lb 2 oz) ground almonds
300 g (10½ oz) sugar
100 g (3½ oz) wheat flour
8 eggs
1 tablespoon vanilla sugar
60 g (2 oz) butter, melted

Base:
125 g (4 oz) butter
2 teaspoons sugar
3 eggs
100 ml (⅓ cup) milk
200 g (7 oz) wheat flour
½ teaspoon baking powder

Garnish:
200 g (7 oz) apricot preserve (orange!)
300 ml (1¼ cup) double cream
30 g (1 oz) icing sugar
1 tablespoon anisette
100 g (3½ oz) shaved almonds

1901 The bridal cake served at the wedding of Queen Wilhelmina and Prince Hendrik

♀ Monbazillac: sweet white wine from the Bergerac.

- Preheat the oven to 150 °C/300 °F/Gas Mark 2. For the top combine the ground almonds and flour. Over hot water beat 6 egg yolks with 2 whole eggs, vanilla sugar and sugar until light. Beat the remaining 6 egg whites to soft peaks and spoon into the egg mixture. Add the melted butter drop by drop. Finally spoon in the flour and almond mixture. Fill the buttered springform. Bake for approximately 60 minutes until set. Remove the cake from the form and cool on a wire rack.
- Preheat the oven to 200 °C/400 °F/Gas Mark 6. For the base cream the butter and sugar and gradually add 3 egg yolks and the milk. Beat the egg whites to soft peaks and spoon into the egg yolk mixture. Finally add the sifted flour and baking powder. Turn the dough into the springform and bake for 30 minutes in the preheated oven. Immediately take the base from the form and cool on a wire rack.
- Place the base on the bottom of the springform. Spread with half the preserve. Slice the almond cake into two horizontal layers. Whisk the double cream, icing sugar and Anisette

until stiff. Spread the layers with half the whipped cream. Reassemble the cake and put it on the base. Glaze the top with apricot preserve. Decorate the middle with rosettes of cream. Spread the side with the remaining cream and press the roasted shaved almonds in it.

DEJEUNER-GALA
du 7 Février 1901.
—
Potage Crème Montreuil
Truite Saumonée à la Russe
Chapons Montmorency
Pâté d'Amiens au Champagne
Chevreuil rôti
Salade Polonaise
Asperges nouvelles
Timbale Sicilienne
Palermitaine glacé
Marquises au parmesan.

7·2·1901

The infinite green kitchen

Vegetarianism of yesteryear

Life was not easy for a vegetarian entering the twentieth century. Coffee and tea, wine and liqueur: all were forbidden. People wanting to know more about the history can visit the Bureau of the Dutch Vegetarian Society in Hilversum where they are smilingly handed Het drie-stuivers kookboek ('The threepenny cookery book', first edition 1901). In it the vegetarian diet is described as 'that which combats strongly the desire for alcohol and other improper cravings'. The horizon was narrow: it was the time of overwrought nationalism.

Vegetarianism of today

Now look at any issue of Leven en Laten Leven ('Live and let live'), the lively veggie magazine of the 1990s and it immediately becomes clear how much vegetarianism has changed: port is drunk with garlic prepared in the microwave oven and one does not limit oneself to dull northern fare, but dares to have couscous and spring rolls. In other words: the movement has turned the culinary way and is inspired by all eating cultures of the world. The green kitchen has become infinitely interesting. That is why at the moment the Society has marked as many as 60 restaurants as 'hospitable for vegetarians'. And that is why you will be able to put together a vegetarian dinner out of the ten specific recipes from all decades in this book. Fact is many people are eating less or no meat at all just for pleasure.

Fast food without criticism!

On deciding to go vegetarian it can be difficult at first to adjust to a different eating pattern. The 'sham minced meat' from Het driestuivers kookboek (made with lentils, fried onion, egg and parsley) tastes nice, but takes time and for most people time is hard to come by at the end of the twentieth century.

So as not always to have to fall back on pita bread with falafel for kosher food, the Israeli firm Tivall in the pioneers years developed beautiful alternatives to burgers on the basis of grains and soy beans. These have been available in the

Netherlands since as early as 1987 in the cooling of super markets. In 1995 the vegetarian cold cuts (slices and pâté) came and in 1997 two protein replacements 'chicken style' and 'beef style' for stir frying followed.

And even the freezer has something to offer. In 1997 the Oetker firm started with an enticing and never before shown assortment of tofu and vegetable snacks, vegetable burgers, a cheese-millet cake, spring rolls, stuffed peppers and even quiche. Plus instant powder for broth, gravy, and sauce. In no time at all it is possible to prepare a feast. Restaurants too are very happy with these products.

The future

The theme for the festive conference in honour of the 100th anniversary of the Dutch Vegetarian Society in 1994 was 'Novel Protein Foods'. This is because of the importance to find new protein sources in reference to the world food situation. At the beginning of a new century we can use a visionary outlook!

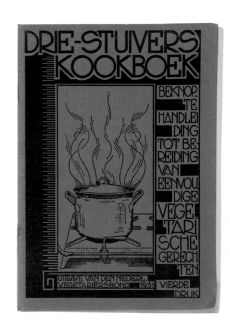

1910–1919
'Our people should learn to eat fish!'

Growing tourism

At the start of this decade life quietly moves on. But then again..., people are starting to get worried about the increasing traffic. The last stage-coach of Van Gend and Loos is put out to pasture. Trains have become extremely popular. In 1909 the Netherlands counted no more than 1500 passenger cars, by 1919 their number had increased to no fewer than 7000! Do not complain, you might say. More guests. At Scheveningen, however, people thought differently. After all, the increased traffic resulted in 'ongoing democratization and a reduction of length of stay'.

In that respect hotel Duin en Daal in Bloemendaal can be seen as a modern trend-setter. In 1911 this hotel markets itself in a sweet booklet with a picture on the cover of Queen Emma, Princess Wilhelmina and Prince Hendrik, and the inside illustrated with advertisements of Victoria water and champagne Moët & Chandon. '(...) at a 7 minute distance from the electrical tram, in which Haarlem station is reached in 12 minutes (return fare 10 cents). (...) We offer carriage housing for coaches, cars and bicycles: possibly the terrain in front of our hotel, about 50.000 m², will incite gentlemen aviators to come and go in their aeroplanes (...).' No wonder they strongly recommend advance booking. At Whitsunday they had to disappoint no fewer than 247 guests. To encourage people to come and visit they offer a guest list with names of all guests of 1910, including their home addresses! One wonders if the people in those days ever were naughty?

Culinary facts

A luncheon menu in the early 1910s at Duin en Daal, shows that broth, steak and egg sunny-side up, cream puff and fruit cost ƒ 1,50 per person. And at Frigge, in Groningen, on Boxing Day 1919, a dinner-concert costs between three and five guilders. In 1916, in Groningen just as in Amsterdam, a Central Kitchen was opened: 8 menus for an average of 11 cents. One would think: 'the way to go'. But people were extremely happy when, in 1919, food scarcity, induced by World War I, was over and the soup kitchens could be closed.

Data from 1910 show the food situation for the common man to have improved dramatically. People could afford meat, fish

---

1910 · Mrs C.J. Wannée writes *Het Kookboek van de Amsterdamsche Huishoudschool*; first reprint already in 1911
1912 · Vitamins (discovered in 1900) are given their mysterious names
· Open Air Museum Arnhem opened on September 6th
· Dutch Society of Housewives founded
1914 · The famous children's books *Pietje Bell* and *Ot en Sien* are published
· Gas lighting is replaced by electricity: Krasnapolsky lights its Winter Garden in Amsterdam
· War is raging in countries around us
1916 · As a result of food scarcity the city of Amsterdam opens a Central Kitchen. Under management of Mrs. Lotgering Hillebrand 188.000 portions a day are served: 'The Central Manger' or 'The Central Trough of Wibaut'. Not a slight accomplishment for those days!
1917 · Food scarcity in the Netherlands. Germany announces an all out submarine war, which, since we are a seafaring nation, hits us hard
· First Annual Fair of Utrecht
· Potato Revolt in Amsterdam, 6 dead, almost 100 injured
· Women's suffrage made possible. The long march by Aletta Jacobs, first Dutch female doctor, finally pays off
1919 · Food and Drugs Act. Aim: to protect the public health against contaminated foods and to promote honesty in the trade Establishment of Dutch Institute for Public Nutrition, forerunner for the *Voorlichtingsbureau voor de Voeding* ('Public Information Service for Food')
· Founding of KLM: first airline in Europe
· Founding of *Horecaf*, successor of the Guild of Hotel Owners

1914 Ot and Sien
'Don't do that, Ot'

and vegetables and sometimes even cheese, eggs and fruit. As a result of the war of 1914–1918, however, the situation once more deteriorated enormously. Although the Netherlands were neutral, food was expensive and the supply of American grain had stopped. Result: bread rationing and distribution coupons.

Restaurant business

At the beginning of the war the *Hotelhoudersbond*, the guild of bed and meal providers in those days, was not overly pessimistic. After all the Netherlands were neutral. However, gradually they started to feel the crisis personally. Levies and taxes increased and in 1916 the guild's magazine reports shortages in the industry. Even worse was the early closing time for hotels and coffee-houses because of the shortage of gas and electric lighting. In 1917 came the ban on fat for fry-ing and baking and margarine, and on dinners in excess of 3 courses. As well as a ban on serving bread with a hot meal. In name of the government the guild organized distribution and a bureau for complaints, and did this so well, also for non-members, that more and more people saw its merit. And that is how the *Horecaf* came about: the Dutch Union of Employers in the HOtel, REstaurant, CAFé and related industries.

Kitchen design

Because of scarcity the hay box is reinstated to save on fuel. A brochure 'Instructions and recipes for a kitchen in wartime' (price 15 cents) explains the principle: 'Take an old carton box (not too small) and fill it with old newspapers or pieces of cloth. An old blanket is very useful too.' The ideal pot has a special bayonet catch (hay box pot). This is how stock is made: 10 minutes on the stove... 6 hours in the hay box. Dried beans: 20 minutes on the stove top... 5 hours in the hay box. During World War II this brochure will be used again.

1917 First Year Fair of Utrecht

Potato salad / Aardappelsla

1917: Potato Revolt in Amsterdam. Initially there was enough rice, but the common people of Amsterdam had no idea what to do with this unknown grain. Barges and shops were plundered by hungry women. They were justly furious because the export of potatoes, meat and butter continued to the war faring countries. In addition they also had to miss their 'cup of comfort' coffee. If there were any potatoes left over at all they could not be fried because of the 'fat scarcity'. People ate sandwiches with sliced potatoes or potato salad. Happy in our time of peace we have added a few shrimps or mussels, which in those days came cheap.

Recipe source: Martine Wittop Koning, *Hoe voeden wij ons thans 't best*, Amsterdam: Elsevier, 1918

2 tablespoons white vinegar
½ teaspoon lemon juice
½ teaspoon mustard
8 tablespoons olive oil
2 tablespoons (fish) stock

600 g (1lb 5 oz) potatoes, boiled in their skins
100 g (3½ oz) white of leek
2 hard-boiled eggs
300 g (10½ oz) shrimps or mussels, cooked

1 head of lettuce
4 tufts of green herbs

• In a salad bowl whisk vinegar, lemon juice and mustard. Keep whisking and gradually add the oil and stock.
• Peel and slice the potatoes. Very thinly slice the washed leek. Mash the eggs. In the salad bowl combine with the shrimps and herbs. Cover the bowl and place in the fridge for 1 hour.
• Pick and wash the lettuce. On 4 plates make a ring of green leaves, spoon the potato salad in the middle and decorate with a tuft of parsley.

☛ Mrs Wittop Koning only mentions parsley, but of course you can also use chervil and tarragon, following the baroness, who created the Colourful salad of Latuw (see page 47).

Parrot tongues / Papegaaientongetjes

A typical Amsterdam joke. Actually just leftovers, but presented in a very nice way.
The name, of course, brings memories of Roman times when people feasted on tongues
of nightingales and larks. However, the name is altogether not that unusual: the Dutch
still eat 'cats' tongues': chocolates or biscuits. Culinary jokes are of all times.

Recipe source: C.J. Wannée Het Kookboek van de Amsterdamsche Huishoudschool, Amsterdam: H.J.W. Becht, 1910

Batter:
30 g (1 oz) soft butter
1 egg
100 ml (½ cup) milk
70 g (2½ oz) wheat flour
½ tablespoon very finely chopped parsley
nutmeg, salt

·

Filling:
about 400 g (14 oz) leftover
cooked veal, chicken, game or fish

• Cream the butter and beat in the egg and milk. Make a
well in the centre of the flour, pour in the milk mixture
and starting from the inside stir into a smooth thick batter.
Season with herbs and salt.
• Cut the leftovers in long triangles. Dip into the batter and
brown in hot oil of approximately 170 °C/ 350 °F.

☞ Very good in combination with deep-fried parsley.

Colourful salad / Salade van Latuw

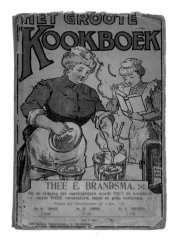

Vegetarians were the first vitamin worshippers. Mrs Valk: 'The more nuts, fruits and uncooked herbs are eaten, the more the eating of meat dishes, the abuse of harmful stimulants such as spices, vinegar and salt, as well as the intake of alcoholic beverages will diminish.' So optimistic! And thus one of the recipes she offered is of a green salad mixed with 'rather a lot of beetroot'. However with a less principal approach baroness Thorbecke was able to top her: she created a salad even a first class chef would feel proud of.

Recipe source: C.L.J.M. Thorbecke, née Cats, baroness De Raet, *Het Groote Kookboek (Lucullus)*, Amsterdam: Gebr. E. & M. Cohen, 1916

1 head of lettuce
400 g (14 oz) colourful mixed salad leaves
½ cucumber

.

6 tablespoons olive oil
2 tablespoons vinegar
piece of garlic
salt and pepper

.

2 hard-boiled eggs

.

fresh herbs, including rosemary, rue, hyssop,
coriander, sage, lemon balm, thyme, marjoram,
basil, burnet, tarragon, borage flowers,
Indian cress flowers, violets, or whatever is available

♀ Pinot Blanc d'Alsac. Fresh and subtle white wine.

• Wash and dry the lettuce and salad leaves. In a salad bowl mix leaves with short shaved cucumber strips.
• Stir a dressing of oil, vinegar, very little garlic, salt and pepper; dribble the sauce over the salad.
• Decorate with egg wedges and herbs of choice.

☞ A very interesting first course, especially in combination with thyme and coarsely grated young cheese and/or strips of boiled ham. Put these on the salad before adding the dressing. Always match added ingredients, such as meats or fish, with herbs of your choice.

Mussel hash / Mosselenhachee

The Central Bureau for the Marketing of Fishery Products, Singel 215 in Amsterdam, in these years published a paper called: *Do eat mussels*. They were shipped in by the government from Zeeland and prices were kept very low because of the meat scarcity: 5 kg for ƒ 0,15. A culinary expert wrote: 'Culinary treasures for those who enjoy these shellfish.' And so people came up with the idea to prepare minced mussels and mussel hash, now forgotten, but in the 1940s during World War II once again appearing in war cookery books.

carrot, celery leaves, onion
1 kg (2 lb 3 oz) mussels (300 g / 10½ oz cleaned)

·

25 g (1 oz) butter
300 g (10½ oz) peeled onion, sliced
30 g (1 oz) wheat flour
salt and pepper
1-2 tablespoons vinegar
salt and pepper

• In a large saucepan cook the cleaned mussels on a layer of carrot, celery leaves and onion with 100 ml (½ cup) of water until all are open (shake thrice). Leave to cool. Remove the mussels from the shell. Strain the cooking liquid through a piece of cloth.

• Melt the butter in a small saucepan, lightly brown the onion. Add the flour and stir until the flour is browned too. Keep stirring and pour in 300 ml (1¼ cup) of cooking liquid. Cook without a lid until a thick sauce is formed. Stir in vinegar and mussels. Season with salt and pepper. Serve with braised red cabbage (with clove) and a little bit of boiled rice.

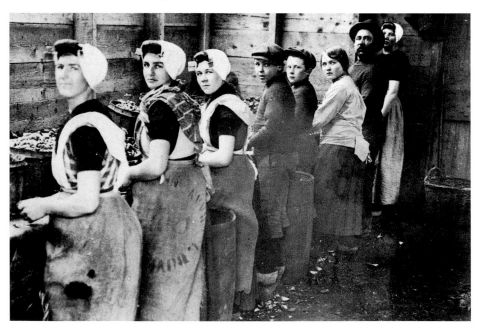

1911 Shelling of mussels at the firm P. Hollestelle

Sameness soup with salty sticks / Eenheidssoep met zoute stengels

During World War I nearly everything had to be bought on distribution coupons. Even eggs. And prices kept rising. Difficult times for housewives! Koba Catenius however optimistically stated: 'There are enough dishes to be made with these governmental articles: dried vegetables for soup, sameness sausages (...), peas, beans, barley, oatmeal.' All better than the 'trough of Wibaut' (the control kitchen), where they served thin hotchpotch without meat. Even the sameness sausage, the ingredients of which one was never sure: goat, chicken, goose, a combination of all. After boiling, minced cakes were made with the meat, and with the broth Koba created a pea soup with leek and mange-tout. We preferred what she called 'an excellent vegetarian soup'.

Recipe source: Koba M.J. Catenius-Van der Meijden, 111 Eenheidsrecepten (Voor stad en land. Voor elken stand), Amsterdam: J.H. de Bussy, 1918 en C.J. Wannée, Het kookboek van de Amsterdamsche huishoudschool, Amsterdam: H.J.W. Becht, 1910

Soup:
celeriac
turnip
leek
carrot
cauliflower
2 tablespoons long-grain rice
2 tablespoons olive oil
1¼ litre (5 cups) vegetable stock
(from cubes)
40 ml (¼ cup) pasteurized egg yolk
(= 2 egg yolks)
100 ml (½ cup) double cream
celery leaves

Sticks:
frozen puff pastry
(defrosted)
1 egg yolk
salt

• Dice the vegetables and cook with the rice in the olive oil. Add the stock and cook until the rice and vegetables are tender (approximately 20 minutes).
• Preheat the oven to 200 °C/400 °F/Gas Mark 6. Cut the puff pastry into strips. Beat the egg yolk with a teaspoon of water and a little salt and spoon over the strips. Line a baking tray with parchment paper and put the sticks 10 minutes in the oven until light brown.
• In a soup terrine beat the pasteurized egg yolks with the cream. Stir in the stock and vegetables. Season with salt if needed. Garnish with coarsely chopped celery leaf.

☛ In the traditional recipe this soup was thickened much more.
☛ Interesting information: after the introduction of the sameness sausages, specialized butchers disappeared from the Netherlands, since they were forced to sell a mixture of different meats.

Eel soup / Palingsoep

Mrs C.J. Wannée freely referred to 'Father Cats' (famous Dutch writer): 'Often a woman has spilled, by unwise cooking / quite a good meal, and so killed the appetite!' and claimed it was better to follow a cooking course than to study numerous cookery books. That was why the Amsterdam Domestic Science School offered a five months cooking course for LADIES (haute cuisine) or MAIDS (common cuisine), and even gave private lessons, if so desired. However, just on paper her eel soup with red chilli, mace, sorrel and chervil already looks enticing.

Recipe source: C.J. Wannée Het Kookboek van de Amsterdamsche Huishoudschool, Amsterdam: H.J.W. Becht, 1910

MENU

HORS D'ŒUVRE À LA RUSSE
Irroy, cachet d'orange
goût américain

REAL TURTLE
BISQUE D'ÉCREVISSES
TURBOT D'OSTENDE POCHÉ, SAUCE MOUSSELINE
Haut Sauterne
SELLE DE VEAU GARNIE FAVORITE
St. Julien
POULARDE FROIDE À LA VENDÔME
Pontet Canet
SORBET AU CHAMPAGNE
BÉCASSINES EN CASSEROLE
Pommard
SALADE RACHEL
COMPÔTE ASSORTIE
CŒUR DE PALMIERS, SAUCE BÉARNAISE
LANGOUSTE EN BELLEVUE
Rauenthaler Berg Auslese
BOMBE SICILIENNE
Mumm, carte blanche
PÂTISSERIE
CORBEILLES DE FRUITS
DESSERT.

Le 20 Juillet 1910.   au Palace Hôtel,
Schéveningue.

1½ litre (6 cups) water
piece of red chilli
mace
salt
400 g (14 oz) thin eel
40 g (1½ oz) butter
50 g (1¾ oz) flour
50 g (1¾ oz) sorrel
50 g (1¾ oz) chervil
40 ml (¼ cup) pasteurized egg yolk (= 2 yolks)

• Bring the water, spices and salt to the boil. Clean the eel and cut the fish in pieces of 3 cm (1¼ in). Wash and cook for 5 minutes until done. Remove the fish from the cooking liquid with a slotted spoon. Strain the liquid.
• Melt the butter in the pan and lightly brown the flour. Keep stirring and gradually add the eel stock. Cook until the soup has slightly thickened. Stir in the chervil and sorrel. Beat the egg yolks in a soup terrine, and whisk in the soup. Season with salt and add the pieces of eel bones removed.

☛ A quicker version: cook 200 g (7 oz) fillets of (smoked) eel for 5 minutes in 1 litre (4 cups) of fish velouté. From the heat stir in a mixture of 20 ml (⅛ cup) egg yolk, 3 tablespoons cream and 1 tablespoon chopped chervil and sorrel.

Salmon in red wine sauce / Zalm in roodewijnsaus

'Our people should learn to eat fish!' And that is why Koba Catenius made a delicious salmon dish. Fish, and especially salmon, was plentiful! In these times it was almost possible to scoop the salmon out of the Bergse Maas, where special flat boats were used for the catch. And Koba prepared it to resemble meat: 'in a red wine sauce'. In classical French Cuisine the dish is called *saumon braisé au vin rouge*, this one *à la bourguignonne*. A dish that did not stick to the doctrine of no-red-wine-with-fish. Luckily some heresy is cherished.

Salmon was often seen on the menu in restaurants, as in Hotel Ponsen in Dordrecht on the occasion of the football match Holland-Belgium on April 2nd 1911.

Recipe source: Koba M.J. Catenius-Van der Meijden, *Vischkookboek*, Amsterdam: E.M. Querido, 1916

500 ml (2 cups) reduced fish stock

300 ml (1¼ cup) red Burgundy

10 peeled shallots

salt and pepper

4 fillets of salmon each 200 g (7 oz)

·

300 g (10½ oz) button mushrooms

8 spring onions

lump of butter

·

4 slices of white bread, buttered

2 tablespoons butter

2 tablespoons wheat flour

♟ Beaujolais Villages. Supple fruity red wine, serve cool if wanted.

• Bring the fish stock and wine to the boil with the shallots and salt and a little pepper. Place the salmon in it and bring the liquid back to the boil. Remove the pan from the heat, put a lid on and let stand for 10 minutes.

• In a pan with lid heat in the butter the cleaned mushrooms with the coarsely chopped white of the onions (save the green!).

• With a pastry cutter cut hearts from the bread. Spread on both sides with butter and fry or grill until golden.

• Place the fish in a buttered warm dish. Cook the red fish stock until reduced by half. Remove the shallots. In a small saucepan brown the butter and flour. Remove the pan from the heat and beat in the fish stock to make a smooth sauce. Heat through while whisking, then pour the sauce over the fish. Arrange the bread hearts, shallots and mushrooms around it. Decorate with the green of the spring onion.

Veal from the Dutch farmer's wife / Kalfsvlees van de Hollandse boerin

Côte de veau à la paysanne was part of a ten-course menu to be ordered for ƒ 3,75 at Hotel Duin en Daal in Bloemendaal. It was served after the turbot and before the chicken with tarragon and the braised pheasant. How did people cope with that much food? Clearly the management was not too sure either since they write in their letter of recommendation: 'simplification of meals if desired' is possible. Servants did not eat at the table, the cost of their meals was ƒ 1,00. Their food was 'equal to that of hotel personnel'. No further specifications.

600 g (1lb 5 oz) loin of veal
salt and pepper
100 g (3½ oz) butter
100 g (3½ oz) cured bacon, in strips
1 onion, diced
200 g (7 oz) green beans
150 g (5½ oz) white of leeks, in 2 inch pieces
100 ml (½ cup) reduced veal stock (jar)

• Preheat the oven to 180 °C/350 °F/Gas Mark 4. Rub salt and pepper into the loin of veal. In a casserole melt the butter and brown the meat on all sides. Add the bacon and onion at the same time. Add the cleaned green beans, cover and cook for a few minutes. Finally add the leek. Pour in the reduced stock.

• Put the covered casserole in the oven until the meat has turned rosé. The cooking time depends on the thickness and quality of the meat.

• Thinly slice the meat. Remove the vegetables and bacon from the cooking liquid, arrange these around the meat. Serve the gravy in a sauce boat and serve with floury boiled potatoes.

☛ The cooking liquid can be thickened with a little potato starch, or by whisking small lumps of cold butter in from the heat. On the farm this was considered too fancy: one ate just 'sju'.

Groeten van Hôtel Duin en Daal.

Lemon rice / Citroenrijst

In 1918 women have to make the most of their means to be able to serve their husbands pleasing dishes. One 'Dutch Housewife' succeeds exceedingly well. For example: after vegetable soup (from cubes) with rice, she serves endive salad with hot sauce and halved eggs, and finishes with *riz glacé*, for the occasion made with citric acid and lemon oil and the remark: 'very pleasant to serve with a vanilla custard'.

Recipe source: *Oorlogskookboek*, Amsterdam: J.M. Meulenhof, 1918, see also C.J. Wannée

100 g (3½ oz) long-grain rice
500 ml (2 cups) water
peel of ½ lemon (no white)
100 ml (1/2 cup) lemon juice
100 g (3½ oz) sugar

• Bring the water to the boil. Add the rice and peel of the well scrubbed lemon, cover and cook on low heat for about 30 minutes until the rice is very soft. Remove the peel.
• Stir in the juice and sugar. Spoon into glasses and cool. Before serving spoon over a thin layer of vanilla sauce or vanilla custard.

☞ Vanilla sauce: bring to the boil 200 ml (¾cup) milk with 25 ml (2 tablespoons) double cream and seeds of half a vanilla pod. Beat 30 ml (2 tablespoons) pasteurized egg yolk with 20 g (4 teaspoons) sugar and some of the hot milk. Thicken over boiling water.

☞ Modern chefs could be inclined to serve this with ice cream. Let simplicity speak for itself, though, and believe our ancestors: the big glassy rice kernels are best with vanilla sauce or a vanilla custard.

The Winter Garden in Krasnapolsky, by the architect G.B. Salm

Dessert for gentlemen / Toespijs voor heren

Aletta Jacobs, the first female doctor of the Netherlands, devoted herself to the emancipation of women. And successfully so! People got used to the idea of female fraternities partying in restaurants. According to a woman of nobility in the preface of a cookery book from 1914, however, women may have changed in the past ten years, men certainly have not. 'As ever, they expect their day of labour to be crowned with a perfectly prepared meal for themselves and their table companions.' In the chapter 'Pudding in Verse' by this noble woman we found how to do this: 'The sauce must be a wine sauce. A spoonful of Cognac will not hurt it and lemon zest makes it attractive. And the aroma, oh my dear Stance, so effective. Of course it has to truly quiver like jelly.'

Recipe source: Lady H. Dólleman-Thierry de Bye, *Heemsteé's Kookboek – Wenken voor het dagelijksch Middagmaal*, Haarlem: H.D. Tjeenk Willinck & Zoon, 1914

1854–1929 Aletta Jacobs

For a steamed pudding mould with lid of 1 litre (4 cups)

butter and breadcrumbs for the mould

125 g stale white bread, crusts removed and in wide strips
100 g (3½ oz) 'bitterkoekjes' or almond macaroons
5 eggs
75 g (2¾ oz) sugar
lemon zest
cinnamon
500 ml (2 cups) milk
100 g (3½ oz) 'boerenjongens' (raisins in brandy)

Frothy Cognac sauce:
80 ml (1/3 cup) pasteurized egg yolk (= 4 egg yolks)
120 ml (½ cup) pasteurized egg white (= 4 egg whites)
150 g (5 ½ oz) soft white sugar
pinch of grated lemon zest
300 ml (1¼ cup) white wine
100 ml (½ cup) Cognac
drop of lemon juice

Garnish:
'boerenjongens' and 'bitterkoekjes'

- Butter the mould and lid, dust with breadcrumbs. Shake out loose breadcrumbs.
- Put the bread and biscuits in separate bowls. Beat the eggs with sugar, lemon zest and cinnamon. Add the milk. Pour some over the bread and some over the biscuits. Leave to soak. Drain the raisins.
- Fill the mould with layers of bread, biscuits and raisins. Start and finish with bread. At intervals pour over the remaining egg milk.
- Over hot boiling water poach the pudding in the closed mould for 1½ hours. Let stand shortly, unmould and serve with warm Cognac sauce. Decorate with raisins and macaroons.
- For the sauce whisk the egg yolks and whites with sugar and zest until foamy. Place over hot boiling water. Add wine, Cognac and lemon juice and whisk until thickened. Serve immediately.

☛ Mrs Dólleman sticks halved raisins to the sides of the mould. We do not think that is emancipated.

☛ Of course you can save time by using small (dariole) moulds. Cover with aluminium foil and put the moulds in a roasting tray with hot water for ½ hour in the oven at 175 °C/350 °F/Gas Mark 4.

The indispensable potato

'Mashing potatoes with fat'

Whatever else may have lacked from the Dutch diet in this century –the potato seldom did. It had to be mashed on the plate unabashedly. This is how around 1910 someone from the Achterhoek (Eastern Holland) explains his diet: 'potatoes dry boiled (mashed), wet boiled (soup), and with sauce and vegetables'. And a little girl keenly says: 'If I were queen I would eat potatoes with sauce and green beans every day of the week.' (Jozien Jobse-van Putten, *Eenvoudig maar voedzaam* ('simple but nutritious'), Nijmegen: Sun, 1995).

It was no different in the cities: the potato was staple food. An Amsterdam 'labourer's wife' happily tells how she eats potatoes four days a week, mashed, every other day with a little bit of meat. Thus it was horrible to suddenly be without potatoes in Amsterdam, only because of bad management! In the summer of 1917 during the Potato Revolt, the situation got completely out of hand. Police and army acted too brutally resulting in dead and injured, especially among the women. Luckily the authorities learned from this to never again deprive the Dutch of their potatoes. In the infamous Hunger Winter of 1944–1945 countless women cycled on their bikes with wooden tires hundreds of kilometres to 'visit the farmers'. Their most wanted catch was a well filled bag of potatoes.

HOE MEN IN AMSTERDAM IN 1917 EEN PORTIE AARDAPPELEN BESTELT

Teekening voor „de Amsterdammer" van Joh. Braakensiek

Aannemen, één portie aardappelen!

products and more precisely potatoes. With those he even needs to restrain himself. He is close to the source with a friend who is a potato grower. This terrine is here to stay and has attracted a lot of attention from colleagues like Robert Kranenborg.

Made from the Donald potato, which he has been using for about four years. Light, floury with yellow coloured flesh. Donald could be Bintje's successor.

Culinary refinement

The meal known as the 'royal food' (potatoes, vegetables and meat, served separately) was to become the normal pattern of an every Dutch family. However, everybody who at the first half of the twentieth century could afford this meal, belonged to those who were going to make it. That can be called an extraordinary development: the potato went from food of the poor at the beginning of the century to the modern food of later years. Not mashed as main ingredient of a dish nor 'with naked feet' (nothing else), but as a side dish, instead of bread. But always more than one potato. How many unbelieving Dutch eyes have not stared at a French plate on which in addition to the meat only two potato wedges were to be found – and instead of vegetables to boot! A rip-off! No wonder the first campers of the 1960s always carried a sack of potatoes in the trunk of their cars. These were places of hardship they were going to visit!

Potato tasters

All those potato eating years have turned the Dutch into connoisseurs. The potato really was about the only culinary subject we could get excited about. One person wanted an 'Eigenheimer', the next a 'Bevelander' and the third the unsurpassed 'Bintje'.

Thus the recent new environmental friendly potato varieties came as a bit of a shock to the principled Dutch potato eater, but he has gotten used to them. For example: mention the word 'Opperdoezer Ronde' to culinary journalist Wim Mey, and he will immediately become ecstatic. He loves them. Nowadays the Dutch can choose from at least 44 different varieties. A challenge for the twenty-first century!

Terrine of Donald potatoes

Jonnie Boer, patron cuisinier of his by now renowned Librije in Zwolle (with two Michelin stars), loves to use Dutch

40 g (1½ oz) sheets of gelatine
1,5 kg (3 lb 5 oz) Donaldpotatoes
salt
2 cloves of garlic
250 ml (1 cup) double cream
400 g (14 oz) smoked salmon, thinly sliced
400 g (14 oz) mayonnaise
110 g (4 oz) drained apple capers
250 g (9 oz) smoked fillets of sprat

• Soak the gelatine in plenty of cold water.
• Peel the potatoes and cut into julienne strips. In salted water cook until just tender. Drain well.
• On low heat simmer the peeled garlic in the double cream.
• Line a rounded terrine mould of 48 cm (19 in) long and 6 cm (2½ in) deep first with plastic foil and then smoked salmon.
• Dissolve the well squeezed gelatine in the strained cream. Spoon the warm garlic cream and mayonnaise into the potato strips.
• Put a layer of this at the bottom of the mould. Cover with a layer of apple capers (stalks removed) and cover again with a layer of potatoes. On top of that – in the width – neatly place the smoked fillets of sprat side by side. Cover with a final layer of potatoes, in such a way that it is rounded slightly above the mould.
• Fold the overhanging smoked salmon over the filling and put it under pressure. Cool for one night.
• Serve each person 3 slices of 1 cm (slightly less than ½ in) with a bouquet of salad leaves in the middle and garlic mayonnaise on the side.

The end of lower-class cookery

Restaurant industry

The First World War resulted in a strong international feeling. The American aid to their allies resulted in an increase of interest for that large young part of the world. When after 1920 scarcity is diminishing, life in the kitchen picks up as well. The subject 'lower-class cookery' disappears from the domestic science school's timetable, leaving only the 'everyday kitchen' and 'refined kitchen', both available to everyone: the

beginning of the democratization of culinary art. However, a lot of people are still opposed to eating outside the home, which is one of the reasons why school nutrition never caught on in this country. Not only supported by the Church, for which the family is the cornerstone of society, but also by domestic science teachers. In 1928 Martine Wittop Koning, after 35 years in the profession, voices the wish 'that our schooling as a function of social work will influence the well-being of the family, economically, hygienically and ethically'.

1920 · First jazz band in Amsterdam, formed by James Meyer
1921 · Opening of the Tuschinski Theatre in Amsterdam
        International Confectioners' Fair in Amsterdam
1923 · Opening of Heck's Lunchroom in Leiden: the very first lunchroom
        in the Netherlands
1924 · Calvé starts with Arretje Nof's fairy-tale books and with beautiful
        plates, bowls and spoons
      · Opening Trade School for the Dutch Confectioners Guild
1925 · Van den Berg introduces Blueband margarine with the most
        expensive advertising campaign up to date (Blueband girl). Jurgens
        hands out a free bar of chocolate with every 150 g package of Lotus
        margarine
1926 · The Netherlands are spellbound by Josephine Baker. She performs
        at Cinema Palace in the Kalverstraat, Amsterdam. Jazz bands pop
        up everywhere and people dance the Charleston. The leg is shown,
        that is in the city
      · Highlight of the year: performance of Paul Whiteman 'the King of
        Jazz' at the Kurhaus
      · Introduction of Gershwin's 'Rhapsody in Blue' (1923)
      · Exhibition of Horecaf, forerunner of the Horecava, in the RAI in
        Amsterdam: no alcoholic beverages, only corked and capped sam-
        ple bottles for the customers
      · Cook booklets for Calvé by Martine Wittop Koning
1927 · Foundation of KEMA in Arnhem
      · Return flight to the Dutch East Indies by KLM-plane 'The homing
        pigeon'
1928 · Olympic Games in Amsterdam
1929 · First Horecaf vocational school at the Gevers Deynootweg at
        Scheveningen

Domestic science teachers stressed moderation, cleanliness, frugality and a homely atmosphere. And the brand new advertisers gladly took this up in their slogans, such as 'Let Blueband help you, and your family will be amazed by your cooking'. This did not go over well in rural areas where people distrusted margarine, calling it 'cart grease'. The difference with the city was still considerable. Farming people from Groningen stuck to their 'concrete' (mash of potatoes and brown beans), while 'stadjers' (city folk) pampered themselves in for example restaurant Riche, taken over by headwaiter Kramer in 1920. It flourished because he catered for private parties. Houses became smaller, the number of servants diminished and the number of cars increased.

A nice anecdote: in 1920 Kramer catered for a royal party at the home of the Provincial Commissioner of the Queen in honour of the opening of the Electra Pumping Station. His extensive menu suggestions proved without avail. Queen Wilhelmina was a moderate eater. When the party was over a farmer from Groningen said in dialect: 'Kramer, could I have another meal, please.' However, even a city the size of Amsterdam still remained something of a village. One could hear the sound of an alarm clock. Sweets could be bought for one or half a cent from a 'sweets table'. One day someone had gotten drunk at café De Vriendschap (corner Nieuwmarkt and Dijkstraat). Manager Pooters put the man to bed in his own home, gave him herring to eat and let him regain himself since he could not come home drunk.

In those days, besides caterers there were still many confectioners who, just as in the previous century, prepared meals in customers' homes. Each chef started his training as a confectioner, and even to this day master chefs such as Leon Ribbens and famous catering firms such as Maison de Boer stress this background. In 1929 super chef Philip van der Stijl started the City Kitchen in Groningen. Here people could buy a subscription for a warm meal brought to the home (ƒ 9,90 for 10 meals). An early forerunner of meals-on-wheels!

Culinary squabbles

After the end of 'lower-class cookery' the culinary art continues on its democratic way. By way of cookery book introductions 'the people' are now included in various subject matters. Mrs Goldenberg of the 'Vocational School for Girls' in The Hague complains how hard it proved to come up with proper 'Dutch' names for her recipes, but stresses she only includes six, at most eight, course menus instead of ten to twelve. The publisher of *Groot Kookboek* derogatively talks about a vocational teacher who did not find it necessary to include luxurious dishes, since they were not suitable for cookery schools. The author also condemns the fact that others are far too much taken by the delusion of the day: 'the modern French kitchen'. Let's after all not forget the elderly with a completely different taste. The attention for the Jewish kitchen is very sympathetic, and is explained by the argument that everybody likes their fabulous cakes, so why not the other dishes as well? In her preface to the seventh edition of *De Vegetarische Keuken* Mrs Valk-Heijnsdijk (vegetarian hotel-restaurant Pomona, The Hague) answers questions of guests. Yes, of course she is opposed to the food industry. People find a fireless kitchen objectionable? Had not a French professor proven dogs died of cooked meat? Mrs Valk holds that raw is the very best, but realizes all those centuries of cooking have estranged man from his true nature.

Cold trout with tartar sauce / Koude forel met tartaarsaus

(Petites truites froides à la hollandaise, sauce tartare)

Obviously a speciality of *Huize Zomerdijk Bussink* (confectioners) served in the Vondelpark pavilion. Not only on the menu for the 'Pioneers on the matter of Electricity' during the Edison Light week in 1929, but in the same year also at a luncheon for the mayor of London when he and his 'sheriffs' visited the mayor of Amsterdam.

Recipe source: menu Confectioners Museum 'Het Warme Land' in Hattem; advisor: Hans Foks, retired chef of the Royal Household; sauce tartare: Escoffier

Cold trout

4 trout, each 250 g (8 oz)

salt

1 bottle of Rhine wine

4 slices of lemon

buttered parchment paper

green of dill

strips of tomato

·

2 egg whites

10 sheets of gelatine (20 g)

lamb's lettuce

Tartar sauce

tablespoon pasteurized egg yolk

(about ½ egg yolk)

1 tablespoon mayonnaise

1 tablespoon vinegar

5 hard-boiled eggs, pushed through a sieve

150 ml (⅔ cup) olive oil

1 tablespoon finely chopped chives

cayenne pepper, salt

Bergerac Blanc. Fruity fresh dry white wine from the Dordogne.

• Wash the trout, place side by side in a wide shallow flame-proof dish and sprinkle with salt. Pour on the wine and top with slices of a scrubbed lemon, pips removed. Cover with buttered parchment paper and keep to the boil for 15 minutes. Cool to room temperature, strip and carefully remove the bones. Do this by cutting the meat from head to tail along the back bone. Take the fillets from the bone, remove the bones and put the fillets back together again. Place the fish on a shallow serving plate or on individual plates. Garnish with a beautiful feather of dill and artistically carved leaves of tomato. Garnish with a collar around head and tail made of finely chopped egg white (left over from tartar sauce see below).

• Slowly bring to the boil the trout's cooking liquid (without the lemon) and 2 egg whites, whisking until the egg white coagulates. Leave for 10 minutes at a warm place. Strain the poaching liquid through a wet, squeezed piece of cloth.

Season 5 dl (2 cups) with salt. Dissolve the soaked and well squeezed gelatine and leave to cool. Spoon the nearly jellied aspic over the fish and leave to set. Decorate with lamb's lettuce. Serve the tartar sauce separately.

• Put the egg yolk, mayonnaise and vinegar in a sauce boat. First whisk in the boiled, sieved yolks and then the olive oil in a thin stream. Season with salt and pepper.

🐟 Everywhere it's aspic time! It could be called modern. In the garnish, the firm Zomerdijk Bussink varied from the recipe, though. *Het Kook- en Huishoudboek* orders green butter: 2 heads of lettuce, a bunch of chervil, tarragon, a handful of sorrel and a handful of spinach are blanched, squeezed, ground and mixed with 250 g (9 oz) of butter, which is piped 'gracefully' onto the fish. And that was the proper way according to Mr Foks.

Chaudfroid of fowl with French salad / Chaudfroid van gevogelte met Fransche salade

So far everybody cosily ate together at one long table (*table d'hôte*). That custom completely disappears after 1920. From then there are the separate tables we still know: the *table à part*. The beginning of the individual modern person. However, it did not spoil the collective fun at Scheveningen. Eyewitnesses recall their parents dancing on the Pier on Sunday afternoons. Also at separate tables the food of the Kurhaus was excellent, considering the menus we came upon, as for example the *buffet froid* from 1925.

Recipe source: C. Goldenberg, M.B. van Doorne-Struwe, *Recepten voor de Fijne Keuken der 's-Gravenhaagsche Vakschool voor Meisjes*, Zutphen: W.J. Thieme & Cie, 1925

A chaudfroid was often made with poached chicken, duck, pigeon and partridge (*chaudfroid de volaille*). They were skinned, boned and cut into equally sized pieces. In those days the Kurhaus used duck, the vocational training school for girls settled on chicken, just like every other domestic science school. The *Haagse Kookboek* still does it to this day.
With white meat a white sauce is in place, with dark meat a brown sauce. We have chosen the easy way out and used chicken breasts, since they are easily turned into portions.

Chaudfroid of fowl

Fowl:
250 ml (1 cup) water
100 ml (½ cup) white wine
bouquet of herbs: leek, parsley and bay leaf
salt
about 400 g (14 oz) chicken or duck breasts
(1 tin of goose liver pâté)

Aspic:
7-10 sheets of gelatine (14-20 g)
400 ml (1⅓ cup) reduced fowl stock (jar)
good pinch of salt

Sauce:
30 g (1 oz) butter
40 g (1½ oz) flour
300 ml (1¼ cup) strained poaching liquid
50 ml (¼ cup) cream
100 ml (½ cup) aspic
1-2 tablespoons pasteurized egg yolk (about 1 egg yolk)

Garnish:
Cooked carrot slices, truffle, garden herbs, tomato, parsley

Children playing on the beach at the Kurhaus at Scheveningen

- Bring water, wine, herbs and salt to the boil. Poach (just below boiling point) the meat with the lid on the pan. This will take about 10 minutes. Remove the skin if necessary and carve the meat into 1 cm (½ in) thick slices. If wanted, when cooled, spread with goose liver pâté.
- Soak the gelatine in cold water. Bring 300 ml (1¼ cup) of reduced stock to the boil. From the heat, dissolve the squeezed gelatine. Stir into the rest of the reduced stock. Season generously with salt and cool.
- Melt the butter in a small saucepan (for duck: brown the butter), add the flour and stir until blended. Whisking rapidly, gradually pour in the strained poaching liquid, cream and aspic. Finally, from the heat, add the egg yolk beaten with a little hot sauce. Pour through a sieve.
- Place the pieces of meat on a wire rack. Cover with the almost cool sauce. Decorate with parsley, carrot, truffle, herbs or tomato. Coat with a layer of semi-jellied aspic. Serve at room temperature.

French salad

- Combine peeled and blanched celery, a few boiled potatoes in strips, small rosettes of blanched cauliflower and strips of blanched carrot, diced pickled gherkin (50 gram / 1¾ oz of each) with finely chopped parsley. Spoon in a sauce made of a generous amount of coarse mustard, salt and pepper, oil, vinegar and soy sauce. Marinate for 2 hours. Garnish with hard-boiled eggs, truffles and aspic.

☛ In those days chaudfroids preferably were served on a pedestal of aspic, rice or even semolina, cooked in water. This offered a better view. Sometimes too it was placed 'against a piece of fruited bread' and garnished with eggs, diced aspic and white mushrooms. We suggest a salad from the Vocational School for Girls.

Carrot soup / Wortelsoep

(Potage grécy)

A soup just as gladly made at the vocational school for girls in The Hague as by vegetarians. The last naturally without beef stock. Instead they used soy sauce and marmite. Surprisingly, the girls are advised to use lots of parsley, whereas *De Vegetarische Keuken* uses it sparsely. Mrs Valk explains: 'Too many herbs, however innocent, such as parsley, chervil, and all alliums, can overpower the natural taste and strongly influence the secretion organs.'

Recipe source: C. Goldenberg, M.B. van Doorne-Struwe, *Recepten voor de Fijne Keuken der 's-Gravenhaagsche Vakschool voor Meisjes*, Zutphen: W.J. Thieme & Cie, 1925, en E.M. Valk-Heijnsdijk, *De Vegetarische Keuken*, seventh revised edition, Rotterdam: Nijgh en Van Ditmar's Uitgeversmij, 1928

250 g (9 oz) carrots, scraped
150 g (7 oz) potatoes, peeled
50 g (1¾ oz) white of leek
1 litre (4 cups) water

salt and pepper
1 tablespoon lemon juice
2 tablespoons double cream
parsley
cubes 'of stale white bread'

- Cook the chopped carrot, potato and leek in the water with a little salt and pepper until very soft.
- Sieve the soup, mash the vegetables, stir the purée into the vegetable broth and season well with salt and pepper (or if you like soy sauce, marmite and salt, no pepper!). Keep hot without boiling. Just before serving stir in lemon juice and cream, and sprinkle generously or sparingly with parsley.
- Our two sources agree about the bread cubes: either fry or grill them.

☛ Nice vegetarian touch: add some roasted hazelnuts.

Clear broth with puffs / Heldere bouillon met soesjes

(Consommé à la Santos Dumont)

In restaurants clear broth is winning from turtle soup. And preferably *en tasse*, in a cup, a novelty the Kurhaus and Krasnapolsky were first to present. This recipe for a strong broth by chef Kooper is not easily found anywhere else: the American in Hotel Amsterdam was to be recommended for such an original chef de cuisine! The cookery book to which he contributed, marks his recipes with a K. And they certainly do not need the advice from the introduction: 'Weak soups and stocks can be righted by adding a few drops of Maggi aroma (always after preparation), an aromatic vegetable extract.' So that's why you find a bottle of Maggi on so many Dutch tables.

Recipe source: H.A. Kooper, *Groot kookboek*, Amsterdam: Vennootschap Letteren en Kunst, 1920

Clear broth

400 g (14 oz) chicken, from the
bone and diced
200 g (7 oz) veal shank
1 head of lettuce
1 large carrot
1 celery stalk
chervil

•

1 unpeeled onion, 1 clove stuck in
6 black peppercorns
2 teaspoons salt
1 litre (4 cups) water

•

carrot slices
2 teaspoons arrowroot or potato
starch
4 tablespoons cooked rice
(truffle and) chervil, as garnish

Puffs (profiteroles)

50 g (1¾ oz) butter
125 ml (½ cup) water
¼ teaspoon salt
75 g (2¾ oz) wheat flour
2 eggs
25 g (1 oz) strong matured cheese,
grated
parchment paper

• Place the meat and bones in a pan with the washed and chopped vegetables. Cover with cold water and bring to the boil while stirring. Add the onion, salt and pepper and simmer for 2 hours. Strain the stock through a wet and squeezed cloth.

• Reheat the stock, in it cook flower-shaped cut out carrot slices until tender, and thicken lightly with a thin paste of arrowroot or potato starch (Kooper used sago) and water. Do not let it boil! Add the small pieces of meat, rice and chopped chervil and maybe a few slices of truffle. Serve in cups with the puffs separately.

• On low heat cook the butter and water in a small saucepan. As soon as the mixture boils lower the heat and add all flour at once. Beat until mixture pulls away from the sides of the pan. Place the dough in a bowl, beat in the eggs, one at a time, until the dough is shiny. Use an electric mixer with the dough-hooks. Stir in the cheese. Line a baking tray with parchment paper, pipe on the dough no bigger than peas. Bake for 5-10 minutes at 225 °C/425 °F/Gas Mark 7.

Stuffed tomatoes / Gevulde tomaten

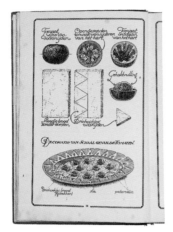

1929 From the AVRO-cookery book

In the 1920s the public radio stations VARA, KRO and VPRO were founded, but the AVRO already had been presenting a culinary pro- gramme for quite a while. Namely by 'microphone-cook' Kers whose AVRO-cookery book, published in 1929, contained recipes such as Eavesdroppers' pudding and AVRO-oranges. We settled on a modern recipe with tomatoes, which came with a splendid working plan. People had been familiar with tomatoes for quite a while, but now whole books were dedicated to them, such as the one by Willy Cornelissen- Schep, *Honderd Amerikaanse Tomatengerechten* (1920). Not only the American Josephine Baker is popular, other aspects of the American culture were discovered as well.

Recipe source: P.J. Kers jr., *AVRO-Kookboek* (part 2), Amsterdam: Algemene Vereeniging 'Radio Omroep', 1929

8 medium sized firm tomatoes (each 120 g / 4 oz)
350 g (12 oz) minced veal
1 egg yolk
2 tablespoons breadcrumbs
salt and generous amount of pepper
100 ml (½ cup) stock or water
breadcrumbs
8 lumps of butter

·

8 slices of white bread, crust removed
butter

·

green salad leaves
parsley

• Preheat the oven to 175 °C/350 °F/Gas Mark 4. Cut the top of each tomato (stalk side under). Scoop out flesh and seeds. Sprinkle the inside with salt and pepper. Combine the minced veal with the egg yolk, breadcrumbs, salt and pep- per. Form into 8 small balls, place in the tomatoes, sprinkle with breadcrumbs and top with a lump of butter.

• Butter a fitting oven-proof dish, add the stock with chopped tomato tops and stuffed tomatoes. Bake for 20 minutes in the preheated oven. Arrange the tomatoes on a plate and arrange a few salad leaves around them.

• In the meantime cut the bread into small triangles. Brown these on both sides in butter and use for decoration.

Mushroom croquettes / Champignoncroquetten

Mrs Valk considers these little dishes 'excellently suited for the conversion to vegetarianism. For those who had gotten used to nerve titillating meat dishes it obviously is a great step into the right direction to have entrées, hors d'oeuvres of meat and fish replaced by dishes with eggs or grains and legumes.' Compared to the mushroom dishes on the menus of those days, her recipe definitely was innovative.

Recipe source: E.M. Valk-Heijnsdijk, De Vegetarische Keuken, seventh revised edition, Rotterdam: Nijgh en Van Ditmar's Uitgeversmij, 1928

100 g (3½ oz) long-grain rice
200 ml (¾ cup) water
400 g (14 oz) button mushrooms
1 beefsteak tomato, peeled
150 ml (⅔ cup) water
1-2 teaspoons soy sauce
1 tablespoon finely chopped parsley
a little marmite
salt

·

30 g (1 oz) butter
1 small onion, chopped
40 g (1½ oz) wheat flour

·

breadcrumbs
3-4 eggs
oil for deep-frying

·

heart of endive
parsley

• Cook the rice in the water until tender (25 minutes, covered). Wash and slice the mushrooms. Cook mushrooms and diced tomato in 150 ml (⅔ cup) water until soft. Pour the cooking liquid in a measuring jug and, if necessary, fill up with water to 300 ml (1¼ cup). Stir in the parsley and marmite.

• In a saucepan melt the butter, lightly brown the onion, add the flour and brown as well. Gradually stir in the mushroom liquid, keep stirring for a thickened and smooth sauce. Heat through with the cooked rice and well drained mushrooms. Season if necessary. Cool.

• Shape the cooled sauce into croquettes. Roll croquettes in breadcrumbs, beaten egg and breadcrumbs again. Deep-fry in oil of 190 °C/350 °F.

• Serve on a salad made of finely chopped heart of endive dressed with oil, lemon juice, salt and a pinch of sugar. Decorate with sprigs of deep-fried parsley. On the side a spoonful of vinaigrette with parsley, if wanted.

☛ These croquettes, nut shaped, are also nice to serve with pre-dinner drinks.

☛ The croquettes can be frozen.

Saddle of lamb with Burgundy / Lamszadel met bourgogne

(Selle d'agneau au vin de Pommard, petits pois – tomates – céleris)

This is one of the dishes served at a dinner presented by the organizing committee to the International Federations of field hockey and football in honour of the IXth Olympic Games. A beautiful dinner, even though it had to be cheap, since the Dutch government, under pressure from the religious parties, had refused subsidy. Therefore no Olympic city either. The athletes had to sleep on boats, in schools and in hotels. No room at all for spectators. That is the reason why flyers were distributed house-to-house so even the smallest bedroom would be made available.

Saddle of lamb was popular in the well-off circles of those days, where then as now field hockey was popular. The ladies from The Hague offer more than 7 recipes.

Recipe source: C. Goldenberg, M.B. van Doorne-Struwe, *Recepten voor de Fijne Keuken der 's-Gravenhaagse Vakschool voor Meisjes*, Zutphen: W.J. Thieme & Cie, 1925, and menu Confectioners Museum '*Het Warme Land*' in Hattem

---

1 kg (2 lb 3 oz) saddle of lamb
salt and pepper
1 teaspoon rosemary leaves
175 g (6 oz) butter
10 shallots
30 g (1 oz) white of leek
100 g (3½ oz) celeriac
40 g (1½ oz) carrot
2 cloves of garlic

•

1 head of celery
100 g (3 oz) peas (frozen)
4 tomatoes
200 ml (¾ cup) red Burgundy
100 ml (½ cup) reduced veal stock (jar)

1928 The ninth Olympic Games are being held in Amsterdam

🍷 Moulin à Vent.
Fruity red 'cru' from
Beaujolais.

• Preheat the oven to 200 °C/400 °F/Gas Mark 6. Rub the saddle with salt, pepper and rosemary. Melt 100 g (4 oz) butter in a roasting tray. Brown the meat on all sides. In the meantime finely chop the shallot, leek, celeriac, carrot and garlic. Turn the saddle bones over, cook the vegetables without colouring. Roast the meat for 30 minutes in the preheated oven. Frequently baste with cooking liquid.

• In the meantime blanch the celery cut into 1½ x 15 cm (1 x 6 in) strips, defrost the peas. Crosswise slit the tomatoes, very shortly plunge into hot deep-frying oil (or longer in boiling water) and open the skin.

• Remove the roasted saddle of lamb from the tray, leave in a warm place. Drain the cooking liquid, return the vegetables to the roasting tray. Pour in the wine and reduced stock. Cook until reduced by half and loosen the bits from the bot-

tom. Mash the vegetables and pour the sauce through a sieve into a small saucepan. From the heat stir in 50 g (1¾ oz) cold butter.

• Melt the remaining 25 g (1 oz) butter in a pan, sauté the celery and cook for a few minutes with a lid on the pan. Season with salt and pepper. Place the meat on an attractive serving plate, arrange the vegetables around it and spoon over a little of the sauce. Serve the rest of the sauce separately. Saddle of lamb needs to be carved at the table.

☞ Other garnishes: fried baby potatoes with onion rings. Naturally, this recipe can also be made with other cuts of lamb. These will have different cooking times.

☞ The original recipe mentions that an 'older animal' should be rubbed with salt and pepper and marinated for 24 hours.

Rolled sole fillets with American sauce / Tongrolletjes met Amerikaanse saus

Everybody, regardless of being a guest at Krasnapolsky, Des Indes or the Kurhaus, seems to want turbot. Even the Dutch Reformed Community of Groningen celebrates its 75th anniversary with turbot. However, a royal menu from 1929 mentions: 'salmon trout with ketchup sauce', and we found a very contemporary dish with sole on a festive menu of July 23rd 1927 in honour of the KLM flight with De Postduif ('The Homing Pigeon'), 'Holland-Indië' return by Lieutenant Koppen: *Tonnelets de soles à la Américaine* (with lobster sauce). Followed among others by braised chicken with *Compote Montreal*. Everything American was the best, even in France, where booklets were written about the American kitchen with addresses for ingredients in Paris.

Recipe source: menu from the collection of the Dutch Confectioners Guild, kept in the library of the Confectioners Museum 'Het Warme Land' in Hattem, and H.A. Kooper, *Groot kookboek*, Amsterdam: Vennootschap Letteren en Kunst, 1920

8 fillets of sole
1 tablespoon lemon juice
salt and pepper
35 g (1¼ oz) butter
100 ml (½ cup) white wine
100 ml (½ cup) reduced fish stock (jar)
100 ml (½ cup) double cream
50 g (1¾ oz) lobster butter
2 tablespoons chopped parsley

1927 First continental charter flight to Jakarta

1 kg (2 lb 3 oz) mealy potatoes
250 ml (1 cup) milk
nutmeg, salt
25 g (1 oz) butter

• Flatten the fillets of sole lightly, sprinkle with lemon juice, salt and pepper. Tightly roll the fillets, skin side in. Place the rolls side by side in a well buttered pan, loose ends down. Pour over the wine and reduced stock and put the pan on the heat. Bring the liquid to the boil and keep it 10 minutes to the boil to poach the rolls. Remove the fish rolls from the pan and keep them warm.
• Cook the cooking liquid until reduced to 3 tablespoons.

Add the cream and heat through. Pour the sauce through a fine sieve. From the heat whisk in the small cubes of lobster butter. Season with salt, if necessary.
• In the meantime cook the potatoes for approximately 25 minutes until soft. Peel and put them through a potato press. Bring the milk to the boil and stir it into the mashed potatoes. Whisk the mashed potatoes at least 5 minutes then add the butter. Pipe a ring of mashed potatoes on an oven-proof plate. Brown in an oven of 250 °C/475 °F/Gas Mark 9. Place the sole in the middle and spoon a little of the sauce over it. Sprinkle with chopped parsley.

☛ A cheaper alternative for sole is lemon sole. However, the rolls easily fall apart after poaching.

Fruit salad / Vruchtensla

The Young Workmen's Federation buys the *Paasheuvel* ('Easter Hill') on the Veluwe hills
(*f* 800,00) for camping activities during which labourers' children are to be educated in
public spirit. A lot of vegetarians spring from the same youth movement, all tuned in to
the new insights of Bircher-Benner's *Fruits and raw vegetables*, which was published in
the Netherlands in 1929. The first camping cookery books spread the meatless message
cheerfully by presenting alongside each meat dish a vegetarian alternative. The following
fruit salad was completely new.

Recipe source: J.H. Bouman, J.V.D Spieghel, *Kookboekje voor kampeerders*, Amsterdam: L.J. Veen's Uitgeversmij N.V., 1929

1 banana
2 oranges
2 apples
50 g (1¾ oz) sugar
1 tablespoon lemon juice

• Dice the fruit and combine with the sugar and juice. Let
stand about one hour.

☛ A camping version we can embellish on, since nowadays we
have a wider choice. One can sprinkle it with roasted shaved
almonds or serve it with ice cream or whipped cream. But
keep it raw! To speak with Mrs Van Deventer, author of
Honderd Vruchtenrecepten (1923): 'Nothing is as good as the
juicy, flavourful, fresh fruit, stewed in sun rays.'

Aunt Heintje's pudding /
Pudding van tante Heintje

In the 1920s many girls still had to fill a notebook with recipes, dictated by their mothers at the kitchen table. Often these have been illustrated in the margin by the little ladies with drawings and sighs of obvious boredom. Our copy is from a novelist, who all the same used hers all of her life and who in her family was famous for the desserts she made from this notebook.

Recipe source: Anna M. Ringnalda, *Kookschrift*, started October 17th 1923

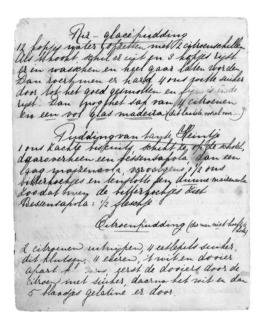

For 4 shallow bowls of 200 ml (¾ cup) each or one large crystal bowl

8 sponge fingers
2 tablespoons Brandy
4 almond macaroons ('bitterkoekjes'), cut in four
2 tablespoons Brandy

2 dessertspoons arrowroot or potato starch
300 ml (1¼ cup) blackberry juice
4 tablespoons sugar
4 dessertspoons Brandy

3½ sheets of gelatine (7 g)
300 ml (1¼ cup) vanilla custard or vanilla sauce
100 ml 'advocaat' (Dutch eggnog)

- Place the sponge fingers side by side in the bowl(s), drizzle with Brandy. The macaroons too are drizzled with Brandy, but in a soup plate.
- Stir a smooth paste of arrowroot and 4 tablespoons of berry juice. Bring the remaining juice and sugar to the boil. From the heat stir in the paste. Once again bring to the boil. From the heat whisk in the Brandy. Spoon the warm sauce over the sponge fingers and cool.
- Soak the gelatine in plenty of cold water. In a small saucepan bring 50 ml (¼ cup) of the vanilla sauce to the boil while stir-

ring. From the heat dissolve the well squeezed gelatine. Stir in the remaining sauce and 'advocaat'. Keep 8 tablespoons separate, pour the rest of the sauce over the cooled berry sauce (start on the outside). If necessary drain the almond macaroons on a piece of paper towel. Arrange on top of the vanilla sauce and cover with the reserved vanilla sauce. Cool in the fridge. Serve at room temperature.

☞ A nice contemporary decoration is made with red currants and a rosette of whipped cream and some leaves of mint.

♀ Muscat de Rivesaltes. Fortified
white (dessert) wine from the
South of France.

☞ The above mentioned version with vanilla sauce and
'advocaat' is our suggestion. In the written recipe cornflour
is used. However, the girl who filled the notebook with recipes (later to be Annie de Moor-Ringnalda) explained
her mother often used custard powder, which was introduced in 1900 and became very popular in the 1920s. One
litre milk (4 cups) was the minimum used, since pudding
servings were larger then. This is how it went:

1 litre (4 cups) milk
80 g (2¾ oz) custard powder
75 g (2¾ oz) sugar

·

50 ml (¼ cup) milk to dilute the pudding

• Blend a paste of the custard powder and some milk. Bring
the remaining milk to the boil, stir in the paste and cook
the pudding while stirring until thickened (3 minutes).
• Keep ¼ litre (1 cup) separate. While still warm stir in some
cold milk and pour over the pudding so that the almond
macaroons show through.

1930–1939
'Cook economically and buy economically'

Restaurant industry

Pessimism all around! Europe is afflicted by economical crisis and political chaos. The Dutch restaurant industry grapples with recession and the 'German throttle law'. The German tourists stay away because of heavy taxes and, much worse since the guilder is expensive, a lot of Dutch people cheaply travel to Germany.

When at the end of the 1930s it became clear which way our neighbours in the East were heading, others refused to drink German wines any longer. The Kempinski wholesale company

took advantage of this and came with good, rather inexpensive Hungarian Riesling. This aversion is easy to understand when one reads how in 1938 the German Consul writes in his rapport to Berlin that German sportsmen and conference attendees continue to stay at the Amsterdam Carlton, although the hotel refused to hoist the German flag and had Jewish owners. You are reading correctly: the war had not even started yet. In 1935 meal prices go up by a quarter because of sales tax, and we see on the menu of Willems in Groningen the charge of ƒ 1,50 for vegetable soup, stewed beef, red cabbage, pastry or fruit. The addition of fillet of sole and cheese with crystallized ginger came to ƒ 2,00, and those who could afford to pay ƒ 3,00 were served fillet of sole with shrimp sauce, and to follow the beef: lobster with mayonnaise and a salad. The Christmas menu in the Doelen in Groningen: ƒ 4,00 for 9 courses. Not bad, really! We have to realize, though, that for many people during the depression of the 1930s even these prices were so high to be unobtainable. In restaurants however, they do their best to be cheerful and jocular on the menu. For the Dutch reserve officers at the Jaarbeurs restaurant in Utrecht:

1930 · Unilever becomes a multinational at the stroke of a pen
1931 · National Crisis Committee installed because of desperate economy
1932 · Founding of Dutch Women Electricity Society
1934 · First issue of woman's weekly *Libelle*
    · The *Uiver* is back home again: 2nd place in the air race London-Melbourne. Crew: Parmentier, Prins, Van Bruggen, Moll
1935 · National Park *Hoge Veluwe* opens. The Hague's City Museum opens. Museum Boymans van Beuningen (Rotterdam) gets a new building
1936 · Wim Kan and Corrie Vonk start the ABC-cabaret
    · Godfried Bomans's first novel *Pieter Bas* is published
    · Snip and Snap replace sick Louis Davids, who still is the key figure of Dutch theatre. He was leader of the Kurhaus Cabaret and discovered as such the talented Wim Sonneveld, who also became his secretary
1937 · Princess Juliana marries Bernhard von Lippe Biesterfeld
    · Founding of Governmental Office for Preparation of Food Supply in Wartime. The lesson of 1914–1918 was not forgotten, but it seemed impossible to imagine worse
    · Opening of first *Broodje van Kootje* sandwich bar in Amsterdam
    · The Netherlands World Jamboree was organized very well Baden Powell himself attended for the last time
1938 · Retailer's Certificate introduced
    · School milk on all schools (surplus of milk)
    · First issue of woman's weekly *Margriet*
    · Princess Beatrix is born
    · First modern, built-in kitchen by Bruynzeel
1939 · Princess Irene is born

1934 The Uiver is welcomed

1934 (left) *Libelle* issue 1, volume number 1

1938 (right) *Margriet* issue 1, volume number 1

'Governor soup with rifle fat' and 'Reservist pudding'. And for the Zuyder Zee labourers at the Weapon of Medemblik the soup is called 'Drill milk diluted with cement water' and the after-dinner cup of coffee comes with 'a pussycat (the hangover will come tomorrow)', the Dutch word for 'hangover' being 'tomcat'

Food at home

Dull food, mended clothes and boredom. An Amsterdam family of nine with father on the dole had to survive on ƒ 16,00 a month, in July 1934. 'Meat was served once a month (to father), a hot meal twice a week: potatoes with 'clamour sauce'. Sugar in coffee: seldom. Milk only for tea. The last eggs were eaten at Easter'. The government took ƒ 1,50 off the monthly allowance. There were 7 dead in the Jordaan Revolt, to no avail.
However, those who were not unemployed still could spend. In 1935 Marion Bekker advises to 'Cook something else for a change!' 'The husband of a solid Dutch housewife will get lost one day in some restaurant with a foreign name, where foreign chefs or mysterious little Chinese men stand behind cookers and where expensive chicken swims in aromatic sauces, fish is served in mud coloured soup and the ever pure floury Dutch potato looses her appearance in everything non-pure and floury.' Apparently Marion was afraid her husband had roving eyes. To keep him home she pleads against 'the Monday cus-

tomary soup, fresh Monday vegetables with potatoes and everyday meat, and a dessert of boredom pudding' (Marion Bekker, *Kook eens iets anders!*, Rotterdam: Nijgh en Van Ditmar N.V., 1935).
In the 1930s weeklies especially for women start to appear, such as *Libelle* en *Moeder* ('Mother'). These too are full with to us rather moralistic advice on sensible nutrition and economic housekeeping. The times asked for it.

Table talk

Mellie Dinger-Uyldert, teacher of modern food preparation and manager of the Hotel Pomona in Rotterdam, wants to help the worrying housewife to 'escape her misery'. She writes in her *Handleiding voor de Moderne Keuken* (1934) how cookery books often are a letdown. Most often the modern nutrition written up by a man is correct, but recipes have not been adapted, most probably since they are collected by women, 'who are hard to pry loose from the old-fashioned way of cooking'. She believes in the modern way: meat does not serve any purpose. From the preface: 'On a diet of raw fruits and vegetables flabby fat girls, who cannot seem to focus, may change into nice lively quick teenagers, while grumpy gentlemen change into friendly uncles.'
About laying the table: 'White is the colour of holiness, cleanliness. That is why tablecloths have always been white. Only in times like ours, in which the intuitive insight has all but disappeared, we see the coloured tablecloths appear (which will not show stains as much!), just like coloured underwear and sheets.' What the last had to do with laying the table? This is the opinion the ladies De Boer and Burger voice to the contrary in their *Tafeltje dek je* (1937): 'Table linens are available in white and colour. Coloured table linens create a cheerful atmosphere, while white ones still are the most beautiful and elegant.' Nothing much changes in a century...

Jellied cured side of pork / Casselerrib in gelei

(met salade de légume, sauce remoulade)

Many chroniclers of these times report extremely dull food. That, of course, is a lopsided exaggeration. For example: this dish appeared on the menu on Wednesday May 10th 1939 at The American Lunchroom, a famous café in the Lange Viestraat 18 in Utrecht. Served with potato salad or French fries for 70 cents... A real treat outside the home, for which cookery books of the 1930s offer mostly a hot version.

Recipe source: card in the menu collection of the Dutch Confectioners Guild, Confectioners Museum 'Het Warme Land' in Hattem; Alice Feijn-Van Smaeck, *Mevrouw kookt*, 's-Gravenhage: H.P. Leopolds Uitgevers-Mij N.V., 1935; A housewife, *Het Coöperatieve Kookboek*, Rotterdam: HAKA; 8th edition Wannée, 1938

12 g (½ oz) sheets of gelatine
400 ml (1 1/3 cup) reduced veal stock (jar)
good pinch of salt
pinch of burned sugar
4 tablespoons Cognac

*

300 g (10½ oz) cured side of pork (cold cuts)
100 g (3½ oz) cooked flageolets, rinsed
200 g (7 oz) haricots verts
4 tablespoons pickled carrot (jar)
mixed salad leaves

Sauce rémoulade

250 ml (1 cup) mayonnaise
1 tablespoon Dijon mustard
1 tablespoon chopped gherkins
½ tablespoon chopped capers, drained
parsley, tarragon, chervil, burnet,
shallot, very finely chopped,
together 1 tablespoon

• Soak the gelatine in cold water. Bring 100 ml (½ cup) of the reduced stock to the boil with a good pinch of salt (gelatine neutralizes flavours) and a little burned sugar for a golden brown colour. From the heat dissolve the well squeezed gelatine. Add the remaining reduced stock with the Cognac and cool until it starts to set.
• Slice the meat and beans into thin strips and together with the flageolets and carrots spoon into the thickening jelly. Divide over 4 fitting moulds. Leave to set in the fridge. Unmould on individual plates and decorate with colourful mixed salad leaves. Serve with sauce rémoulade.
• For the sauce rémoulade combine all ingredients.

☞ Actually, the correct spelling is Kasselerrib: from Kassel. Source: *Het Coöperatieve Kookboek*.

Eggs from Het Loo / Eieren van Het Loo

A much favoured dish at the royal table. Royal in its simplicity. And without doubt of French origin – Larousse still offers this recipe for poached eggs: *oeufs à la Béarnaise* – but Wilhelmina liked to keep it national and simple. Since tarragon flourished in the excellent kitchen garden of Soestdijk Palace, her summer residence, that was not too difficult. And when the need for it struck in early springtime a member of the royal staff would go and fetch it from palace Het Loo.

Recipe source: card in the menu collection of the Dutch Confectioners Guild, library Confectioners Museum 'Het Warme Land' in Hattem, based on *Larousse Gastronomique*

250 g (9 oz) peeled potatoes, not mealy
1 tablespoon milk
nutmeg, salt and pepper
½ teaspoon butter

4 soft boiled eggs
tarragon leaves

Tarragon sauce (sauce Béarnaise)
50 ml (¼ cup) white wine
1 tablespoon tarragon vinegar
1 tablespoon chopped shallots
½ tablespoon chopped tarragon
salt and pepper
100 ml (½ cup) pasteurized egg yolk (= 5 egg yolks)
125 g (4 oz) soft butter

tarragon leaves

Rotterdamsche Lloyd

• Slice the potatoes, barely cover with water and cook until soft. Drain. Mash the still warm slices with milk, seasonings and butter. Form into 4 oval sized pedestals and bake for 15 minutes in the oven at 200 °C/ 400 °F/Gas Mark 6.
• In the meantime soft boil the eggs in 6 minutes. Plunge into cold water and peel. Divide on to the mashed potato pedestals, coat with tarragon sauce and decorate with whole tarragon leaves.
• For the tarragon sauce cook the wine with vinegar and seasonings until reduced by half. Strain the liquid and cool. Put a saucepan over hot water, add the yolk and whisk in the spiced wine until the sauce thickens. Remove the pan from the water, whisk in melted butter a drop at the time and add a few coarsely chopped tarragon leaves.

Green perch / Baars in 't Groen

Werumeus Buning, one cannot avoid mentioning him. He truly was the first to write in a newspaper, *De Telegraaf*, in a different way about food, no longer how it was supposed to be. Just about the nicety of it, without slipping into dogmatic lectures. Slightly pompous, but that has to be a reflection of his time. His 1928–1939 columns were collected in 1939. From that book we present this recipe together with his advice: '... and especially do not forget those well buttered perch sandwiches of black rye bread between thin white bread with crust removed! I know people who like to eat perch just for those'.

Recipe source: J.W.F. Werumeus Buning, *100 Avonturen met een pollepel*, Amsterdam: H.J.W. Becht, 1939

100 g (3 oz) runner beans, cut
2 leeks, in strips
thyme, tarragon, chervil
parsley, celery, chopped
dash of vinegar
generous amount of salt and pepper
600 g (1 lb 5 oz) fillet of perch
butter
salt and pepper

·

4 thin slices of sandwich bread, crust removed
2 thin slices of black rye bread
parsley butter

• Blanch the vegetables in a little herb stock with vinegar, salt and pepper. Drain the vegetables. Brush the fillets of fish with butter and quickly grill them.
• Thickly spread the white bread on one side with parsley butter, place one slice of rye bread between 2 slices of white bread and cut into triangles.

☛ Werumeus Buning serves the fish warm in vegetable liquid and tells us to please remember to eat the vegetables as well. Especially the runner beans, he says: 'add a lovely peppery taste to it all'.
☛ We advise to serve the perch cold, in the following way: Combine the vegetables. Divide on to 4 plates and put the fillets on top. Serve with the sandwiches.

🍷 Montravel. Dry white wine from the Bergerac.

Watercress soup / Waterkerssoep

(Crème cressonière)

Taken from the menu of April 1932 in honour of the 50th anniversary of the newspaper *De Standaard*. Plover's eggs, watercress soup, salmon trout and chicken in wine, and for dessert orange ice-cream soufflé. In our days still appetising. What a difference to 50 years earlier! Abraham Kuyper, founder of the paper and shown on the menu, celebrated his 25th wedding anniversary in 1888 with a twenty-course meal...

Strangely enough this soup is not to be found in the vegetarian books. Not even in the nice, non-dogmatic *Het vegetarisch middagmaal* (1937) by Martine Wittop Koning. Mellie Uyldert tells us this is because the herb watercress with its strong cleansing effect was not for sale here. It had to be gathered in the wild. Do you think the letter setters of *De Standaard* went to the fields themselves?

Recipe source: menu in the collection of the Historical Documentary Centre of Dutch Protestantism (1800–present), Free University Amsterdam

1 litre (4 cups) milk
1 onion with 1 clove stuck in it
herb bouquet (parsley, bay, thyme)
salt and pepper
3 tablespoons rice flour

2 tablespoons butter
2 bunches watercress
200 ml (¾ cup) double cream

1937 World jamboree in the Netherlands. Soup in the open

• Bring the milk to the boil with the onion, herbs, salt and pepper. Stir the rice flour with a little cold milk to a smooth paste and stir into the boiling milk. Simmer the milk for 3-15 minutes (depending on the type of rice flour; see further) to thicken.

• In the meantime, in an other saucepan melt the butter. On low heat for a few minutes cook the watercress and mash in a blender just before serving. Stir the puree in to the rice crème. Push the soup through a sieve, add the cream and season with a little salt.

☛ In the Netherlands it is hard to get rice flour. It is mostly sold parboiled for toddler's porridge. It can be made by grinding rice to a powder in a blender. The cooking time of this will be the long one.

Tomato broth / Tomatenbouillon

'Cook economically and buy economically!' An advertisement in the oh so severe econo-
mising book by Mrs Lotgering, however, wants people to daily use the 47 piece Wedgwood
dinner-service (f 39,95). Our lovely broth of tomatoes would look rather
nice in it with its white beans, potato cubes, small meatballs, onion and parsley.

Recipe source: R. Lotgering Hillebrand, *Kook Voordeelig*. More than 300 recipes for simple food suitable for a frugal household,
Amsterdam: H.J.W. Becht, 1935

1 litre (4 cups) meat stock
1 bay leaf
1 chopped onion

·

100 g (3 oz) waxy potatoes, diced
200 g lean pork, minced
salt and pepper

·

100 g (3 oz) cooked white beans
2 tomatoes, peeled, seeds removed, diced

· Heat the stock, bay leaf and onion until the onion is tender.
· Bring to the boil water and diced potatoes. Season the
  minced pork with salt and pepper and form into small balls.
  Cook with the potato for 15 minutes. Rinse in a colander and
  add to stock.
· Finally add the rinsed white beans and pieces of tomato and
  heat through. Serve immediately.

☞ Naturally, the recipe in *Kook Voordeelig* lets us soak the beans
  ourselves (500 g/1 lb 2 oz!, no wonder this soup is called
  nutritious), after which they are cooked for 1½ hours, when
  1 kg (2 lbs 3 oz) tomatoes and the other ingredients are
  added and cooked until soft. That way the soup becomes a
  meal on its own. We used the same ingredients, but with a
  lighter result. Mrs Lotgering served it with bread.

Indonesian fried rice / Nassi Goreng

In the 1930s this Indonesian dish was often served. The American Lunchroom in Utrecht, for example, had 'Nassi Goreng with all the trimmings' as a day special (*f* 0,90). We also find the recipe on the cooking calendar of the Guild of Societies of Housewives in the Dutch East Indies, for the benefit of the unemployed. For the first time in the real authentic version, served with forty Indonesian dishes. In the company of the very traditional Dutch oatmeal soup, sturgeon from Kampen and Dutch rusk pudding.

Recipe source: *Menu's en recepten.* Published by Vereenigingen van Huisvrouwen in N.O. Indië, 1934. Facsimile publication Amsterdam: Raven Press, 1992

250 g (9 oz) chump end of pork
salt and pepper
vegetable oil

·

250 g (9 oz) rice

·

1 onion, sliced
3 eggs, salt

·

3 red chillies (Lombok peppers), seeds removed
1 red onion
1 clove of garlic
small piece of trassi

·

sliced cucumber
(large cooked shrimp)

- Sprinkle the meat with salt and pepper and cook for 20 minutes in a little oil until done. In the meantime cook the rice according to the packet instructions.
- In a frying pan brown the onion rings. Remove from the pan and make an omelette with the beaten eggs.
- Chop the chillies, onion, garlic and trassi. Add to the meat and heat through. Add the rice and heat while stirring to form a homogenate mixture. Pile the rice on a serving plate.
- Top with the onion rings and slices of cucumber and maybe some shortly fried shrimp around it.

- Trassi is a fermented shrimp paste, also called terasi or trasi. Usually, nasi goreng (fried rice) is made from leftover cold boiled rice and leftover meat.

Escalopes of veal Boukamp / Kalfsoesters Boukamp

(Filets de veau Florentine)

This recipe was created by confectioner-chef Boukamp. According to the introduction by Mr De Graaf of Bath-Hotel Baarn the objective of the book was to create attractive and appetising dishes on a meagre budget. He recommends the subject matter to 'the young generation, that have a calling to choose this difficult though principled subject as a profession'. On the menu of Badhotel Baarn we find a large roast of veal Westmoreland 'with piccalilli sauce' in June 1939 for the Brotherhood of Notaries in the Netherlands. Sounds good, but we rather follow Boukamp, who already in 1939 tells us that the time of overflowing dishes 'will be out of fashion for the time being'. Even so we cannot take the 'meagre budget' too serious seeing how much Boukamp loved truffles.

Recipe source: C.H. Boukamp, *De hedendaagse keuken*. Manual for chefs including the ritual and vegetarian cuisine. Deventer: published in conjunction with the Dutch Confectioners Guild by N.V. Uitgevers-Maatschappij Æ.E. Kluwer, 1939

1939–1940 Mobilization. On the picture was written:
'either onion, beans or hash, I like it all and eat no less!'

500 g (1 lb 2 oz) peeled potatoes, not too mealy
50-100 ml (¼–½ cup) milk
½ teaspoon salt
pinch of grated nutmeg
pinch of pepper
1 egg yolk
lump of butter

·

1 kg (2 lb 3 oz) spinach
100 ml (½ cup) double cream
salt and pepper
butter
(4 slices of white bread
2 hard-boiled eggs)

75 g (2¾ oz) clarified butter
8 escalopes of veal (each 50 g / 1¾ oz)
flour, salt and pepper
50 g (1¾ oz) boiled ox tongue, cut in strips
sliced truffle or 1 teaspoon truffle oil
100 ml (½ cup) reduced veal stock (jar)
1 teaspoon arrowroot or potato starch

🍷 Tokay Pinot Gris. Very spicy strong
wine from the Alsace.

• Slice the potatoes and cook in a little water until soft. Drain
and stand uncovered. Whisk in seasonings, egg yolk and butter to make a light mash. Pipe rosettes of mash into a buttered oven-proof dish. Brown the rosettes in 20-30 minutes
in an oven at 225 °C/425 °F/Gas Mark 7. Or serve plain just as
chef Boukamp did; in which case mash the potatoes with 100
ml (½ cup) milk and pasteurized egg yolk.

• Wash the spinach and cook on medium heat until wilted.
Chop coarsely and press out the water. Cook the cream down
to half and stir in the spinach. Season with salt and pepper.
Place a large lump of butter on the spinach. According to
Boukamp this will protect the colour.

• Coat the escalopes with flour and sprinkle with a little salt
and pepper. In hot butter brown the meat on both sides in
about 8 minutes. Shortly sauté the strips of ox tongue and
divide between the escalopes. Top with a slice of truffle or
drizzle with truffle oil.

• Spoon the spinach on the dish with the potato rosettes,
put the meat on it, and if wanted garnish with wedges of
hard-boiled egg and 'heart shaped croutons fried in clarified
butter'.

• Combine the cooking liquid and reduced stock, thicken it
with a smooth paste of arrowroot and water. 'Pour over the
gravy while passing the plate'.

☞ Instead of escalopes of veal, use medallions or chops.
☞ Clarified butter is made by melting butter, pouring off
the foam and carefully pouring the fat into a pan, throwing
away the watery liquid.

Whiting fillets from Gouda / Goudse Wijtingfilets

(Tortillons de Merlans Région)

Th.N. van Stigt, chairman of Horecaf, writes a lyrical introduction to a collection of recipes for Dutch products: 'the land of blue skies and succulent pastures'. How right he was, since the participating chefs were outstanding. Hence his wish: 'May the fame radiating off the Dutch restaurants to the rest of the world be heightened by the preparation of these recipes and the adaptation of "true" dishes.' This recipe was created by P. Minderman, chef de cuisine at the Carlton hotel in Amsterdam.

Recipe source: G.J. Kamps, B. v.d. Laan, F.A. Lamers, P. Minderman, *Economische Zuivelgerechten* (no city of publishing mentioned): Dutch Dairy Bureau, 1936

- Cut the cleaned leek in finger long pieces. Cook in a little salted water until tender, drain well or squeeze out the water.
- Put the flour in a saucepan, whisk in the milk and butter and, when smooth, the cheese. On low heat whisk to a smooth and thick sauce. Add the leek, rice, parsley and horseradish, season with salt and pepper.
- Butter a flame-proof dish. Spoon the cheese ragout in the middle of the skin side on the fillets. Fold the fish over the filling: first the wide side than the tail side. Place the fish seam side down in the dish. Pour over the cream, add halved mushrooms, cover and cook on low heat for 10 minutes.
- Spoon the cooking liquid into a saucepan. Cook it down until lightly thickened, stir in the egg yolks and cheese plus the mushrooms.
- Puree this sauce in a blender. Arrange the leek around the fish, pour the sauce over and sprinkle lightly with breadcrumbs. Top with a few lumps of butter and brown in the oven at 200 °C/400 °F/Gas Mark 6. Just before serving sprinkle the leek with finely chopped parsley.

4 thin leeks
salt

65 g (2¼ oz) wheat flour
125 ml (½ cup) boiling milk
25 g (1 oz) butter, melted
nutmeg
40 g (1½ oz) grated mature Gouda cheese
1 tablespoon chopped leek
1 tablespoon cooked rice
1 tablespoon chopped parsley
1 tablespoon grated horseradish
salt and pepper

·

butter
800 g (1 lb 12 oz), 8 fillets of whiting, skin removed
salt and pepper
150 ml (⅔ cup) double cream
4 button mushrooms

·

1 egg yolk
2 tablespoons grated mature Gouda cheese
breadcrumbs
lumps of butter
parsley

Pancakes with apricots /
Roomstruif met boerenmeisjes

The agricultural domestic science education, given by driven ladies who were convinced farming people were very much behind times, was a real phenomenon in the countryside. The lessons were an outing for farmers' daughters, who did not mind hearing about canning – up until then everything conserved was in brine or dried – and who laughingly, dressed in a white coat with matching hat, were not against preparing a 'curried dish' or a Moscovic biscuit cake' for once. And then it was back to normal again. They only remembered the desserts. Generations later 'wentelteefjes' (French toast) and Dutch rusks in berry sauce were still on the menu, served after the regional dishes the cooking teachers did not approve of. There were exceptions, for example this dish from the province of Brabant to which vanilla seeds were added.

Recipe source: C.L.W. Rakhorst-Schokkenkamp, *Kort en Bondig Kookboekje*, Zwolle: W.E.J. Tjeenk Willink, 1937

6 eggs
500 ml (2 cups) milk
50 g (1¾ oz) sugar
seeds of 1 vanilla pod
150 g wheat flour
pinch of salt
butter for frying
icing sugar for dusting

·

300 g (10½ oz) apricots in heavy syrup
1 tablespoon arrowroot or potato starch
1 tablespoon Apricot Brandy
sprigs of mint

· Separate the eggs, beat the yolks with sugar and vanilla and whisk into the milk. Beat the egg whites.
· Blend the sifted flour and salt, gradually whisk in the milk and spoon in the beaten egg whites. In a 18 cm (7 in) frying pan in hot butter bake 6 pancakes on one side until dry on top (4 minutes per pancake, in a professional kitchen the

pancakes are dried under a medium grill). Pile the pancakes on top of each other, brown sides under. The last pancake is placed brown side up. Dust the pile with icing sugar. Divide into 8 wedges and serve 2 per person with a warm compote of apricots, made the following way:

· Cook the apricots in 200 ml (¾ cup) of their syrup. Thicken with a smooth paste of arrowroot and 1 tablespoon of syrup. Just before serving stir in the liqueur. Serve tepid. Garnish with a sprig of mint.

☛ One may also use the real 'boerenmeisjes': brandied apricots
1938 Volendam girls eat rusks with aniseed comfits on the occasion of the birth of Beatrix

Chocolate roll with ice cream /
Chocoladerol met roomijs

Martine Wittop Koning was the empress of the domestic science schools and convinced defender of happiness in the home in the first half of this century, She wrote more than 80 books, translated many others, and was not above working for the business community. As long as she approved of their products. Thus, she wrote in the 1930s for Maggi, Calvé, Flipje of Tiel, Planta, Haust ánd Droste. Whereby the firm Droste honestly states on the front page: 'we present this booklet free of charge wishing to increase the use of the well known Verpleegster (Nurse's) Cacao powder'.

Recipe source: Martine Wittop Koning, *52 recepten voor het bereiden van Chocoladespijzen met Droste's Verpleegster Cacao, Haarlem, 1934*

Cake:
3 eggs
75 g (2¾ oz) sugar
45 g (1½ oz) self raising flour
1½ heaped tablespoon cacao powder
pinch of cinnamon
caster sugar

·

Ice cream:
200 ml (¾ cup) double cream
40 g (1½ oz) icing sugar
150 ml (⅔ cup) pasteurized egg white (= 3 egg whites)
1 tablespoon Kirsch

·

Garnish:
icing sugar
Kirsch to taste

♟ Banyuls. Red dessert wine from the South of France.

• Preheat the oven to 175 °C/350 °F/Gas Mark 4. Line a baking tray with parchment paper, also the sides. Place a mixing bowl in a bowl of hot water. Break the eggs into the mixing bowl. Add the sugar and whisk with an electric beater until the mixture holds a ribbon.
• Gradually sift the flour onto this mixture and carefully fold it in with a large smooth spoon. Spread the dough evenly onto the lined baking tray. Bake for 15 minutes. Sprinkle the top with icing sugar. Place a clean tea towel on the cake. Turn onto a flat surface. Remove the paper from the cake. Sprinkle with sugar and roll up the cake with the aid of the towel, starting at the short side. Cool.

• Lightly whisk the double cream and sugar. Beat the egg whites to stiff peaks. Combine both with a large smooth spoon and fold in the Kirsch.
• Spread over the unrolled cake. Reroll the cake. It does not matter if small tears appear. Wrap the roll in aluminium foil and freeze. 15 minutes before serving take the roll from the freezer. Unwrap and dust with icing sugar. Diagonally slice and drizzle with Kirsch.

☛ Mrs Wittop Koning filled the roll with a smooth mixture of 125 g (4 oz) icing sugar, 60 g (3 oz) butter, and a little seed from a vanilla pod. Of course there was no freezing in those days!

Dining with cheese

Happy with cheese

Cheese was here even in prehistoric times. And through the ages we have truly enjoyed it, as is obvious from the tasteful breakfasts to be found on the paintings from the Golden Century, with bunches of grapes and goblets of wine, an atmosphere so nicely described on a signboard of an Old-Dutch cheese shop:

Neemt 'blinde' kaas en 'siende' broot
Dan heb je kost voor hongersnoot,
En heb je dan ook wijn die springht,
Soo wort je vrolick als je drinkt.

('Choose "blindly" cheese and "seeingly" bread
no longer will you have cause for hunger,
and if to accompany there is a lively wine,
you will be happy while you drink.')

That is the reason why so many families proudly have been named after cheese and bread. In the 1950s the cheese farmers from Zuid-Holland sometimes pityingly said: 'In The Hague, they alternate the cheese from one slice of bread to the other.' The Netherlands continue to surprise the world with yet another variety of cheese.

Moreover, cheese became one of the pillars of our economy. Those who want to know what was done in this area at the start of the twentieth century, should visit the rebuild Frisian dairy factory Freia in the Openlucht Museum in Arnhem – a really impressive sample of Dutch craftsmanship.

Cheese enters the kitchen

From the above you might deduce that cheese has always played an important role in Dutch cuisine. But no, that did not start until the beginning of the twentieth century.
In *Het Kook- en Huishoudboek* from 1908 mostly foreign cheese is mentioned. And even in 1931 'a housewife', correspondent for the woman's page of the newspaper the Algemeen Handels-blad, writes in her *Encyclopedie voor de keuken*: 'We only eat cheese in a sandwich. Although it has been often tried to include

cheese in hot dishes (...). Some of these dishes are eaten abroad (especially in Italy), but in our country they are not accepted.' However, the four top chefs who in 1936 have been snared by the Dairy Bureau to write the booklet *Economische Zuivelgerechten* are not afraid of a little foreign cuisine: in addition to cheese soup from Alkmaar they calmly offer the grilled French onion soup, that became very popular in the 1960s.

Twenty years later things have changed quite a bit. Henriëtte Holthausen: 'If you realize how many varieties of cheese we know and how many dishes we can prepare with all these, it will not surprise you that (...) the Romans held cheese (Latin *caseus*) in such high esteem that barbarians were only blamed for two things namely the fact they lead immoral lives and knew nothing about cheese.' (*Spreekuur in de keuken*, 1958) Well, at least you know what to order so as not to be considered an immoral barbarian!

Cheese has the future

In the meantime the Dairy Bureau continued its culinary mission in the Netherlands. In the 1970s the Bureau started with extremely successful cooking schools and published the book *Kookook*, a marvellous all-round piece of work, that, in conjunction with hundreds of campaigns in the restaurant business from the 1960s on, was responsible for including cheese in the hot meals in wide circles of the population. The result: famous chefs of our day, such as Robert Kranen-borg and Cas Spijkers, like to work with Dutch cheese. And an increasing amount of top restaurants serve a plateau with Dutch cheese for dessert.

At the start of a new century we can add this: it is obvious that cheese has a future because of its beneficial image. Never boring, because always different. Easy to keep even in bad conditions, especially Dutch cheese. Here a recipe with both a past and a future:

soft. Add the diced celeriac to the soup with the remaining grated cheese and maybe a little salt. Sprinkle with finely chopped chives. Serve with toast cut in small squares.

Roasted peppers with crayfish tails and new goat's cheese / Geroosterde paprika's met rivierkreeftenstaartjes en jonge schapenkaas

A Recipe by Marijke van Essen, patron cuisinière in Leeuwarden. Trained at 'Kaatje' and Jean Beddington, she soon realized she was not suited to work for a boss. She explains to Ton de Zeeuw why: 'I am too conceited. As is my style of cooking: what I have in my head my hands have to be able to immediately copy. I do not want to have to explain it first.' And she succeeded very well indeed. In 1999 restaurant Van Essen was named the best of Friesland by magazine *Lekker*. This is what she says about goat's cheese: 'It is a very soft and tasty round cheese. In Friesland we look forward to it in the springtime.'

8 large peppers, yellow, red and green
4 tablespoons olive oil
3 tablespoons red wine vinegar or half vinegar and half lime juice
black pepper from the mill
coarse sea salt from the mill

.

salad leaves
chervil
24 crayfish tails
1 fresh goat's cheese (250 g / 9 oz)

- In a hot oven (about 250 °C/475 °F/Gas Mark 9) roast the peppers until black on all sides. Rinse under cold streaming water and peel off the skin. Remove the inside and chop the flesh into large chunks.
- Put the chunks of pepper in a bowl with the oil, vinegar, salt and pepper. Marinate for at least one hour.
- On 4 plates arrange a few salad leaves. First place the pieces of pepper on it and then the crayfish. Top with slices of goat's cheese and sprinkle with chervil. Put sea salt and pepper on the table and serve with wholegrain bread.

☞ Alternative for crayfish: scampi or Dutch grey shrimps.

Cheese soup from Alkmaar / Alkmaarse kaassoep

Recipe source: F.A. Lamers, chef de cuisine of the New or Literary Society 'De Witte' in The Hague in: *Economische Zuivelgerechten*, Zuivelbureau, 1939

50 g (1¾ oz) butter
1 chopped onion
50 g (1¾ oz) flour
1¼ litre (1¼ quarts) milk
50 g (1¾ oz) grated matured Gouda cheese
1 small celeriac
100 g (3 oz) grated matured Gouda cheese
salt
chives
toast

- In a saucepan melt the butter, cook the onion until soft and add the flour. Stir and gradually pour in the milk. Whisk to a lightly thickened soup. Add the cheese and cook for approximately 15 minutes, stirring occasionally. Strain the soup.
- Peel and dice the celeriac and cook in a little water until

1940–1949
Meagre rations

Restaurant business

After the setback of 1940 the restaurant business recuperated in the following two years. People could not travel abroad because of the German occupation, and very few goods were for sale. So they went out for dinner, in spite of blackouts and all sorts of regulations, such as jacket potatoes, the surprise menu 'Take potluck' and one meal with meat at the most.

1940 · Invasion of the Germans
   · Radio Orange broadcasts from London with Lou de Jong
   · Glass School Leerdam starts
   · Tom Poes replaces forbidden English and American strips in newspaper De Telegraaf
   · Tea, coffee, bread, butter, soap, tobacco, textiles on coupons
1941 · Rationing of meat, eggs, milk and potatoes
   · Founding of 'Voorlichtingsbureau voor de Voeding' (Public Information Service for Food)
1942 · Noordoost polder ready for habitation
   · Discontinuance Horecaf (club catering industry)
1943 · Princess Margriet born in exile
   · Cabaret artist Buziau is incarcerated for quite some time and stops thereafter. He had been logging a portrait of an important Nazi around stage asking: 'Will I hang him or put him against the wall?'
1944 · Railway strike: no more food transport into big cities
   · Cessation of gas and electricity: cooking on 'majo-stove', if there was food to be had at all
1945 · End of February first Swedish food transport
   · April: food droppings
   · May 5th: comeback of The Dutch Swing College Band
   · Sunday afternoon May 6th at 17.00 hours signing of capitulation charters in Wageningen
   · Wilhelmina lands in Zeeland
   · Founding of Institute for Vocational Training Restaurant business
1947 · Birth of Princess Marijke (later: Christina)
   · Re-foundation of Horecaf
1948 · Inauguration Queen Juliana, September 6th
   · Four Olympic gold medals for Fanny Blankers-Koen
   · Restaurant business order: restaurants need to economize

Preferably, of course, without a coupon. Which resulted in sampling the lesser known lamb or game (partridge, for example) or fish. Up to 1944 the Netherlands did not lack in food. To get hold of it, however, took a boringly long time and there were also times when there was only one of the same thing to be had.

Especially in the beginning of the war restaurants offered variation. Thus, in 1941 melon in port was the first of a ten-course feast in the Poort van Kleef in Apeldoorn, with six superior wines, just prior to the September ordinance, in which Jews no longer were allowed in public places. Wine could be served since it did not come under the rationing of alcoholic beverages (the Governmental Bureau felt that the scarce sugar did not belong in Dutch jenever).

In 1943 the restaurant business too is going down. It is the time of the enforcement of strict restrictions, which make it impossible to continue.

1948 Exam nerves: mass attendance of future café owners

Hunger

In the cities in1945 around the clock of 12.30 p.m. restaurants serve a plate of watery soup and a few potatoes. From 11.30 am on the guests are sitting at the neatly laid tables, quietly watching each other. The ration in western Holland went down to 500 calories in January 1945. Hunger trips on bicycles with wooden tires. Hours of queuing for coupons and soup kitchens. Anne H. Mulder writes: 'There are only two ingredients left: sugar beets and tulip bulbs, endlessly varied to overcome their taste. Stewed sugar beets, raw grated sugar beets, sugar beets with essence, home-made sugar beet syrup, fried tulip bulbs, roasted tulip bulbs, biscuits made of tulip bulbs.' All prepared on the majo or wonder stove, a cylinder of iron sheeting with a few draft-holes at the bottom, for which only a few chips of wood were necessary.

Even in the big cities, regardless of the hardship, people had saved a little something for the liberation festivities, and when capitulation came the long hidden bottle of champagne finally could be opened. Liberation was also celebrated in the living room with the last slice of Swedish white bread, the last home baked rye bread, the last sugar beet mash. Or, as in the restaurant Frigge in Groningen: with buttermilk and orange syrup.

Hunger was not over yet, though, and engineer Louwes of the Governmental Bureau for Food Supply warned: 'Distribution will have to be maintained for a long time to come.' Indeed up to the 1950s people continued to eat very soberly. For example, our famous athlete Fanny Blankers-Koen was not entertained with a dinner in honour of her 4 gold medals. She said: 'That was not necessary! One just went on. How I got my energy? Every day one spoon of cod-liver-oil and a plate of beans. My father's advice. And I followed it as long as possible. We sportspeople were given Ovomaltine by the NOC: horrible! My favourite dish? Hash of boiled potatoes, raw endive and bacon. I do not mind pancakes either.'

'New insights'

Mrs A. Geurts could smell business! Already in 1940 a second edition of her Oorlogskookboek appeared. Scarcity did not exist yet, but she foresaw its coming, so back to the hay box or cooking with thick wads of newspaper, just like in 1914–1918. Also at the beginning of the war, C.J. Ooms-Vinckers wrote Ons Dagelijksch Brood in Oorlogstijd ('Our daily bread in wartime'). In it professor Julius from Utrecht finishes his preface with a suspect nationalistic appeal: 'Good luck with the work and remember your Dutch duty!'

However, better times are coming. In 1948 Mrs Ooms gets the opportunity to revenge herself with her Standaard Kookboek, including more than one thousand meals and dishes. In the introduction she writes: 'We have been brought up by parents and teachers who had little understanding of the new insights on the home and public domain (vacuum cleaner, electric washer, iron, cooking on gas and electricity).' News was scarce because of the war and that is why Mrs Ooms explains everything explicitly: 'On swallowing the food, pulp passes the pharynx and arrives in the oesophagus.' That is why she gives the following spring dinner: tomato soup and cream / cod, sour sauce, potatoes, apple sauce / roast with spinach and carrots / toast and biscuits with fish paste. Oh well, she must have thought on reflecting this bizarre menu, it'll all turn to pulp anyway...

However, she was right in foreseeing that everybody realized the world would never be the same as before 1940. Belief in the good of the people was gone and the world became hard and cynical. The first atom bombs had fallen and it was clear that for the first time technology had enabled man to destroy himself completely.

This also resulted in people starting to feel freer to enjoy as long as they (still) could. The Calvinistic sobriety ideal of before the war had lost its credibility. Merchandise was available, even food and drinks, and people were ready to be informed of what was to be had.

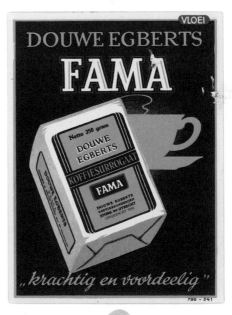

Russian egg / Russisch ei

(Oeufs à la russe)

After 1945 this was an incredibly popular first course. No wonder: the potato had been missed for too long and eggs were rare. In addition, it was nice to be able to prepare something in the pre-war manner. In the Kurhaus, according to *commis de garde manger* Jan Krems, this is how it was done: A basic salad with fish, potatoes and vegetables; on top eggs halved in the width, covered with ravigote sauce; garnished with lettuce leaves, and anchovies and capers on top of the eggs. However, there was another pre-war preparation that had a revival in many restaurants: the vegetarian version of confectioner-chef Boukamp for one of his luncheons.

Recipe Source: C.H. Boukamp, *De hedendaagsche keuken*. Manual for chefs including the ritual and vegetarian cuisine. Deventer: published in conjunction with the Dutch Confectioners Guild by N.V. Uitgevers-Maatschappij Æ. E. Kluwer, 1939

---

4 extremely fresh eggs

2 tablespoons vinegar

20 g (⅔ oz) salt

·

boiled carrots, potatoes, green beans, together 250 g (9 oz)

3 tablespoons vegetable oil

1 tablespoon vinegar

1 tablespoon capers

parsley, tarragon, chervil, chives

salt and pepper

·

cucumber

tomatoes

vinegar

salt and pepper

·

mayonnaise

capers

• In a large saucepan bring to the boil 2 litre water (2 quarts) with salt and vinegar. Break in the eggs, lower the heat and keep the water 2–3 minutes to the boil (poaching). Remove the eggs with a slotted spoon and plunge into cold water. Trim the edges with scissors and cool the eggs.

• Combine the diced vegetables with a sauce made with the next ingredients (ravigote or vinaigrette sauce) and pile in the middle of a glass serving plate. Arrange the eggs around it and garnish with a ring of peeled and sliced cucumber and tomato, drizzled with a little vinegar and sprinkled with salt and pepper.

• Spoon the mayonnaise over the eggs and sprinkle with capers.

1945 Food droppings in Amsterdam

Sardines of The Gilded Turk /
Sardientjes van de Vergulde Turk (sardines en boîte)

One of the most expensive dishes on the menu of The Gilded Turk in Leiden, recorded on November 3rd 1948: ƒ 2,25! While a hot three-course lunch went for ƒ 2,50. This delicacy was served in the tin, exactly like the then very popular haddock liver, and with buttered toast. We use a garnish of marrowfat pea salad from a leaflet dating November 1946. For 3 cents one could buy ideas to augment ones meagre rations of egg, meat and fish.

Recipe source: *Peulvruchten*, 's-Gravenhage: Commission for Advice on Home and Family Planning in conjunction with the Public Information Service for Food, 1946

the heart of a head of endive
1 jar of pickled beetroot (about 200 g)
1 jar of young marrowfat peas (approx. 200 g)
4 pickled gherkins
oil, vinegar
mustard
salt and pepper
2 tins of sardines

•

4 slices of toasted white bread
butter

• Very thinly slice the cleaned and well dried endive. Place in the middle of a serving plate with the beetroot on top.
• Combine the drained marrowfat peas with the diced gherkins, oil, vinegar, mustard, salt and pepper. Spoon around the beetroot and top with the sardines. Or do as shown on the photo. Serve with bread and butter.
• In 1946 'ersatz' pepper was used, and mashed potato and, for sauce, the cooking liquid of the beans.

♈ Muscadet de Sèvre et Maine sur lie.
Fresh dry tingly wine from the
Loire.

Queen's soup / Koninginnesoep

A must during the war! We found the soup on several menus from 1941 and twice on a hand-written menu from early 1946. Cookery books printed during the war years always referred to it as "Chicken soup with crème de riz' or 'with flour' (potage à la reine). The Germans had ordered menus only to be in Dutch or German, not French. And what better than to oblige them? Queen's soup it was.

Recipe source: F.M. Stoll, W.H. de Groot, *Recepten Huishoudschool Laan van Meerdervoort in 's-Gravenhage*, De Gebroeders Van Cleef, 11th revised edition, August 1943. With supplementary sheet: Suggestions for these times, containing pea cake and (boiled) rye bread

- Bring the water, reduced stock, chicken, seasonings, leek and salt to the boil. Simmer covered for 1 hour. Strain the liquid through a wet and squeezed fine cloth.
- Melt the butter in the pan, add the flour and lightly brown it. Gradually add the stock, keep stirring for a smooth soup. Cook for a few minutes. Add diced chicken meat and season with Bordeaux and cream. Bring to the boil once more. Sprinkle with tarragon.

☞ We use reduced veal stock instead of the original 250 g shin of beef, which is less suitable for this soup. Moreover, making the broth with shin would take three hours.

1 litre (4 cups) water
400 ml reduced veal stock (jar)
500 g (1 lb 2 oz) chicken leg
tarragon, chervil, thyme
1 small leek
salt

·

35 g (1¼ oz) butter
35 g (1¼ oz) flour
50 ml (¼ cup) white Bordeaux
50 ml (¼ cup) double cream
½ tablespoon finely chopped tarragon

1945 Wilhelmina returns to the Netherlands

Sorrel soup / Chiffonadebouillon

(Consommé Chiffonnette)

Mia de Kok used the Dutch name for this soup just as she meticulously did with all her recipes, on regulation of the *Kulturkammer*. She used sorrel and lettuce and, because of rationing, water and flour. Derived from a real French broth. Our own Culinary Encyclopaedia characterizes *chiffonade* as 'garnish for soup made of very thin strips of lettuce, sorrel or a combination of both, lightly fried in butter'. Restored to honour on the menu of Hotel des Pays-Bas in Utrecht, for Christmas 1949.

Recipe source: card in the menu collection of the Dutch Confectioners Guild, Confectioners Museum 'Het Warme Land' in Hattem; broth: Mia de Kok, Koken...Nu, Recepten voor Distributie en Oorlogstijd, Wageningen: Zomer & Keuning, 1942

Hotel „De Nederlanden"
WINSCHOTEN
CAFÉ-RESTAURANT   Winschoten, *Mei* 19*40*.
Telef. 134
STALLING / AUTO-GARAGE

Nota voor *de Orts Commandant*

1940 van J. RUIBING

1940 Bill from Hotel de Nederlanden to the Ortskommandant, for missed income during the occupation

2½ litre (2½ quarts) cold water
500 g (1 lb 2 oz) soup bones
1 carrot, scraped
1 onion, 2 cloves stuck in
1 bay leaf
black peppercorns
salt

100 g (3½ oz) dark green salad leaves (Romaine)
100 g (3½ oz) sorrel leaves
lump of butter
1½ tablespoon arrowroot or potato starch

• In a pan without lid make a broth with the water, bones and seasonings. Simmer gently, preferably 12 hours or more (oil cooker!). Strain the broth through a damp, fine cloth; it should be about 1 litre (4 cups).
• Shred the vegetables and soften in a little butter. Thicken the soup with a paste of arrowroot and water and add the vegetables.

☞ For a vegetarian version follow Martine Wittop de Koning: 2½ teaspoons marmite and a piece of mace with 1¼ litre (1¼ quart) water. Follow the recipe.

☞ This broth has been seasoned with foreign spices, hard to come by during the war. Mia de Kok leaves them out.

Eggs for Churchill / Eieren voor Churchill

'Oeufs frites, sauces tomates'. That was the name of the dish on the menu of the luncheon for Winston Churchill on his visit to Queen Wilhelmina, May 10th 1946. To be sure, the palace would have preferred a Dutch menu, but since that had been the rule during nazi times, French menus were back in fashion immediately after the war. The main course was tournedos with mushrooms and mange-tout, followed by chocolate soufflé, fruit and coffee.

Recipe source: card in the menu collection of the Dutch Confectioners Guild, Confectioners Museum 'Het Warme Land' in Hattem; and Oeufs frites à la Française, sauce tomate, Escoffier, Ma cuisine, Paris: Flammarion, 1934

1½ kg (3 lbs) beefsteak or plum tomatoes
3 tablespoons olive oil
parsley
piece of garlic
salt and pepper

olive oil
4 extremely fresh eggs
salt
parsley

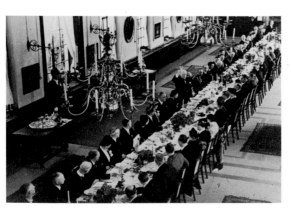

1946 Winston Churchill visits the Amstelhof in Amsterdam

• Remove the seeds from the quartered tomatoes. Put the wedges in a saucepan with the oil, seasonings and salt. Cover the pan and simmer for 20 minutes. If necessary cook the liquid down. Push the sauce through a fine sieve. Season with salt.
• Pour 1 cm (½ in) of oil in the bottom of a small non-stick frying pan and heat. On a saucer break one egg at the time and slide into the oil. Tilt the pan and immediately spoon the egg white over the yolk so that it is completely covered. Hold the egg together with two spoons. Drain on paper towels. Sprinkle with a little salt.
• Serve hot with the hot tomato sauce. Garnish with deep-fried sprigs of parsley.

☛ If you leave the sauce a short while, cover with a little butter to save the colour.

Spicy fish cakes / Kruidige viskoekjes

Mrs Ooms on war restrictions: 'Superficially judged this should lead to a deterioration of our meals. However, that is not necessarily so, it may even be possible to gain richness and variety of food.' Later she will be proven right by historian Trienekens. She and her colleagues were the first to successfully promote the now popular fibrous diet. Apart from that, the potato fish cakes of Mrs Reiding deserve not to be forgotten. Garnish: turnip tops, prepared according to the demand of time. By the way, from the overviews given by Mrs Ooms it appears she only knew parsley, celery leaf and chervil to be fresh herbs.

Recipe source: C.J. Ooms-Vinckers, A.J. Reiding, *Ons Dagelijks Brood in Oorlogstijd*, no place of publication, 1940

100 g (3 oz) waxy potatoes
400 g (14 oz) fillet of fish
1 egg
1 tablespoon finely chopped parsley
nutmeg
salt and pepper
breadcrumbs
butter

·

750 g (1 lb 10 oz) young turnip tops
lump of butter
50 ml (¼ cup) milk
½ tablespoon cornflour

• Cook the sliced potatoes in a little water until tender (approximately 20 minutes). Steam until dry. Bring the fish to the boil in a little salted water. In a bowl mash the fish and potatoes with the egg and seasonings. Make four patties, coat with breadcrumbs and brown on both sides in butter.

• Remove the roots from the turnip tops, wash and chop the tops and wash again. Cook the tops with a little lump of butter for 10 minutes in a covered pan and cook the liquid down with the lid removed. Stir a paste of milk and cornflour and add to the tops. Keep stirring and cook shortly. Season with salt and spoon the tops around the brown fish cakes to complement the taste.

Dinner of pike perch, parsley sauce, carrot and potatoes / Dinerschotel van snoekbaarsfilets

(met peterseliesaus, worteltjes en aardappels)

In 1940 fish could be bought without coupons and people were happy to do so, judging by this rhyme:

'n Gestoofd of 'n gebakken visje,
'k Geloof niet dat 'k veel meer geven kan
En ... je slikt ut en bikt ut.
Staat op 't laatst zelfs stom verbaasd,
Dattut even goed gesmaakt heeft,
Als 't uitgebreid diner van laatst.

('Fish stewed or fried,
I believe that's all I can give
And ... after swallowing
It surprises even myself,
How it tasted just as good
As a full course meal.')

However, during the occupation less and less fish was brought in, which is why cookery books offer ideas for fresh water fish, which people could catch themselves. Noticeable is that even in those days people copied from others. This dish is given by Mia de Kok (see before) and is nearly identical to the one found in the *Oorlogskookboek*.

Rhyme: Paul Arnoldussen, Jolande Otten, *De borrel is schaarsch en kaal geworden, Amsterdamse Horeca 1940-1945*, Amsterdam:

Bas Lubberhuizen, 1994. Recipe source, also: A. Geurts, *Oorlogskookboek*, 2nd edition, 1940

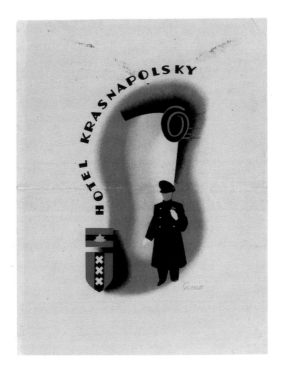

400 ml (1⅓ cup) water
head and bones of pike perch
onion, carrot, parsley
(mace, thyme, peppercorns)
½ teaspoon salt
1 kg (2 lb 3 oz) fillets of pike perch, with skin
8 pieces of thread

·

300 g (10½ oz) peeled potatoes
300 g (10½ oz) peeled celeriac
200 g (7 oz) carrots
200 g (7 oz) mange-tout
200 g (7 oz) leek
butter

·

40 g (1½ oz) butter
50 g (1¾ oz) flour
400 ml (1⅓ cup) fish stock
about 2 tablespoons milk
2 tablespoons finely chopped parsley

♀ Riesling d'Alsace. Elegant fruity
wine from the Alsace.

- In a large saucepan cook the water with the head and bones of the fish and seasonings. Simmer, covered, for 20 minutes. Pour the liquid through a sieve, bring it to just under boiling point. Sprinkle the skin side of the fish with mace, thyme, salt and pepper. Fold the fillets in half with the skin side in, and tie with a piece of string. Poach the fillets for 10 minutes in the fish stock and remove from the pan with a slotted spoon. Remove the threads and keep the fish warm.
- Cook the sliced potato and diced celeriac very soft and mash into a soft puree. Season with salt and a little butter. Pipe a decorative ring on a serving plate, place the fish in the middle.
- Cook the carrots and mange-tout separately in a little water and a small lump of butter. Add to the plate.
- In a small saucepan melt the butter and lightly brown the flour. While stirring add the strained fish stock (about 400 ml / 1¾ cup). Keep stirring until the sauce thickens. Season with milk and parsley and pour over the fish.

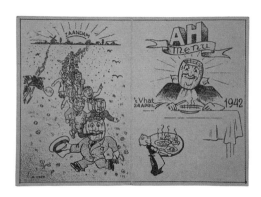

Grandmother's chicken /
Kip op grootmoeders manier (Poulet Grand-mère)

Right through the 1940s chicken remains favourite. In 1941 the Confectioners of Utrecht celebrate their 40th anniversary with Grandmother's chicken. In 1948 The Gilded Turk served *Coq au vin à l'Indienne* (at *f* 5,50, more expensive than pheasant) and in 1949 we find *Poulet roti* on the menu of the Kurhaus. We realize chicken was highly regarded when we see chicken with mushrooms and peas was served during the midday meal on December 27th 1949 in the royal palace in Amsterdam on the occasion of the transfer of sovereignty of the Dutch East Indies.

Recipe source: card in the menu collection of the Dutch Confectioners Guild, in the libraby of the Confectioners Museum 'Het Warme Land' in Hattem; and Auguste Escoffier, *Ma Cuisine, 2500 recettes*, Paris: Flammarion, 1934

butter
1 tablespoon finely chopped onion
200 g (7 oz) minced beef
1 chicken liver, diced
2 tablespoons breadcrumbs
1 tablespoon finely chopped parsley
nutmeg, salt and pepper
1 roasting chicken of 1 kg (2 lb 3 oz)

·

1 tablespoon butter
50 g (1¾ oz) lean bacon
20 pickling onions or halved shallots
400 g (14 oz) peeled potatoes, diced
parsley

• In an oven-proof casserole melt the butter and cook the onion until soft. In a mixing bowl knead onion, minced meat, liver, breadcrumbs, parsley, seasonings and salt for a stuffing of the chicken. Rub the chicken with salt and pepper. Stuff the chicken and close the cavity with a wooden stick.
• Melt a little butter in the casserole, add the chicken. Simmer on low heat (or an oven of 160 °C/325 °F/Gas Mark 3) for half an hour. Turn occasionally. The chicken will become slightly brown.
• Cook the bacon and onions in a little butter. Add to the chicken with the potatoes and simmer another 45 minutes. Sprinkle with parsley and serve from the casserole.

☛ Serve with rhubarb compote or various dried fruits and green beans.
☛ This recipe is ideal for a Römertopf cook pot. Soak the (old) pot in cold water (modern pots do not need this treatment any longer) and put it in a cold oven. Heat the oven to 250 °C/475 °F/Gas Mark 9. After half an hour add the potatoes, bacon and onion. Cook for another 45 minutes.

1948 Juliana during her inauguration as queen

Bavarois with candied fruits / Chipolatapudding

In the dark winter of 1944 a lot of people turned to cookery books, like musicians to reading a score, to savour all the delicacies of yesteryear. Some people even started a card index with recipes that at that moment could not possibly be prepared. For example this pudding: everything the Council for Nutrition had forbidden went into it. That is why after Liberation we see an outbreak of this pudding on the menus. The bavarois version was much preferred.

Unnoticed by the occupiers this pudding was smuggled into *Het Haagse Kookboek* of 1943 under the title 'Diplomat pudding' next to 'Pudding made of frothy skimmed milk'. That is the recipe we have based ours on, enough for 10 servings! The general feeling must have been: if something which is that good is prepared, guests should be invited. And that still holds since in the 75th edition of the same book (1995) the recipe has not been changed.

1½ litre (6 cups) mould

16 g (½ oz) gelatine
100 ml (½ cup) Maraschino
12 sponge fingers
60 ml (¼ cup) pasteurized egg yolk (= about 2 egg yolks)
125 g (4 oz) sugar
500 ml (2 cups) milk

90 ml pasteurized egg white (= about 2 egg whites)
250 ml (1 cup) double cream
50 g (1¾ oz) glacé cherries, diced
25 g (1 oz) candied orange peel, diced
25 g (1 oz) steeped raisins

• Rinse the mould with water and turn it upside down. Soak the gelatine in plenty of cold water. Place the sponge fingers side by side on a plate and pour over the Maraschino.
• Beat the egg yolks with half the sugar. Bring the milk with the remaining sugar to the boil. Stir a little milk into the egg yolk mixture, add to the remaining milk and while stirring cook on low heat until thickened. From the heat dissolve the well squeezed gelatine.
• Let the sauce cool and start to set. Fold in the beaten egg whites and fruits. Stir occasionally until quite thick. Fill the mould with 4 layers of 3 sponge fingers and pudding. The first and last layer must be pudding. Set in the fridge. Decorate with whipped cream if wanted.

Mandarin ice soufflé / Mandarijnen-ijssoufflé (soufflé glace)

'A wife who cooks well,
is highly regarded by her husband!'
This is the slogan on the title page of a cookery book published in 1943 (Wilma Münch, *Het Kook- en huishoudboek*, 4th edition, Van Dishoeck: Bussum 1943), when even surrogates were only to be obtained on coupons. Each book published in those days automatically was suspect. But seeing under practical advice: 'Jewish salt not dangerous', one could expect everything to be all right. And here too, there are clever recipes to get around all the misery. For example the preparation of ice cream in a Dutch rusk container, which was then placed in a bucket of ice blocks and salt. After the war mandarins returned on the market. But a generation had sprung up that had never seen these fruits. Children regarding them as apples did not hesitate to eat them, peel and all.

Recipe source: menu of Hotel des Pays-Bas, Christmas 1949, kept in the library of Confectioners Museum

'Het Warme Land' in Hattem, collection of the Dutch Confectioners Guild

4 *individual soufflé dishes of 150 ml (⅔ cups) and*
4 *pieces of thrice folded tin foil. With sticky tape secured*
around the top of the dishes to give a collar of 2 cm (1 inch)

·

80 ml pasteurized egg yolk (⅓ cup)
120 ml pasteurized egg white (½ cup)
(= equivalent of 4 medium sized eggs)
100 g (3 oz) soft white sugar

·

200 ml (¾ cup) double cream
4 tablespoons mandarin liqueur

·

4 tablespoons mandarin segments,
fresh or from a tin
4 tablespoons mandarin liqueur

· Whisk the egg yolks and whites with sugar to hold a ribbon.
· Whisk the double cream and carefully fold in the mandarin liqueur. With a large smooth spoon fold the mixture into the beaten eggs.
· Fill the moulds to the edge of the collar. Put in the freezer for at least 3 hours. 15 minutes before serving remove the moulds from the freezer to the fridge.
· Macerate the mandarin segments in the liqueur. Remove the collars. Place the moulds on small plates and decorate with drunken mandarin segments.

➤In those days one could eat raw eggs without a problem. Nowadays there always is a risk of salmonella, which is why we advise you to buy pasteurized egg, sold at wholesalers and delicatessen.

♟ Muscat de Beaumes-de-venise. White dessert wine.

Fish on the menu

Wonderfully light

'Fish leaves a person unchanged.' An age-old proverb. At that time not meant to be very flattering: fish did not give one the satisfied feeling necessary in a time when survival depended on a heavy diet. However, even before research had really gone into it – the science

of nutrition did not start until the twentieth century – it was known how easily digestible fish was (1 hour) in comparison to fowl (2 hours) and meat (3 hours).

That is why this old proverb needs rehabilitation! Fish is light and we now know its importance to our well-being. Ideally, every business lunch should be made up of raw vegetables and fish, so as not to doze off doing business! And we now hear about all the extraordinary qualities of fish oil – 'it protects the heart, combats depression and rheumatism' – all of which we get for free.

Fish – the favorite food

At the end of the nineteenth century it was still possible for dr. A.J.C. Snijders to write in his book *Onze Voedingsmiddelen* ('Our foodstuff'): 'Fish, enjoyed in many ways, has always been a favourite food in a country rich in fish as the Netherlands, both by the rich and the poor.' Those 'many ways' were rather disappointing, though. People had very little imagination. The Public Information Service for Food hired no less than seven domestic science teachers to school the Dutch. Later this evolved in the founding of the Bureau of Fish, which has always been active in the promotion of ideas for good and tasteful fish dishes, often in co-operation with the best chefs of the Netherlands.

Once again fish has become 'popular'. That is why we offer one fish recipe for each decade. Nowadays, we can purchase – also thanks to the efforts of the Fish Bureau – quite a number of hereto unknown fish: tilapia, catfish, sea wolf, monkfish (in the past often just thrown back after the catch). However, the kitchen princesses of the early twentieth century were not too bad either: Mrs Wannée of the Amsterdam domestic science school offered recipes for halibut, whereas Mrs A. Simonsz (*Geillustreerd kookboek*, 1901) recommends bass and gurnard.

Only on Fridays?

Because of the numerous Roman Catholic days of fasting, Friday was called fish-day. For some, though, every day was fish-day. At the end of the nineteenth century there were Frisians of whom it was said: 'In the cellar, in the chimney, on the walls and in the cupboards, everywhere there is fish to be found.' (Jozien Jobse van Putten, *Eenvoudig maar voedzaam* ('Simple but nutritious'), Nijmegen: Sun, 1995). An Amsterdam journalist wrote about an early breakfast of fried flounder and a cup of coffee. In Zeeland people ate fried kipper on Sunday mornings resulting in fumes in church that were rather extreme. In the 1940s fish played an important role, since people were delighted to have fish that came without coupons.

Dutch herring

According to legend, the city of Amsterdam was built on herring bones. From ancient times on herring has been enormously popular in Holland. A country like this, lying open to the sea, obviously has a long history of fishing. Herring especially has been caught for many centuries. As early as almost one thousand years ago Dutch fishermen hauled in so many herring that their catch was spoiled before it could be eaten at all. We know from ancient documents that around 1100 AD people tried to prevent this by salting the herring heavily. To no avail. Moreover, the herring lost its taste in the process. Therefore up to this day the Dutch reverently commemorate their compatriot Willem Beukelszoon from Biervliet who invented the 'haringkaken' (gutting) in 1350: the throat is cut away together with the gills and some of the intestines, except the pancreas which in combination with a modest amount of salt produces enzymes that enhance the fermentation which lends tenderness and taste to Dutch herring. Modern cooling and preservation techniques have made it possible to keep the tender, yet firm state of 'new' herring much longer than before.

Dutchmen become real gluttons when offered 'maatjes' herring. Even our British friends with whom we fought several battles over herring fishing rights do not have a better word for Dutch herring than 'matie' or 'mattie'. They do not know what it means. 'Maatje' means virgin ('maagdje'), because the Dutch want their young raw herring without roe.

For some 50 years the first new 'matjesherring' has been landed in the harbour of Scheveningen, close to the Hague. Then 'Vlaggetjesdag' (Flags' day) is celebrated, the official start of the new herring season around late May or early June. The ships are beflagged and everybody critically samples the 'maidens', her Majesty the Queen first of all.

What do others think of Dutch herring? Some time ago a journalist of *Saveur*, a leading culinary magazine in the States, visited several herring countries of Europe: Sweden, Denmark, Norway and the Netherlands. He tasted all the inlaid 'sill/sild' of our Scandinavian friends. But about Dutch 'matjesherring' he wrote: 'I taste a creamy fishiness utterly different from everything I've ever had. This is real herring!'

1950–1959
'How is the Camembert today?'

Restaurant business

Wina Born, in preparation to her later leading role among Dutch culinary journalists, characterizes the 1950s as 'static' in her booklet *25 jaar Nederlandse Restaurantgeschiedenis* ('25 years of Dutch restaurant history'). There were three groups: the

1950 · Opening of the Keukenhof
 · *Visvrouw* ('Fish selling woman'), painting by Co Westerik, receives Jacob Maris award
 · Foundation of Dutch Bartenders Club
1951 · Start of emigrant flow to the United States of America
 · Price of bread, fat and margarine raised
 · Sculpture *Dokwerker* ('Longshoreman') unveiled
 · Opening of first tourist hotel Grand Hotel at Scheveningen
 · First Albert Heijn supermarket
1952 · Coffee no longer on distribution coupons
 · Opening first student restaurant in Delft
1953 · Consumers Organization established
 · Flood... Purses open, dikes closed
 · 'Schijf van vijf' ('Basic Four') introduced by Public Information Service for Food
1954 · Jeen van den Berg wins 'Elfstedentocht' (skating marathon) and Jan Hein Donner becomes Dutch chess champion
 · Wim Kan is on the radio at New Year's Eve for the first time
 · Founding of Dutch Club for Chefs de Cuisine
 · First Bilderberg Conference in De Bilderberg, Oosterbeek
1955 · Founding of Trading Association for the Restaurant Business
 · Wessel Ilcken and Rita Reys: Jazz behind the Dykes
1956 · First Old Age Pensions and colour televisions
1957 · Corrie Brokken wins European song contest with 'Net als toen' ('Just like then')
 · Six Dutch restaurants receive 1 Michelin-star and two restaurants 2
 · First specialized fair for the restaurant business (Horecava) in RAI in Amsterdam
1958 · First paperback to arrive on the market
 · Flagship *Rotterdam* launched
 · Six more Michelin-stars presented, one to Hotel Prinses Juliana in Valkenburg
1959 · Wina Born starts as culinary journalist for women's weekly Margriet
 · Teddy Scholten wins song contest with 'Een beetje' ('A little bit')
 · Brigitte Bardot: even her dresses are fashionable

classical French restaurant, restaurants for the common people with green beans and apple sauce, and the then already inevitable Chinese restaurant. It is true, after the Liberation restaurants more and more felt the competition from exotic eating-houses. That was to be blamed on the customer's 'snobbism', was the opinion of the Consumers Organization. However, those foreign places to eat, especially the Chinese, often were family businesses and quite a bit cheaper. In the 1950s an Amsterdam student could afford nasi at 'Aunt Mia's' on the Oudezijds Achterburgwal or the Binnen Bantammer, but a huge steak at Die Port van Kleve was out of the question. And since this new generation of students primarily were the ones to eat out, a lot of emphasis was placed on exotic food, even though one had no money yet to travel abroad.

There was, for example, the Fromagerie Crignon (still in existence) behind the New Church on the Dam, where cheese fondue was served and one could hear a bragging connoisseur

1953 Throughout the years the presentation of the essential food groups has changed, but the message has remained the same

proudly crow: 'Waiter, how is the Camembert today?' It is also the time for 'country wine' to become popular. However, after the war wine was still so unusual that one bottle was ordered by four, while listening to French chansons by Juliette Greco or Nicole Louvier.

The Horecaf came with solid advice to its members: 'Serve less limited meals and less monotonous meals, but do not return to the very copious pre-war meals. Look for quality, not quantity. Allocate a full place for fish on the menu.' Dutch jenever as an aperitif was to be maintained (not quite successfully, sherry was on its way), the wine cult had to be redeveloped. In the meantime Michelin-stars were given to restaurants where chefs used fresh ingredients rather than products from tins, which was another stimulus to quality improvement.

During festive occasions one could count on hefty servings, despite Horecaf's warning. After all people no longer suffered from hunger. It did not lengthen the menu, though. For example, the first course was a large plate of smoked salmon, smoked eel, crab or lobster, haddock liver, artichoke bottoms with vinaigrette, palm hearts with mayonnaise, sardines, caviar, several pre-war mayonnaise salads, eggs stuffed soft as butter, rye bread with creamed cheese and a few radishes, gherkins and tomatoes. Nowadays we would call that a cold buffet. In the Kurhaus this was served on a rotating plateau with small silver dishes. This copious start did have its advantages: according to some restaurant owners people did not notice what came to follow (oral information by Jan Krems, then commis de garde manger, Kurhaus).

In some places, like in the American Lunchroom in Utrecht, it was possible to order an hors d'oeuvre on a plate so large that a one-and-a-half-year-old would have been able to crawl on it. And sometimes they unabashedly did so under the eyes of their busily talking parents.

In 1951 Culinaria is published, a culinary and gastronomic specialist journal. The editorial staff realizes that things have to change and also that the role of Carême and Escoffier should be shared by others: 'We have to take into account the modern way of service, with embellishment and garnish tuned to the cultural feelings of the modern guest, with new insights into nutrition, and a lot more, so much so that we cannot familiarize ourselves with without proper scientific information.' Yes, a lot had changed after the war, although at first the slightly insecure older generation did not realize just how much.

1953 The dikes break. All of the Netherlands is affected by the flood

Eating at home

Although the professional world had taken a serious attitude, writers and speakers about food and drink took a far more frivolous approach. The tone of cookery books changed. 'To eat, love, sing, digest – those are four acts of the comic opera called life,' according to Rossini in Spreekuur in de keuken ('Consultations in the kitchen'), recipes in the evening paper NRC by Henriëtte Holthausen, who immediately confesses never to cook from a recipe herself. No endless stories about what is good and healthy, on the contrary. Mrs Van Lanschot and Van Limburg Stirum in their Introduction to Lekker Eten slightly anxiously write: 'First of all we call on the kindness of all experts on cooking and nutrition since we are neither one nor the other. We are two women who like to eat well, have no servants and therefore do our own cooking.'

Edmond Nicolas went a bit further. This influential biochemist became the first KRO television chef and had quite a number of radio-talks to his name in the programme 'Mocders Wil is Wet' ('What Mother wants is done') before he turned to television in the early 1950s, He claims in Het extra Kookboek that he has eaten his best meal with a housewife who had never held a cookery book, who was helped by a kitchen princess who could not read. And how his worst omelette ever, had been prepared by a diploma holding cooking teacher. The kitchen at home is turning into something daring!

Crab salad / Krabcocktail

(met grapefruit)

Even without knowledge of the correct spelling people were fond of it: on one menu from those days we found it spelled 'crap coctail'. The ladies Van Lanschot and Van Limburg Stirum classify it under the heading 'Warm weather – cold food'. According to them this salad of lobster, crab or shrimp is also good for ''n kluifke op de bleek', which is Brabant dialect for a garden buffet. The ladies make the sauce by mixing 'a large jar of mayonnaise' with double cream, tomato ketchup and Cognac, restaurants also used sherry, just as the ladies did in the sauce of their second book.

Recipe source: C.M. van Lanschot, C. van Limburg Stirum-Van der Willigen, *Lekker eten, recepten voor hen die kunnen koken*, Den Haag: H.P. Leopold, 1953, same authors, *Kookboek Tesselschade-Arbeid Adelt*, Amsterdam, 1957

150 ml (⅔ cup) double cream
1 tablespoon tomato ketchup
1 tablespoon mayonnaise
1½ tablespoon Cognac
or 3 tablespoons dry sherry with a drop of lemon juice

·

4 green salad leaves
200 g (7 oz) crab
500 ml (2 cup) tin of grapefruit segments in light syrup

· Whisk the cold double cream not too stiff. Combine with the ketchup, mayonnaise and Cognac.
· Divide the washed and dried salad leaves into 4 glass coupes. Flake the crab and divide over the coupes (keep some nice pink pieces for garnish) together with the grapefruit segments. Spoon over the sauce and garnish with pieces of crab.

🐟 Although in the 1950s grapefruit segments came from tins, nowadays it is also possible to use fresh ones, of course.

🍷 Bordeaux Blanc Sec. Dry white wine.

Hors d'oeuvre varié

The hors d'oeuvre varié had replaced the many courses of yesteryear, even at home, where so many courses had never been served. A dinner with many small first courses became extremely popular.

Recipe source: *Verwachte en onverwachte gasten*, edition of 'De Betuwe' N.V., N.V. Corn Products Company, N.V. Oliefabrieken T. Duyvis Jz., Maggi's Producten Maatschappij N.V., no place of publication, 1959; and Henriëtte Holthausen, *Spreekuur in de Keuken*, Baarn: Het wereldvenster, 1958

For a simple small plate of hors d'oeuvre, on salad leaves

Cervelat boats

12 slices of cervelat, not too thinly sliced
6 tablespoons mixed cooked vegetables
(peas, diced potato, diced carrot)
2-3 tablespoons mayonnaise
parsley rosettes

• In a frying pan cook the cervelat slices until the edges curl. Remove from the pan and cool. Spoon the mayonnaise into the vegetables. Just before serving divide the vegetables over the salami boats. Garnish with parsley. Place the snacks together with the others on the plate, do not wait too long to serve, or they will loose their crispiness.

Cheese salad

piece of cucumber
vinegar, salt and pepper
200 g (7 oz) new hard cheese, diced
1 green pepper
1 small onion
pinch of caraway seeds
spoonful of mayonnaise

• Shave thin slices of cucumber and marinate for a short while in vinegar, salt and pepper. Combine the cheese and very thinly sliced pepper with the thin onion rings and caraway seeds. Divide on to boat shaped salad leaves. Garnish with strips of cucumber and a little mayonnaise. Put the cheese boats in the middle of the plate.

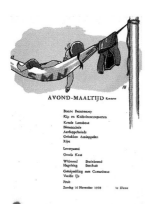

1954 On board of the KLM Constellation people also enjoy small snacks first courses

Stuffed tomatoes

4 small tomatoes
100 g (3½ oz) tinned salmon
1 tablespoon mayonnaise
1 teaspoon Dijon mustard
hard-boiled egg wedges

• Cut the tomatoes crosswise three times (stalk side under). Spoon out the seeds, fold the leaves outwards (Mrs Holthausen calls this a 'water lily').
• Blend the mayonnaise and mustard, combine with the salmon flakes, but reserve 4 nice small pieces. Fill the tomatoes and garnish with a piece of reserved salmon and a wedge of egg.

☛ Sweet peppers were very new then, and often bought in tins.

1954 The kitchen of the KLM-constellation

Clear oxtail soup / Oxtail clair

A very popular dish, judged by how often we found it on menus, although not immediately recognized by everyone. In 1959 a guest of the Americain in Dordrecht added the Dutch translation to the menu: 'ossestaartsoep, helder'. No wonder it was not prepared at home very often and that Henriëtte Holthausen in her book for the working woman, uses tins of oxtail soup; it entails a lot of work. Please, do not forget the Madeira!

Recipe source: Henriëtte Holthausen, *Spreekuur in de keuken*, Baarn: Het Wereldvenster, 1958

50 g (1¾ oz) lean bacon, diced
1 onion, cut in half
4 small carrots
1 leek
a piece of oxheart cabbage
2 celery stalks
500 g (1 lb 2 oz) oxtail in pieces of 5 cm (2 in)
2 tablespoons tomato purée
generous amount of black peppercorns, salt
1½ litre (6 cups) boiling water
parsley, thyme, tarragon, chervil

·

very finely chopped parsley
1 glass of Madeira

• Preheat the oven to 250 °C/475 °F/Gas mark 9. Place the bacon in a wide oven-proof saucepan. Put the onion and coarsely chopped vegetables on top and finally the pieces of oxtail. Place the pan uncovered in the oven for 40 minutes. As soon as the meat starts to brown add the tomato purée, a generous amount of crushed peppercorns and salt.

• Remove the pan from the oven, pour in the water with the green herbs. Simmer approximately 2 hours on very low heat. Strain the stock through a damp, fine piece of cloth. It may be necessary to clear the broth with 1 beaten egg white in the following manner: cool the stock and on low heat bring back to the boil with 1 beaten egg white stirred in. Strain as before. Season with salt if necessary. Remove the meat from the bones. Place between two plates (under pressure) in the fridge. Dice the meat and just before serving add to the broth, together with the parsley. Season with Madeira or put small glasses of Madeira on the table for everybody to serve themselves.

1951 The first Albert Heijn supermarket. An increasing amount of food is sold in tins

Creamy mushroom soup / Champignon-roomsoep

It is quite remarkable to see how every soup that became popular in the 1950s immediately had a dried or tinned version. Maybe with the idea of war still lingering: never to be caught empty-handed again.

In 1950 a small leaflet was published by Le champignon Lutèce. In those days only foreign mushrooms were available in the Netherlands, which is nearly incomprehensible nowadays, after the enormous flight the cultivation of mushrooms took in the 1960s. The monthly period *De Volksgezondheid* ('The National Health') mentions this most well known of all fungi in its May edition: 'Cultivated mushrooms are a welcome addition to the everyday menu and are recommended for those who lack appetite or undergo lengthy rest cures. Since fresh mushrooms contain so much fibre they are also recommended for the treatment of constipation and obstruction. Mushrooms cooked with lemon, onion and vinegar are a good remedy for obesity.' These are still the times where taste has to be excused by health!

A recipe for *velouté* is also given, in which mushrooms are cooked in milk, drained and thrown away, according to a good French custom. We follow *Het Haagse Kookboek* (24th edition, 1952), which leaves them in, but we use the *crème de riz* by Escoffier, translated in the same year, since there is no need for a strong taste of stock when using tasteful mushrooms.

1 litre (4 cups) milk
1 onion with 1 clove stuck in
white peppercorns
2-3 teaspoons salt
bouquet of parsley, bay, thyme
4 tablespoons rice flour
(for toddler's porridge, the version to be cooked)

250 g (9 oz) white mushrooms, sliced
100 ml (½ cup) double cream
nutmeg
chives

• Bring the milk to the boil with the onion, herbs, salt and pepper. Make a paste of rice flour and a little cold milk and stir into the milk. Heat the milk for 3 minutes until thickened. Strain.
• Add the cleaned and sliced mushrooms and cook for 5 minutes. Stir in the cream. Season with chives and nutmeg.

☞ Also see Watercress soup (1930s).

Pastry shell with chicken ragout / Kippenpasteitje

If, in the 1950s, one wanted to put on airs, pastry shells were served. Of course that was not the reason for the confectioners to put them on the menu for their official dinner of June 10th 1952, that is called occupational pride. According to Heleen Halverhout it can be seen as traditional Dutch food for festive days. She wished the recipe in her booklet would serve as 'a piece of Holland' for all those people who were leaving the country to emigrate to Australia and America. The ragout soon was sold in tins. In those days a new pan was also brought on the market: the pressure cooker, and Heleen advises to use it for the chicken.

Recipe source: Heleen A. M. Halverhout, *Traditionele recepten voor de Feestdagen*, Bussum: Uitgeversmaatschappij C.A.J. van Dishoeck, 1955; we replaced the mushrooms with peas. Also see R. Lotgering Hillebrand, *Snelkookpanrecepten*, Amsterdam: Van Perlstein, Roeper Bosch N.V., 1955

Heleen A. M. Halverhout

Traditionele Recepten

voor de Feestdagen

100 g (3 oz) minced veal, salt
50 g (1¾ oz) peas (frozen)
300 ml (1¼ cup) water

600 g (1lb 5 oz) soup chicken
50 g (1¾ oz) onion
40 g (1½ oz) carrot
1 bay leaf
pinch of saffron
a little thyme
parsley
lemon zest
peppercorns
salt
.

40 g (1½ oz) butter
50 g (1¾ oz) flour
500 ml (2 cups) chicken stock
1 tablespoon white wine
50 ml (¼ cup) double cream
20 ml (4 teaspoons) pasteurized egg yolk (= 1 egg yolk)

4 pre-baked pastry shells
4 sprigs of parsley

1958 The Rotterdam is launched. The flight of emigrants started in 1951 will continue for quite a while

• Form small balls of the minced veal and salt. Cook for
5 minutes with the peas in 300 ml (1¼ cup) water. Strain
the stock.
• Joint the chicken and put the pieces with the seasonings and
cooking liquid of minced veal in a pressure cooker without
its grid. Cook for 25 minutes under pressure (normal pan
1½ hours, under water). Take the meat from the bones.
Strain the stock through a moist piece of cloth. Add water
to make 500 ml (2 cups).
• Melt the butter in a saucepan and lightly brown the flour.
While stirring add the stock and keep stirring for a thick
and smooth sauce. Season with the wine, egg yolk beaten

with the cream and a little hot sauce. Stir in the meat balls,
peas, chicken meat and maybe a little salt. Heat the sauce
without boiling.
• Heat the pastry shells according to the packet instructions.
Fill with the ragout. Put the lids on and decorate with a sprig
of parsley. Serve on a folded serviette.

☞ The official recipe requires 150 g (5½ oz) mushrooms
instead of peas. Blanch and drain the sliced mushrooms
and add to the ragout with the meatballs.
☞ Instead of a whole chicken take 300 g (10 ½ oz) cooked
chicken meat and 500 ml (2 cups) of stock.

113

Asparagus with Hollandaise sauce / Asperges met hollandaisesaus

A golden oldie! It also appeared on the menu of the Amstelhotel in Amsterdam on the occasion of the opening of the international exhibition 'The Sugar' in April 1952. The sauce is very Dutch, although the French tried to steal it from us. It was written up in the first Dutch cookery book printed on Dutch soil, an appendix to the medical book of Carolus Battus, Dordrecht 1593.

Recipe source: card in the menu collection of the Dutch Confectioners Guild, to be found in the library of the Confectioners Museum 'Het Warme Land' in Hattem

16 white asparagus
salt

·

4 slices of bone ham
2 hard-boiled eggs

·

1½ tablespoon water
1½ tablespoon white wine vinegar
3 crushed black peppercorns
85 g (3 oz) butter
30 ml (2 tablespoons) pasteurized egg yolk (= 1 egg yolk)
salt, (cayenne) pepper, lemon juice

• After buying, place the asparagus in cold water to stay as fresh as possible. Rinse and remove the wooden piece from the bottom of the stalk. Peel the asparagus with a vegetable peeler, start just below the tip. Put peel and pieces of stalk in a pan, cover with a clean cloth, put the asparagus on top with the salt and enough cold water to cover. Bring to the boil, lower the heat and keep the water just below boiling point for 10 minutes. Remove the pan from the heat and leave for 15-20 minutes. The asparagus should be soft, but firm.

• Cook the water with vinegar and peppercorns until reduced by half. Melt the butter, remove the foam and only use the clear fat (clarifying!), keep it tepid. Place the reduced liquid in a larger pan with boiling water (au bain-marie). Whisk the egg yolks in and keep whisking to form a lightly thickened light sauce. Also, gradually whisk the tepid butter in. Season with salt and (cayenne) pepper and if needed lemon juice.

• Drain the cooked asparagus. Place on a warm serving plate. Fold the slices of ham over the bottom end. Garnish with a line of mashed hard-boiled egg yolk, mashed hard-boiled egg white and chopped parsley. Spoon a little of the hollandaise sauce around and serve the remainder in a sauce boat.

☛ Without a doubt a pinch of sugar went into the cooking liquid for the asparagus, because this was customary in those days and especially at the Sugar exhibition. Connoisseurs of our days reject this.

♟ Pinot Blanc d'Alsace. Fresh light spicy white wine from the Alsace, the pre-eminent white asparagus wine.

Lemon sole with North Sea shrimps / Tongschar met Noordzeegarnalen

The menus of these years were overflowing with sole, their size still large enough to fill an oversized plate. It nearly goes without saying that in February 1958 the Dutch Club of Chefs de cuisine in the Kurhaus was treated by chef J.Th. Heering to *Paupiettes de sole Caroline*. According to Mr Anton Jansen, who for years reigned the Kurhaus, this name is not about the sauce, but about the garnish. He prefers Dutch shrimps and a few feathers of dill. Carême's famous words are featured as slogan on the menu: 'People who know how to eat, are as scarce as culinary artists.' Unfortunately sole is even more scarce nowadays, so we propose lemon sole.

Recipe source: Escoffier: *Filets de sole Marguery*. Also needed are mussels, see next recipe source for the title of the translated book.

200 ml (¾ cup) reduced fish stock (jar)
200 ml (¾ cup) white wine
20 g (¾ oz) butter
30 g (1 oz) flour
salt
200 ml (¾ cup) double cream
50 g (1¾ oz) butter

·

8 fillets of lemon sole
salt and pepper
4 tablespoons reduced fish stock
150 g (5½ oz) Dutch shrimps
chives
fresh dill

·

baby potatoes
butter, dill

• Cook the stock with the wine down to 300 ml (1¼ cup). Melt the butter in a small saucepan, brown the flour lightly, whisk in the reduced liquid. Keep stirring and cook to make a smooth sauce. Stir in the cream. From the heat whisk in the cold butter in small cubes.
• Thickly butter a flame-proof dish. Bring 4 tablespoons reduced stock to the boil. Fold the fillets of fish lengthwise (skin side in) and place in the dish. Sprinkle with salt and pepper, and poach for 5 minutes. Halfway through carefully turn the fish over. Sprinkle with the shrimps and herbs. Spoon over the sauce. Place the dish under a hot grill: not to brown, but to glaze. Garnish with feathers of dill.
• Serve with boiled baby potatoes with a little butter, sprinkled with dill.

Three chairmen of the Dutch Club of Chefs de cuisine, from left to right: J. Geervliet, A.J. Hekkelman, H. Anderweij

Fillet of beef in the fashion of the market gardener's wife / Ossenhaas van de tuindersvrouw

(Filet de boeuf jardinière)

From the menu at Soestdijk April 1956: a cold dish of ham with champagne Dom Perignon 1947; clear broth; fillets of sole in white wine sauce with Batard Montrachet; roasted fillet of beef with several vegetables and the wine Chateau Cos d'Estournel 1937; coffee, ice cream, fruit. The French influence is not only visible in the choice of excellent wines. The best chefs completely focused on Escoffier, whose famous manual they had translated and adapted. In this period fillet of beef was put on the menus so frequently that Het Haagse Kookboek laments: 'Since restaurants so often need fillet of beef, the private customer often needs to be satisfied with a different cut!' We give you the recipe for a larded fillet of beef à la jardinière. With lots of different vegetables. A custom also held upright in true Dutch eateries with many other combinations of meat.

Recipe source: Escoffier, *Handboek voor de Keuken*, adaptation of *Le Guide Culinaire* by P.F. Loncke, F.G. Swidde. With a preface by F. Lehman, chef de cuisine, and with the assistance of J.Th. Heering M.C.A., chef de cuisine Kurhaus Scheveningen, A.C. van der Linden, chef de cuisine Royal Palace Soestdijk, W.E.L. te Meij M.C.A., retired chef de cuisine Esplanade, Utrecht. Amsterdam: Universum, 1952-53

Serves 8
1¼ kg (2 lb 12 oz) fillet of beef, cut from the middle
salt
150 g (5½ oz) butter

For the potato stacks (pommes fondantes):
potato slices of 1½ cm (1 in) thick
butter for frying
brown sauce or marmite for brushing

Suggestion for vegetables:
200 g (7 oz) endive with bacon
200 g (7 oz) chicory
200 g (7 oz) cauliflower
200 g (7 oz) green beans
4 small tomatoes
4 dessertspoons cooked peas
1 slice of cheese
200 g (7 oz) white mushrooms, butter
salt and pepper, melted butter

1950 The largest garden of the Netherlands, The Keukenhof

🍷 Pécharmant. Strong red
wine from the Bergerac.

• Preheat the oven to 275 °C/500 °F/Gas Mark 9. Rub the meat with salt. In a frying pan melt the butter and brown the meat quickly on all sides. Place the meat in a roasting tray, pour the butter around it. Roast the beef for 10 minutes in the middle of the oven, basting regularly with cooking liquid. Put the meat on a warm plate and leave for 15 minutes. In this way lesser juices will seep out during carving.

• In the butter brown and cook the potatoes slices until tender. Brush with brown sauce or marmite. Make a stack on a plate and keep warm. Cook all vegetables. Fill the tomatoes with the peas and place a quart of a slice of cheese on top. Grill until brown. Brown the slices of mushroom in butter. Season with salt and pepper.

• Carve the meat at an angle in thick slices and put these in their original shape on a serving plate with the *pommes fondantes*. Arrange the beef with separate sections of the different vegetables and glaze with melted butter. Stir a little water into the cooking liquid and cook it down a little. Serve in a sauce boat.

☛ In former years the meat was larded with 100 g (3½ oz) strips of pork fat. For this purpose salted fat from the back was used, which when cut parallel to the rind is strong enough to be inserted into the beef with a channelled larding needle. This way the meat would not dry out during cooking. We no longer do this, since meat is more tender nowadays and larding tends to loosen the meat juices.

☛ Instead of fillet of beef one can also use roast beef from the loin.

☛ In the photograph you can see a pedestal cut from white bread. The sides have been decorated and the bread deep-fried.

117

Crêpes Suzette / Crêpes Suzette

'Cooking at the table' becomes very fashionable. This is asking a lot of the service personnel, since people could want a main course (for example tournedos Stroganoff) as well as a dessert flambéd at the table. Lydia Winkel, the boisterous cookery writer of the newspaper *Het Parool*, missing unfamiliar dishes in Dutch cookery books, gives a recipe for crêpes Suzette. She does her utmost to convince her readers cooking is not a 'sour duty', but can be as creative as 'reading, playing music and sewing dresses'. Well, that did not come as a surprise to J.Th. Heering, chef de cuisine of the Hotel Kurhaus at Scheveningen: he had known for a long time. He created a playful version: 'Pancakes Madame Butterfly', a real work of art. He folded a spoonful of solid frozen vanilla ice cream into the crêpes before flambéing them. That way cooking can even give you a high!

Recipe source: *Lydia's Recepten Winkel*, Amsterdam: N.V. E.M. Querido's Uitgeversmij, 1957, and C.M. van Lanschot, C. van Limburg Stirum-Van der Willigen, *Kookboek Tesselschade-Arbeid Adelt*, Amsterdam, 1957

8 *crêpes*
75 g (2¾ oz) wheat flour
2 eggs
pinch of salt
250 ml (1 cup) milk
butter

·

2 oranges
30 g (1 oz) butter
1 tablespoon sugar
6 tablespoons Cointreau

1959 Cooking at the table at Hotel Krasnapolsky

• In a frying pan of 18 cm (7 in) diameter prepare the pancakes.
• Scrub the oranges and from one orange peel the zest without the bitter pith. Finely chop the zest. Combine the zest with the sugar, butter and juice of both oranges. Melt the mixture in a warm pan and coat the pancakes on both sides. Put the pancakes back in the pan, pour over the Cointreau and flambé.

☛ Chef Heering used Curaçao and pure alcohol.

Semolina pudding / Keeke's flaméri

(met bessengelei en kersen)

From his preface to *Lydia's Recepten Winkel* (previous recipe) we know journalist Henri Knap became mortally ill just by hearing the word '*toetje*' ('dessert'). It made him think of 'slimy semolina pudding', that never ceased to appear on the Dutch table. He was born in the wrong country, because the Dutch have always been extremely fond of '*toetjes*'. And no-one has been able to ban them from our table, not even good old Gaylord Hauser, who in those years tried to conquer the market with his dubious slimming theories.

Recipe source: every cookery book from domestic science schools in the 1950s. Homely version of someone who endlessly prepared semolina pudding, and her family loved her for it.

Individual moulds of 150 ml (⅔ cup) or one mould of 1 litre (4 cups)

·

3 sheets of gelatine (6 g)

·

500 ml (2 cups) milk
60 g (2 oz) semolina
75 g (2½ oz) sugar
seeds from a vanilla pod
1 drop bitter almond oil

·

100 ml (½ cup) pasteurized egg white (= about 3 egg whites)
225 g (8 oz) red currant jelly
2 tablespoons Kirsch

·

fresh cherries

- Fill the mould(s) with cold water. Soak the gelatine in plenty of cold water.
- Bring the milk to the boil, add the semolina while stirring. Cook until the mixture becomes a thick porridge (5 minutes), stirring occasionally.
- In the meantime whisk the egg whites to stiff peaks. Into the porridge stir the sugar, vanilla seeds and drop of almond oil. From the heat dissolve the well squeezed gelatine. Fold in the egg whites.
- Empty the mould(s) and pour in the pudding. Let set in the fridge.
- Unmould the pudding and serve at room temperature. Garnish with a ring of red currant jelly with Kirsch and a ring of cherries, stones removed.

☛ In the photograph you see beautiful home made jelly cubes of blackberry juice. The jelly should not be too stiff. The adding of Kirsch will turn it into a kind of sauce that goes extremely well with the texture of the pudding and creates a wonderful taste sensation.

1960–1969
Flower power and bistro

Dining together, in good harmony

In 1989 The University Department of Human Food, in Wageningen, analysed food advertisements of this century. The 1960s show a tremendous change. Words like tasty and

cosy appear far more frequently than the word 'healthy', known from the forties and fifties. This is the period in which tins, jars and bottles are highly praised. And on reading the book *Eet goed, al goed* ('Eat well, all well') by Wina Born and Harriët Freezer (Arbeidspers, 1968) – beautifully illustrated by Peter Vos – we get an impression of just how popular tins were: game soup followed by crab salad with olives, pickled peppers, jellied chicken, anchovies and artichokes...

This development did worry the Public Information Service for Food and the Commodity Boards. In 1964 they commissioned a food paperback titled *Dat is lekker* ('That is nice'), which is packed with healthy dishes. The name Lydia Winkel is on it, but one justly doubts a large input from her side. She passed away that year and would never have backed up the Introduction: 'May this book (...) contribute to be an improvement (...) of popular food(!).'

Food advertisements emphasize the social aspect of eating together. And that way the advertising boys put their finger on the wishes of people with a little increase in wealth: longer and more elaborate dining.

1963 An evening with Wim Sonneveld

Exotic fare at the home table

People started to travel, although not very far. The food paperback *Lekker* informs us that kebab is meat on a skewer, to be found in Eastern Europe, the Balkans and Asia, and is made of beef, lamb, small sausages, pieces of pineapple and mushrooms. Henriëtte Holthausen takes us on a trip 'with chicken around the world', but it is highly unlikely her publisher allowed her to go to Egypt, since she describes the national Egyptian dish of brown broad beans (ful medames) as a white bean dish.

For many first time campers the *Kampeer en Caravan Kookboek* by Wina Born was a reliable guide. People started trekking around Europe by car, which became more and more common property in those years. And since French bread was unknown as yet, some took their own potatoes to France.

The enlightened already cooked with wine, again lead by Wina Born, or made pizza following the recipe of *Het Haagse Kookboek* (55th edition, 1968), and, furthermore, spicy macaroni dishes, a product the Dutch in years before had only used in sweet porridge with raisins.

The common fare still remains popular. Mrs Lotgering Hillebrand (*Toetjesboek*, 3rd edition, 1969) writes: '(...) a dessert is very pleasant, a little festive and there is no reason our daily meal should not be that', and she continues to offer apart from chocolate fondue, recipes for buttermilk porridge and bread porridge. Not everybody was watching their weight. Henriëtte Holthausen, for example, writes in her apple cake recipe in *Meisje kun je koken* ('Girl, can you cook'): 'Girls, do I need to add that this is delicious with double cream whipped with lots of soft white sugar?'

There was a different public as well. Alternative people who wore turtlenecks and were social critics. Provo's provoke, the occupation of the Maagdenhuis (Amsterdam University) 'democratizes' the Dutch universities. The hippie scene went into macrobiotics with yin and yang, a trend that later proved to be very unhealthy.

Restaurant business

In the meantime people at top restaurants still ate traditionally French. Dr J.M. Fuchs in his *Van eten en drinken weten* ('Knowing about food and drink'; early 1960s) describes what could be ordered at top locations. Not bad! *Tortue Lady Curzon* with Madeira from 1870, *Filets de sole Czarine*, *Selle de veau Winsor* and strangely enough *gingembre* for dessert and mocha with Cognacs and liqueurs (plural!).

Completely non-traditional was Frans Fagel's new bistro. According to a charter in a Moscovite fastfood restaurant the designation 'bistro' was introduced early in the previous century in a fast food place in Paris by victorious Russian soldiers. They called 'Bistro, bistro' ('Quick, quick!') to the waitresses in the cafés. Speed was definitely not Frans and Janny Fagel's concern – they foremost wanted their guests to be able to dine in a convivial atmosphere, on something slightly different. With onion soup and escargots on the menu, in those days imported from Paris. After a few hours of fasting in a tray with salt they were cooked for 2 hours and served in a thick sauce of parsley, celery, dill, onions, butter and Alsatian wine (*à l'alsacienne*). And bear meat from Poland, imported by a customer who went there for timber. Successful with the guests, who were made up of academics, medical people and businessmen.

There also were eateries for 'guest workers' to be found, among whom the Turks. Wina Born tells about a few shrewd businessmen, who soon employed belly dancers, which is how the Netherlands discovered shish kebab. This is the start of the multicultural cuisine.

Kitchen design

Suddenly the kitchen is much better equipped. Books are published with titles such as *Koelkastboekje* ('Refrigerator booklet') and *Mixed grill* (Heleen Haverhout). A quote on the cooker: 'We can have all in one: good burners, a spacious oven with a high temperature and a separate build-in grill. This is what every housewife wants.' Henriëtte Holthausen mentions the following 'luxury appliances for the kitchen': refrigerator, electric mixer, electric meat mincer, pressure cooker, electric fruit press, coffee grinder (preferably electric). And Miss J. Straatsma gives a splendid overview of all new gadgets (with drawings) in *De moderne keuken* ('The modern kitchen'; Utrecht, 1963), plus recipes for milkshakes, popular since they were served at Ruteck's, Heck's and other simple cafés that no longer exist.

In hindsight it is almost unbelievable that the modern mechanized kitchen has become public property only such a short while ago.

Dips and crisps / Dipjes en Chipjes

'These dips are a wonderful starter for any party', Hugh Jans writes. It is the American variation on hors d'oeuvre, which we do not seem to be able to forget. Together with blanched broccoli (new!) or raw vegetables or jumbo shrimps, they become a first course, but with the addition of little meatballs, frankfurters, with breadsticks, baguette and crisps we are approaching a main course. It had to be simple, since the housewife often was 'on the work force' as well. The sauces were served in 'cosy' bowls, the base often 'spruced up' ready-bought sauce from a jar. See the index for other sauces.

Recipe inspired by Wina Born, Lily van Pareren, Hugh Jans, *Feest, tips en recepten voor partijtjes thuis en buiten.* Amsterdam: Albert Heijn n.v., 1968

Sour cream dip

250 ml (1 cup) thick sour cream (crème fraîche)
1 tablespoon finely chopped parsley
1 tablespoon finely chopped chives
⅛ teaspoon curry powder
pinch of paprika
salt

• Blend all ingredients.

Cheese dip

250 ml (1 cup) mayonnaise
2 tablespoons grated mature cheese
1 clove of garlic, crushed
tabasco to taste

• Blend all ingredients.

Chutney dip

250 ml (1 cup) mayonnaise
2 tablespoons mango chutney
2 spring onions

• Stir the minced chutney and onion into the mayonnaise.

1965 Enough is happening in the theatres of the 1960s. Opening night for the musical *Heerlijk duurt het langst* ('Delicacy is the best policy') by Annie M.G. Schmidt

Cucumber dip

1 cucumber
250 ml (1 cup) yoghurt
dried mint
salt and pepper

• Squeeze the coarsely grated cucumber and combine the pulp with yoghurt drained in a cheese cloth, the mint, salt and pepper.

Smoked eel with shrimps, anchovies and horseradish mayonnaise / Gerookte paling met garnalen, ansjovis en mierikswortelmayonaise

In 1960 the Horecaf (club catering industry) celebrated its 70th anniversary from May 12th to 23rd inclusive.

They did so with an international exhibition Salon Culinaire: Guest and Host. This event was sufficiently important for journalist Bibeb to come with a book (same title) in which famous Dutch people share their experiences of the restaurant business. The recipe is of a first course, found on the menu of the International Restaurant La Palette. Smoked fish – variation: trout or salmon or a combination of the two – with toast became so popular in these years that it was even offered to the royal couple in the Havenrestaurant in Amsterdam (1962). The most simple version is to be found in a book by Maja Krans: eel with parsley and lemon, an excellent combination that we gladly borrow.

Recipe source: Maja Krans, *Koken voor twee* ('Cooking for two': a title never seen before, to have 16 editions!), 1st edition, 1966. Also menus kept by Confectioners museum *'Het Warme Land'* in Hattem and Culinary Museum Mariënhof in Amersfoort

150 g (5½ oz) lambs lettuce
garden cress
radishes

·

300 g (10½ oz) smoked eel
50 g (1¾ oz) cooked Dutch shrimps
8 anchovy fillets
2 tablespoons very finely chopped parsley
1 lemon
1 tablespoon grated horseradish
2 tablespoons mayonnaise
salt and pepper

·

toasted white bread
butter

• Divide the washed lettuce onto 4 plates. At the edges place a rosette of garden cress and a few thin slices of radish.

• Cut the eel in thin strips. Place the strips in a circle in the middle of the lettuce and garnish with a ring of parsley, a ring of shrimps around them, and 2 anchovy fillets (soaked in ample water for half an hour in order to loose the salt – in those days they used milk!). Decorate with wedges of lemon. Serve with a sauce of horseradish and mayonnaise. Serve with toast and butter.

Dutch and other fish soups / *Scheveningse en andere bouillabaisse*

Kitchen master Willem E.L. te Meij, one of the members of the executive committee for the international exhibition '70 years of Horecaf' writes in a newspaper article in 1960: 'A little variation makes dining more pleasant.' He assumes 'the young housewife will hide her cookery books in a far and dark place' and that she will react to the recipe pages of her 'woman's weekly' only with an 'oh dear, what lovely pictures!'
To give her some new ideas he offers this recipe.
The same fish soup, but prepared the French way, was made by Hans van Mierlo, founder of the political party D'66, about six years later more popular than ever. On television he proclaimed to be able to make a very good bouillabaisse indeed. Unheard of for a politician!

Scheveningen

30 g (1 oz) butter
½ chopped onion
1 clove of garlic
40 g (1½ oz) flour
1 litre (4 cups) fish stock
100 g (3½ oz) soup vegetables
1 tablespoon shrimp butter
1 fillet of sole
100 g (3 ½ oz) fillet of turbot
1 tablespoon pearl barley (cooked)
50 ml (¼ cup) cream

baguette

• Melt the butter in a soup pan and soften the chopped onion and crushed garlic. While stirring add the flour. Gradually stir in the stock. Keep stirring for a smooth and thickened soup.
• Add the vegetables and cook until tender. Stir in the shrimp butter and poach the small pieces of fish. Add pearl barley and cream, and serve with baguette.

1966 Beatrix and Claus break the tradition by marrying in Amsterdam instead of The Hague

The Scheveningse bouillabaisse is a typically Dutch translation of a strong and flavourful Mediterranean soup. The Dutch sometimes did dare a little more, witness Hugh Jans in *Samen lekker koken* (Amsterdam Arbeiderspers 1963, 1969). We adapted his version to species of fish that were available on the market in those days. He has the fishmonger fillet the cod, sole, mackerel, pike perch, carp and fresh eel. He buys shrimp, but also squid and crab (separately cooked), and makes stock of the heads and bones with water and a little wine. This is what follows:

100 ml (½ cup) olive oil
1 large onion
1 leek
3 cloves of garlic
1½ litres (6 cups) fish stock
2 tablespoons tomato purée
1 piece of orange peel without bitter pith
2 tablespoons finely chopped parsley
pinch of saffron powder
1 bay leaf
thyme
(Pernod,) salt and pepper

rings of squid, fish fillets, shrimp, crab meat
toasted French bread spread with garlic

• In a large pan heat the olive oil. On low heat cook the onion and leek until tender. Stir in the crushed garlic and add the stock, tomato purée and seasonings. On high heat bring to the boil.

• Carefully slide the rings of squid and fillets, firm ones first, into the pan: they should stay whole. Finally add the crab and shrimp. Do not stir.

• Place the toasted French bread in soup plates, divide a little fish over it. If wanted season the stock with a little Pernod, salt and pepper and pour it over the fish. Or serve the fish separately with the following sauce: *rouille*, made in a blender by combining 2 cloves of garlic, 2 red peppers (a novelty in those days), a soaked and squeezed slice of bread, 2 tablespoons of olive oil and enough fish stock to make a thick sauce.

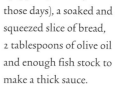

Parisian onion soup / Parijse uiensoep

1961 Chez Francois, the first
bistro in the Netherlands

What a sweet time! When at the end of a party the very civilized hostess thought: let's put an end to it... she served soup. An 'elegant hint', says Wina Born, but also 'a heart rendering goodbye'. Her first – and excellent! – choice is Parisian onion soup. 'Onion soup is extremely suited to land on the ground again after drinking a pleasant glass!' *Potage à l'oignon* was also served at the Salon Culinaire: Guest and Host (price per bowl *f* 2,00), but was not new for the Netherlands, where in the 1930s this soup was to be found as *potage viveur* in *Economische zuivelgerechten* ('Economical dairy dishes'). Obviously, this also was a popular dish in Frans Fagel's bistro. After Wina Born had written *Koken met wijn*, it could happen that even Dutch country kitchens started to smell like Paris.

4 heat proof bowls
400 g (14 oz) peeled onions, halved and thinly sliced
2 tablespoons butter
300 ml (1¼ cup) dry white wine
800 ml (3 cups) meat stock
75 g (2¾ oz) Gruyère cheese (or other rather spicy cheese)
4-8 slices of baguette

• Melt the butter in a heavy pan. Cook the onion transparent and soft. Pour on the wine and stock. Simmer, covered, on low heat for 20 minutes.
• Grate the cheese, toast the baguette on both sides. Preheat a grill.
• Spoon the soup into 4 bowls. Place a slice of bread on top. Sprinkle with cheese and brown under the grill.

☛ Adding wine is Wina Born's idea in *Koken met wijn*, 3rd edition, Amsterdam/Brussels, 1967. Without the wine the soup is nice too, just take extra stock.

☛ Another piece of advice from Wina Born is to sauté a few cloves of garlic with the onion and spice the soup up with a little cayenne pepper (from: *Feest, tips en recepten voor partijtjes thuis en buiten*. Amsterdam: Albert Heijn n.v., 1968).

☛ These days sometimes one tablespoon of tomato purée is added with a little thyme. All are variations on the recipe of this 'sixties-soup'.

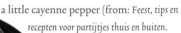

Cheese fondue / Kaasfondue

Madly popular in the 1960s, especially with students on festive occasions. The Netherlands want to eat 'differently' as well as informally. Mrs Lotgering Hillebrand is tuned into this, and in 1963 she writes 200 *Oude en nieuwe recepten, die men niet in elk kookboek tegenkomt*. In it she presents both cheese fondue and fondue bourguignonne, a dish for which pieces of meat are deep-fried in hot oil at the table, resulting in a trip to the cleaner's the next day, in order to get the smelly clothes cleaned.

The Dairy Commodity Board also sees possibilities. On December 20th 1961 it puts a full-page ad in the newspapers recommending fondue made of Dutch farmers' cheese: 'meant to be consumed late in the evening when there is a call for something very gratifying.' Mrs Voorhuis, in *Fijne hapjes van Margriet* (1964), also serves fondue as entremets during supper.

Per person
·

head lettuce
olive oil, vinegar, garlic, salt and pepper
·

½ clove of garlic
1 glass of dry white wine
75 g (2½ oz) Gruyère or Dutch Leerdammer cheese, coarsely grated
75 g (2 ½ oz) Emmentaler or Dutch Maaslander cheese, coarsely grated
about 1 tablespoon arrowroot or potato starch
½ shot glass of Kirsch
pinch of nutmeg
·

baguette

· Dress the lettuce with a vinaigrette made with three times as much oil as vinegar, a little garlic, salt and pepper.
· Rub a pan with half a clove of garlic, add the wine and heat to the boiling point. Add the cheese and stir with a wooden spoon at low heat until all cheese has melted. While stirring make the figure 8.
· Thicken this unappetising mass with a paste of arrowroot and water. Transfer the fondue to a *caquelon*, stir in the Kirsch and put the pan on a methylated spirit burner, on which it will bubble softly. Dust with a little nutmeg. Everybody dips a piece of bread on a long fork into the fondue. Serve with white wine or tea together with the salad.

☞ Often recipes use cornflour instead of potato starch: don't do this, because you will get cheese sauce instead of cheese fondue.
☞ Traditionally, the whole melting process should take place in the earthenware pot (*caquelon*), but this modern method saves time.

1969 Students occupy the Maagdenhuis, Amsterdam

Flambéd scampi / Geflambeerde scampi

(Scampi Flambés Belle Alliance)

Alphons II Stevens (Alphons I was the founder), in the 1960s the owner of the famous hotel and restaurant Prinses Juliana in Valkenburg, attended a course on flambéing in Switzerland in those days. Flambéing was fashionable, and Juliana, which in 1967 joined the prestigious Alliance Gastronomique Néerlandaise, took the lead. The present managing director, Paul Stevens, has very fond memories of that period: 'It was still possible to surprise people, because my father himself went shopping in Paris.' Prinses Juliana also had a real life lobster tank (homarium) and its own herb garden, in itself surprising enough.

This is what Wina Born writes in 1967 about the dish with fresh prawns from the lobster tank, the recipe of which is given below: '(...) like pink ceiling angels on an Italian painting surrounded by a feathery soft cloud of creamy sauce with a dash of Calvados and some sharp seasoning.'

No wonder dr. J.M. Fuchs also mentions these heavenly flambéd scampi in *Van eten en drinken weten* (Amsterdam, 1963). He adds that the Michelin guide recommends the detour necessary for visiting the Prinses Juliana. And people still feel it is worth doing so: this restaurant has had a Michelin-star for 40 years in a row! Here the original recipe, checked by master chef Otto Nijenhuis, these days chef of Prinses Juliana.

---

100 g (3½ oz) shallots
100 g (3½ oz) carrots
2 bay leaves
1 tablespoon tarragon leaves
1 tablespoon parsley leaves
sprig of thyme
25 g (1 oz) butter

12 fresh scampi (as a main course 24)
50 ml (¼ cup) Cognac

50 ml (¼ cup) Calvados
2 glasses of dry white wine

.

20 g (¾ oz) butter
25 g (1 oz) flour
2 ripe tomatoes
100 ml (½ cup) double cream
salt and pepper

.

parsley
boiled rice to serve

♀ Riesling d'Alsace,
the 'king of wines',
dry and fruity.

- Clean the vegetables, finely chop them with the herbs and
  cook them in 25 g (1 oz) butter.
- Add the fresh scampi and cook for a few minutes. Flambé
  with Cognac and Calvados. Pour over the wine and simmer
  for 5 minutes on low heat. Remove the scampi from the pan.
- In a small saucepan melt 20 g (2 tablespoons) of butter, stir in
  the flour and lightly brown it. While stirring add the scampi
  cooking liquid with the diced tomato and the cream. Cook
  this sauce down for 10 minutes (to about 200 ml / ¾ cup).
  Season with salt and pepper and push through a sieve.
- Pour the sauce on a warm serving plate, place the shelled
  scampi in the sauce, sprinkle with parsley. Serve with dry rice.

Alliance
Gastronomique
Néerlandaise
1967-1982

(Lemon) sole Véronique / Tong(schar) Véronique

Already to be found in Escoffier's *Guide Culinaire*, a book published in 1902: the story goes that a certain chef Malley of the Ritz in Paris created it for a party. He ordered a young sous-chef to prepare it while he himself went for a walk. On his return it appeared that the excited sous-chef had become father of his first daughter, named Véronique, hence the name. Who knows if this is true? Anyway, it became a famous dish of the Ritz hotels, where the rich went to be pampered and Escoffier became famous. Why this dish suddenly became popular again in the 1960s? According to Johannes van Dam, an Amsterdam culinary journalist, that might tie in with the renewed popularity of Escoffier after a new translation of his book *Handboek voor de keuken* in the 1950s. It certainly was not because there were enough fresh grapes to be had. John Fagel tells how in those days grapes came from tins. At least it gave the dish an appearance of luxury, something we desperately wanted in those days.

Recipe source: menu of Hotel Apollo in Amsterdam, September 14th 1964, Turbot Véronique, kept in Culinary Museum Mariënhof in Amersfoort; in 1969 Dorp de Kaag served the fish 'in white wine sauce, with grapes, mashed potatoes and carrots'. Furthermore, Sole Véronique in Lydia Winkel, *Culinaria van ver en dichtbij*, Amsterdam: C.J.A. Ruys, 1963

25 g (1 oz) butter
8 fillets of (lemon) sole, each about 75 g (2¾ oz)
lemon juice
salt and pepper
200 ml (¾ cup) white wine

·

50 g (1¾ oz) butter

·

250 g (9 oz) skinless grapes

· Prehcat the oven to 200 °C/400 °F/Gas Mark 6. Butter an oven-proof dish. Drizzle the fillets with lemon juice and sprinkle with salt and pepper. Fold the fillets and place in the buttered dish. Pour over the wine. Cover with a buttered piece of parchment paper and poach the fish for 12-15 minutes in the preheated oven.

· Pour off the cooking liquid. Arrange the fillets in an overlapping circle in the dish, leaving the inside empty.
Cook down the cooking liquid to syrup thickness, and from the heat beat in cold cubes of butter. Pour the sauce over the fish and place under a hot grill to lightly brown the top.
· Just before serving spoon the skinned and pipped grapes in the middle.

☛ Serve this dish with short crust crescents and a salad or soft vegetables.
☛ In the 1960s sole with tinned fruit, called Tong Picasso, was extremely popular. A Dutch creation using every imaginable variety of tinned fruit: pineapple, tangerine, grapes or a mixed cocktail and often also curry sauce. In our time, this fried sole with browned almonds and fried fresh fruit can be ordered at the Oesterbar ('Oyster bar') on the Leidseplein in Amsterdam.

Spanish pork tenderloin / Spaans varkenshaasje

(Filete de cerdo valdecabras)

Not only spurred on by the sudden travel and trekking, but also because of the television programme by Ben J. Kuyper the Dutch are beginning to enjoy the Indonesian, Austrian, Scandinavian and Spanish cuisine. Cookery books are published claiming to be 'Het neusje van de zalm' ('The best there is').

After a stay of a year and a half in Spain, F.J.M. Wientjes returns with a Spanish chef, and decides people in Dutch restaurants would like the taste. In the Grand Hotel in Zwolle, that carries his name, one can order beautiful sherries, with, of course, *tapas*. In the 13th century a Spanish king ordered the serving of a mouthful of food with every glass of wine. His name rightly was Alphons the Wise. With tapas as a starter, the meal can only be Spanish!

We have chosen the often ordered main dish, pork tenderloin... with mushrooms! Do not worry, that is the only ingredient to remind us of our national pork tenderloin.

Recipe source: Richard Nieman, *Buitenissig eten Buitenshuis*, Den Haag: W. van Hoeve, 1964

🍷 Rosé de Provence, elegant rosé wine, always offering freshness with spicy dishes.

50 ml (¼ cup) olive oil
4 pork tenderloin, each about 150 g (5 ½ oz)
salt and pepper

·

300 g (10 ½ oz) onions
8 tomatoes
1 clove of garlic
150 ml (⅔ cup) reduced fowl stock
pinch of crumbled saffron threads
½ teaspoon finely sliced red chilli or tabasco to taste

·

200 g (7 oz) white mushrooms
(25 g / 1 oz) truffle
100 ml (½ cup) Madeira
salt and pepper

· Heat two thirds of the olive oil and cook the meat, rubbed with salt and pepper, until tender. Remove from the pan and keep warm.
· Chop the onion and cook until translucent in the remaining olive oil. Peel the tomatoes, remove the seeds, add to the onion with the crushed garlic and cook to a pulp. Add the reduced stock and saffron with the pieces of pepper or tabasco, cover and simmer for 10 minutes.
· Reheat the oil in the meat pan. Cook the mushrooms (and sliced truffle), pour on the Madeira. Cook to reduce the liquid by half. Add the sauce and heat a little longer, season with salt and pepper.
· Diagonally slice the meat and spoon over the sauce.

☞ Truffle is beautiful, but not necessary. Nice to try as an alternative: Chinese black truffle, sold at farmers' markets and Chinese wholesalers. Very reasonably prized!
☞ Serve with fried baby potatoes and green beans cooked with thin strips of red pepper, garnished with strips of raw ham.

Raspberry puffs / Frambozensoezen

Fruitgeneugten ('Fruit delights') is the title of folder No. 1137 presented by the Public Information Service for Food on July 10th 1961. This is how it begins: 'Fruit belongs to the ancient foods. We may easily assume that people living on this earth in long gone days used to bring into their caves a meal of berries or edible greens in addition to the catch of fishing or hunting. (...) It does not matter whether we eat fruit because we like it or because it is healthy. Most important is eating it.' Obviously it was compulsory, although luckily most recipes made you forget this.

Recipe source: Folder 1137, kept in the Culinary Museum Mariënhof in Amersfoort

8 puffs
100 ml (½ cup) water
salt
40 g (1½ oz) butter
50 g (1¾ oz) wheat flour
2 eggs
·
500 ml (2 cups) raspberry ice cream
200 g (7 oz) raspberries
100 ml (½ cup) whipped and sweetened double cream
icing sugar

• Bring the water with the butter and a little salt to the boil. Add the flour all at once and stir until the dough pulls away from the sides of the pan like a ball.
• From the heat beat in the eggs, one at a time, until completely absorbed.
• Spoon or pipe 8 small mountains onto a buttered baking tray, not too close together. Bake the puffs in a preheated oven of 200 °C/400 °F/Gas Mark 6 for approximately 20 minutes until brown and done. The puffs are done when they feel light.
• Open the oven door slightly for the puffs to cool before removing them from the oven. Snip open with scissors just above the middle. Fill with a ball of ice cream. Put the puffs on a plate, decorate with cream. Loosely spoon raspberries over and around and close the puffs. Dust with icing sugar.

🍷 Rosé d'Anjou, medium dry wine from the Loire region.

Sherry trifle / Sherry-trifle

Koninklijke Rotterdamsche Lloyd

The sherry years! Do not hesitate to call them that. Albert Heijn was instrumental in the introduction of this aperitif to the masses. Sweet sherry, though. They said: 'Call it dry, but make it sweet.' Sherry became popular enough for many ladies to become addicted to it, especially in the area 't Gooi, where diligent coppers, when school was out, posted to give tipsy young mothers traffic tickets. Tempting excuses were invented, like a slimming diet of sherry. They say even Queen Juliana tried it. Urged on by the slogan of the Public Information Service for Food: *houd je lijn aan het lijntje* ('watch your weight')!

Those who would not drink sherry used it in a real English trifle. Fondly consumed in Hilversum, at least according to the columnist and poet Nico Scheepmaker, who named his daily column in the GPD-newspapers after trifle: *Trijfel*. A prehistoric dessert, that in 1964 even got all the way to the menu of the famous restaurant De Witte in Amersfoort, under the reign of Ernst Hastrich, one of the founders of the Alliance Gastronomique. An exclusive dessert!

250 ml (1 cup) milk
25 g (1 oz) sugar
2 egg yolks
1 tablespoon cornflour

250 ml (1 cup) double cream
1 tablespoon vanilla sugar
1 tablespoon lemon juice
1 tablespoon Cognac

8 thin, round slices of plain cake
raspberry jam
medium dry sherry
200 g (7 oz) ripe strawberries

• Bring the milk to the boil with half the sugar. Beat the egg yolks with the remaining sugar and cornflour. Whisk in the boiling milk. Pour the mixture into the pan. On low heat, while stirring, cook to a thick cream. Cool this cream completely.

• Whisk the double cream and vanilla sugar not too stiff. Keep whisking and add the lemon juice. Fold in the Cognac.

• Spread 4 slices of cake with raspberry jam and put the remaining slices on top.
Line the bottom of 4 glass coupes with the cake and nicely soak in sherry. Divide the sliced strawberries onto the cake and pour over the custard cream. Top with drunken cream.

Spicy kitchens in the Netherlands

Anything exotic is exciting!

The Dutch have felt this way since ages. The rich of the Middle Ages ate dishes that strongly resembled what is now called the Arabic cuisine, which, in its turn, was influenced by the age-old spice trade (via Ethiopia and Oman) with the Indonesian Archipelago.

When new travel routes to the East were discovered and the East Indies Company was founded, the Dutch started to experiment with pepper, cloves, nutmeg and cinnamon. Never in authentic dishes, but always added to the already known local dishes. Partaking in the real Oriental cuisine was still a long way off for us.

Spices from far-away places were too expensive for the common people. Moreover, a lot of bizarre tales were told about spices. In her cookery book *Aaltje* (1887) Odilia Corver writes about the eastern spices: 'It is good to use these in great moderation... The continuous use of hot spices may sometimes cause stomach paralysis.' But when, in the twentieth century, the steamboat made it possible for an increasing number of Dutchmen to travel to Indonesia, and spices were shipped home in large amounts, it became more and more commonplace to grate nutmeg onto cauliflower and endive, to be generous with the peppermill and to liberally sprinkle rice porridge with cinnamon.

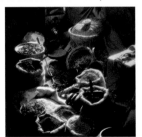

It starts at 'The Chinese'

Almost each year of the twentieth century Indonesian cookery books are published, which at the same time were a bit Chinese as well, since many Chinese emigrated to Indonesia from the 13th century onward. They did so with their noodles and for Muslims forbidden pork. The Chinese are born emigrants. Around 1918 there were four Chinese rooming houses to be found on the Binnen Bantammer in Amsterdam,

and in 1928 the famous Chinese chef Cheung started his first eating place in Rotterdam, in 1933 followed by his restaurant Het Verre Oosten ('The Far East') on the Laan van Meerdervoort in The Hague. After returning home, also ladies who had looked over the shoulder of their 'kokkie' in the former colony tried to recreate the cherished Far Eastern kitchen, such as Mrs Catenius-Van der Meijden, highly praised in Paris, with her *Groot nieuw volledig Indisch kookboek*, and Mrs Keijner with her *Kookboek voor Hollandse, Chinese en Indonesische gerechten*.

The growth

Nowadays, Chinese restaurants are to be found in many villages and cities. Eating at 'The Chinese's' has become such an intricate part of Dutch culture that it is hard to imagine differently. Nevertheless, the beginning was difficult, as told by Boudie Rijkschroeff in a PhD thesis on this subject. This is the reaction of a journalist to a Chinese meal in 1931 in the newspaper *Algemeen Handelsblad*: 'Different components were mixed together in one dish, heaven knows which. I asked to be served a glass of beer, which did not improve anything. (...).' Not withstanding this, 30 Chinese restaurants were in operation in 1945, and 225 in 1966. This was the result of the repatriation from Indonesia after independence.

At the moment eastern spices are undeniably part of the Dutch cuisine. One of the most important contributors to this has been Beb Vuyk, with her *Vrij Nederland* column in the 1960s called 'Eet een beetje heet' ('Eat a little spicy'). With the arrival of people from Turkey, Morocco and Surinam, the spice palette broadens even more. In the 1980s many Dutch people attended 'ethnic' cooking classes. At the moment the Netherlands have an enormous range of foreign restaurants.

Boiled beef with Sichuan pepper / Gekookt rundvlees met Sichuanpeper

A recipe developed in the test kitchen of 'Verstegen Specerijen' in Rotterdam, founded in 1886 by Mr J.H. Verstegen himself. One of the first seasonal trendsetters of the Netherlands. Mr Peter Dumont, whose recipe we give below, is part of the team of 'food specialists' who continuously are on the look out for new trends to sell to their customers. Taste spies, who often make long journeys and subsequently, at trade fairs, show you how to prepare the niceties at the flick of a hand, that they have discovered for you.

The main ingredient for this dish is Sichuan pepper. The Sichuan kitchen, from the inlands of China, is known to be very hot because of the effect of their local pepper, the fagara. The taste sensation of ordinary pepper is instant; this pepper, however, is nearly tasteless, but develops a very special, hot taste sensation later.

Sauce:	Meat:
2 tablespoons vegetable oil	300 g (10 ½) oz fillet steak or
1 whole Sichuan pepper	entrecôte
½ teaspoon fermented black	6 leaves of head lettuce
beans, crushed (buy in a toko)	100 ml (½ cup) water
2 tablespoons onion, finely	¼ teaspoon ground Sichuan
chopped	pepper
1 teaspoon garlic, finely	½ teaspoon dried ground garlic
chopped	
1 teaspoon dried ground ginger	
(djahé)	
1 tablespoon black bean paste	
(buy in a toko)	
125 ml (½ cup) water	
salt	

• Heat the oil in a wok. Quickly sauté the pepper, remove from the wok and chop. Cook the remaining sauce ingredients for a few minutes in the wok. Add the pepper with a little salt.
• Cut the beef in very thin slices (machine). Tear up the salad leaves. Bring the water and pepper to the boil. Cook the slices of beef until they change colour. Drain well and heat in the sauce. Arrange the meat and sauce in a dish with the torn up lettuce around it, and sprinkle with chopped garlic.
• Serve with boiled rice and pickled cucumber.

Indonesian chicken / Ayam Paniki
Chicken in aromatic sauce

An Indonesian dish from the Menado region by 'kokkie' Hilda, who for almost 30 years has been chef of Rijsttafel Restaurant Wisma Hilda (Hilda's Residence) in Haarlem. She started with a cafeteria, but in the sixties someone fortunately asked her to prepare something 'East Indian'. And she prepared an authentic Indonesian dish, without taking into account the fear that some Dutch have for that delicacy. The best policy is: taste it!

1 small chicken
2 tablespoons lemon juice
salt and pepper
.
2 tablespoons vegetable oil
1-2 tablespoons sambal ulek
approximately 2 cm (1 in) fresh ginger, finely chopped
2-3 tablespoons chopped onion
1-1½ tablespoon garlic
2 tablespoons vegetable oil

100-200 ml (½-¾ cup) coconut milk
.
1 pandanus leave
¼ teaspoon turmeric (curcuma)
1 stalk of lemongrass (sereh)

• Cut the chicken in pieces, rub with salt, pepper and lemon juice. Put aside.
• Combine the following five ingredients and ground to a paste in a blender. Gently heat the paste in the oil. Add the chicken pieces and finally the coconut milk – a little at a time – and the pandanus leave, turmeric and lemongrass. Simmer for 45 minutes, covered. Taste and smell if the taste is right. Serve with white rice.

☞ Pandanus leave is also known as daun pandan. It is a leave with a slight vanilla aroma, sold in Asiatic specialty shops (tokos); they may be replaced by curry leaves.

1970–1979
'Nouvelle cuisine, possible in our country?'

Different from others!

If there is a conclusion to be drawn from the eat books of the 1970s, it is the revolution around the table at home. How else can we explain the market for a recipe-collection called *Menu*

1970 · Musical *Hair* with naked actors is shocking
· Tomato campaign: 'theatre needs to be socially relevant'
· Dolle Mina's occupy Nijenrode
· Kabouters in the Civil Council of Amsterdam. Love and Peace in Kralingen
· First North Sea quick-fish restaurant opens in Rotterdam
· Four teaching locations of the Dutch Dairy Bureau
1971 · First McDonald's opens in Zaandam
· Albert Heijn publishes the series of *Volkomen kookboeken*
1972 · First menu in Braille at station refreshment room in Vlissingen
· Report by the Club of Rome places question marks at western consumption drive
1973 · After strong criticism from foreigners on French cuisine Henri Gault writes his 'manifesto' in the *Gault-Millau* magazine: *Vive la nouvelle cuisine française!*
· The film *Turks fruit* (based on Jan Wolkers' novel) in Dutch cinema's
· Oil Crisis! Sundays without cars and, consequently, with empty restaurants
· The Dutch Vegetarian Society starts a recipe-line: the Slimming Line
1974 · First issue of gossip magazine *Story*
· With the introduction of the Witkar it is hoped to launch a new era for Amsterdam
· Opening Café Jan Primus in Utrecht: 30 special beers
1975 · Teach In wins song contest with 'Dingedong'
1976 · Doctoral degree for G.H. Jansen on thesis: *De eeuwige kroeg: hoofdstukken uit de geschiedenis van een openbaar lokaal* ('The eternal pub: chapters from the history of a public house')
· Jan Hekkelman wins the Silver Chef's Hat, trophy of the most important chef's competition, organized by Nestlé on the Horecava
1977 · Restaurant classification by ANWB
· Dries van Agt and Hans Wiegel design a coalition agreement during dinner at Le Bistroquet in The Hague, while enjoying 'a pleasant Bordeaux', as Dries confided
· Cas Spijkers wins the Silver Chef's Hat during the Horecava, where also a symposium is held, moderated by Jaap Klosse. The title is: 'Nouvelle cuisine, possible in our country?'
1979 · Opening of Music Centre Vredenburg in Utrecht
· 50th Anniversary of the Hotel Management School in The Hague

(1973), published in 130 weekly instalments, supervised by Wina Born? She writes: 'Recipes for anyone (including men who like to wear the apron on Sundays) who likes to happily withdraw into the kitchen, forgetting all worries. And, what's more, recipes that differ from others.' A nice match for the indignant protest, often heard in those days: 'Het enige recht van de vrouw is het aanrecht!' ('Woman's only right lies in the kitchen!')

The Public Information Service for Food still tries to put an end to all sorts of detestable habits: fat and sugar are no longer allowed, we have to restrict ourselves to 'pure' vegetable margarine, our biscuits may contain no additives. Nevertheless, we start to 'gourmet', bake quiches, collectively buy the series of enormously instructive *Volkomen kookboeken* ('Perfect cookery books') at Albert Heijn. This name was slightly pretentious, but tongue-in-cheek in remembering historic books with titles such as: *De volmaakte Hollandse Keukenmeid* ('The perfect Dutch kitchen maid', 1761).

1977 Cas Spijkers wins the Silver Chef's hat

Apart from this, we as a people are starting to 'snack' (potato crisps and mini meatballs) and the consumption of beer and wine shows a hefty increase. The result: training circuits and reducing clubs, plus the dr. Atkins-diet, milk-diet, points-diet, chicken-cure, Beatrix-cure, Callas-cure and the bikini-diet. All to be able to continue using the car.

Restaurant business

In the early 1970s the restaurant business is slack, especially right after the Oil Crisis. Business picks up tremendously after 1976. The number of restaurants increases with 130 percent to a total of

1970 Scene from the musical Hair

approximately 6000, counting a lot of bistros. Most spectacular is the rise of top restaurants: exclusive dining becomes a status symbol. Chefs de cuisine become national heroes. This must be a reflection of the fact that 10 percent of the households is made up of 'dinkies' (Double-Income-No-Kids couples). This is the time that in France a ban is placed on heavy sauces by Henri Gault. His manifesto of October 1973, published in the magazine *Gault-Millau* with the title: '*Vive la nouvelle cuisine française*' is presented as the Ten Commandments. And thus, France's gastronomy regains its prestige – and its tyranny. Because we have known! A culinary journalist tells us how, after finishing a 'nouvelle cuisine plate' with two peas and three mange-touts in a top restaurant, he always went out for a bag of French fries to still the empty feeling in his stomach. A lot of people are displeased with the slices and breasts of half

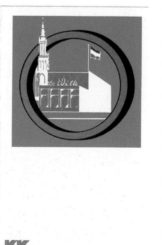

raw meat and almost raw vegetables. However, everyone loves a glass of Kir to begin with – sherry is out – and they enjoy the first 'amuses', which reach us via Belgium.

Food under discussion

At the same time, the report of the Club of Rome creates a nervousness, just as reports on additives do, and the ecological movement (spelled: ekologiese, instead of the correct ecologische), macrobiotics and biodynamics are getting a stronger voice. Wholefood shops with unsprayed vegetables and fruit, often run by communes, are an addition to the old fashioned reform shops, where one particularly bought bread and sport biscuits made by Demeter. Supermarkets introduce an 'alternative corner'.

Lucas Reijnders, in conjunction with several others, writes the book: *Voedsel in Nederland: gezondheid, bedrog, vergif* ('Food in the Netherlands: health, deceit, poison'). A new approach, no longer only about the small country called the Netherlands (the authors themselves label it a luxury problem here), but focused on the world food situation. People are opposed to 'cotton wool bread', but still eat twice as much white bread than wholemeal bread. Additives multiply. Apprehension exists about pesticides. The public becomes environmentally-minded. Many people regard meat as a luxury and a laborious method for food production.

Nut pâté / Notenpaté

DINER

HOLIDAY INN
LEIDEN
13 NOVEMBER 1976

AANGEBODEN DOOR
SIKKENS VERKOOP NEDERLAND NV
DOE-HET-ZELF SECTOR

'Eating at a sewing machine table', *Lekker 1977* sulks, a special issue of Panorama magazine 'to celebrate the Festive Season'. This is a reference to the sudden increase of bistros all over the country. The names of dishes and drinks are written up on a blackboard with chalk, people pour their own wine and very much enjoy eating from a wooden plate (especially pâté). Eric Esurio, who goes all over Amsterdam in search of meals cheaper than ten guilders, describes the garnish: with baguette, lettuce, strips of red pepper and a slice of lemon, sprinkled with paprika, and all this for ƒ 3,00. French-like!

This is so very much the fashion that people start giving 'pâté -parties' at home. Ria Holleman informs us in *Pastei & Pâté* (Bussum/Antwerpen, 1973) that very nice pâtés can be had at the butcher's, but they'll never want to tell you how they made them. She does. And we varied on her theme.

1 litre (4 cups) pâté mould with lid

.

100 g shelled walnuts
100 ml (½ cup) Cognac
butter
250 g (9 oz) pork tenderloin
150 g (5½ oz) pork liver
250 g (9 oz) pork belly
750 g (1½ lbs) spiced sausage minced meat
1 egg
2 teaspoons onion juice (from a garlic press)
2 drops of garlic juice
1 teaspoon coarsely ground pepper
¾ teaspoon salt
4 bay leaves

.

50 g (1¾ oz) shelled walnuts
sliced leek
50 ml (¼ cup) Cognac
pinch of burned sugar
6 sheets of white gelatine
salt
pickled onions and gherkins

• Macerate the walnuts in the Cognac. Stir occasionally. Butter the mould. Preheat the oven to 175 °C/350 °F/Gas Mark 4.
• Dice the tenderloin and liver. Cut 4 strips of fat 15 cm (6 in) long from the pork belly. Put aside. Dice the remaining pork belly. Combine all meats with the sausage minced meat. Stir in the egg, garlic, salt and pepper, and finally the walnuts with Cognac. Fill the mould with this mixture and press it down, it will protrude as a shallow dome. Cover the top diagonally with the strips of fat, press down and place the bay leaves in between. Put the lid on and weigh down if possible.
• Place the mould in a roasting tray, filled with water to halfway up the mould. Bake in the bottom of the oven for 2 hours.
• Pour the cooking liquid into a saucepan, sieve through a wet cloth into a measuring cup. Add Cognac and water to make 250 ml (1 cup). Put a weight on the pâté mould and cool for one hour.
• Remove the fat from the top, in its place put the walnuts. Soak the gelatine in plenty of water. Bring 50 ml (¼ cup) water with a pinch of burned sugar to the boil while stirring. From the heat dissolve the well squeezed gelatine and stir into the sieved cooking liquid. Season well with salt. When this 'aspic' starts to set, spoon it over the pâté. Cool in fridge. Serve with pickled onions and gherkins. And baguette.

Cake of sole and vegetables / Taartje met tong en groenten

'Gâteau de filets de sole aux légumes', this is the way it is included in the magazine of Gault and Millau in June 1979, then called *Nouveau Guide* and in existence for six years. The creators of the nouvelle cuisine condescend to visit the 'Benelux'. They focused on some young patrons-cuisiniers, whom they felt gave a promising interpretation of the nouvelle cuisine. Someone like John Halvemaan. A little arrogant, for sure. Why would this stubborn Dutchman, who always knew precisely what he wanted, suddenly adhere to Gault's Ten Commandments? After sneering the Dutch who dauntlessly continue to eat their 'fatty cabbage' while John 'is looking for the taste of the new', the French gentlemen arrive at the right conclusion: the 'independent, nonconformist' chef is extremely gifted, something to be realized right after eating his cake of sole and vegetables.

🍷 Muscat d'Alsace, very refined white wine from the Alsace.

4 moulds of about 11 cm (4¼ in) in diameter and 2 cm (¾ in) high

·

4 fillets of sole, each 100 g (3½ oz)
salt and pepper
4-8 large leaves of iceberg lettuce
200 g (7 oz) of mixed vegetables in season
2 tablespoons herbs (parsley, basil, tarragon, chives)

·

melted butter
4 egg yolks (100 ml / ½ cup)
100 ml (½ cup) double cream
salt and pepper

· Preheat the oven to 120 °C/250 °F/Gas Mark 2.
· Carefully flatten the fillets of sole and sprinkle with salt and pepper. Diagonally cut each fillet in half. Blanch the salad leaves and pat dry. Carefully remove the bottom of the core. Dice the vegetables, blanch all separately. Finely chop the herbs. Combine with the vegetables.
· Butter the mould with melted butter. Line with lettuce leaves so that the leaves hang over the rim. Into each mould place 2 fillets side by side, let these hang over the rim as well. Divide the vegetables onto the fish, seasoned with salt and pepper.
· Beat the egg yolk and cream, season with salt and pepper. Divide this mixture over the moulds, fold sole fillets over the vegetables and lettuce over the fish. Cover with aluminium foil. Bake for 40 minutes in the preheated oven.
· Place the moulds upside down on plates, unmould carefully. Serve the cakes tepid with a beurre blanc or lobster sauce.

Beurre blanc (butter sauce)

· Cook 100 g (3½ oz) shallots with 400 ml (1⅓ cup) dry white wine down to two thirds. Finely mash in a blender. Heat the puree. From the heat whisk in 100 g (3½ oz) butter. Keep whisking to form a creamy thickened sauce. Gradually whisk in another 100 g (3½ oz) cold, diced butter until the sauce has the right consistency. Season with salt and pepper.

☛ See for lobster sauce 'American sauce', 1920s (p. 70).

Kate's mustard soup / Kaatje's mosterdsoep

In 1977 mustard soup is a must in every contemporary restaurant, also at Kaatje bij de Sluis in Blokzijl – started three years earlier as a small bistro. However, the original Anneke and Fons van Groeningen soon no longer fit that simple concept. In 1977 they amaze the culinary world with their Seven-course Meal, small lovely dishes to take you through the evening. Even copied in France as *Menu Dégustation*. No more than a year later they receive a Michelin-star. Nowadays, 25 years after opening, they proudly carry two stars. Guests in their stately hotel can even order a seven-course breakfast.

Edzard Delstra (in those days chef de cuisine) and André Mol (present chef de cuisine) are creators of daring dishes, such as clear quail broth with chrysanthemum petals. André still clearly remembers the simple mustard soup. An adventure in taste.

1 litre (4 cups) fowl stock
75 g (2¾ oz) chicken breast, skinned
100 ml (½ cup) double cream
2 tablespoons coarse mustard (from Zwolle)
salt

- In a large pan bring the stock to the boil. Place the chicken breast in it and cook until tender in approximately 5 minutes. Remove the meat from the stock and dice it.
- Cook the broth down to about 750 ml (3 cups).
- In a bowl whisk the cream until stiff. Add the cream and mustard to the boiling stock. Whisk well. Season with salt.
- Divide the diced chicken into 4 warm soup bowls, pour the soup over and serve immediately.

1973 Pubs and restaurants expect to be hit hard by 'car-less' Sundays. One restaurant owner tries to make the best of it by offering a special menu for cyclists.

Mild sauerkraut soup / Milde zuurkoolsoep

Chef Jon Sistermans, who creates this soup at the end of the 1970s while working at Ile de France in Amsterdam (with Michelin-star), later excels in de Kersentuin (Amsterdam, opened in 1980), where he runs a very special kitchen (also with Michelin-star) in a long-standing collaboration with manager Joop Braakhekke. The menu is poetic in atmosphere. It contains sentences such as: 'To make a clear symphony of all ingredients that the world has to offer, craftsmanship, good taste and love are vital.' Both gentlemen have proved to possess that love in their later careers. Since 1994 Jon has been running one of the Netherlands' best restaurants: the famous Mariënhof in Amersfoort, situated in a late fifteenth-century cloister complex. And besides being patron of his restaurant Le Garage in Amsterdam, Joop became the most popular television chef of the 1990s.

A typical September dish when sauerkraut is first on the market. It is important to use naturally prepared sauerkraut, since only then its mild taste can be the intriguing base for this soup.

·

250 g (9 oz) traditional sauerkraut, squeezed
1 litre (4 cups) fowl stock
2 cloves of garlic, crushed
2 bay leaves
200 g (7 oz) goose liver, diced
salt and pepper
dash of sherry (Madras)

·

8 nice bread croutons of ¼ cm (¼ in)
100 g (3½ oz) goose liver, diced

1920 Arrival of white cabbage at the auction-mart

• Combine sauerkraut, stock, garlic, bay leaves and goose liver and simmer at low heat for 30 minutes. Remove the bay leaves. Cream the soup in a blender. Season with salt and pepper and a dash of sherry.
• Place the croutons and cubes of goose liver in the soup and serve immediately.

☛ Jon himself explains that chicken livers may be used instead of goose liver. The taste, however, will be less refined.

Little omelettes of Mother Nature / Omeletjes van Moeder Aarde

The aversion against the bio-industry, the fear for antibiotics and growth hormones, and the awareness that a lot of grain for the poor and hungry in the world is lost in meat production, turns many people into vegetarians in the 1970s. Sometimes this is taken very far, as with the Kushi-Institute in Amsterdam, where they practise macrobiotics (only grains and vegetables). There is hardly any appetising dining to do there. Eric Esurio goes to sample it, but leaves the macrobiotic Sensei Oshawa Centre in the Amsterdam Rozen-straat put off by the religious atmosphere and with an empty stomach; he hurries to the Fromagerie Crignon to have cheese fondue. It does not have to be that bad, though. Harry du Bois reports how it is possible to have a three-course vegetarian menu for ƒ 10,00 at De Werfkring at the Oude Gracht in Utrecht, in an 'alternative, playful atmosphere' that is very restful. No waiters, no menu, nice and uncomplicated. No wonder De Werfkring still exists. In the meantime, also De Hoefslag in Bosch en Duin, the place Wulf Engel created a furore in those years, serves a vegetarian 'menu dégustation'.

Recipe according to instructions from: F. Moore Lappé, *Eten van Moeder Aarde*, Amsterdam/Brussel: Elsevier, 1974

Filling for 4 omelettes:
100 g (3½ oz) (brown) rice
100 g (3½ oz) brown lentils
1 tablespoon olive oil
100 g (3½ oz) finely chopped vegetables (leek, carrot, celery)
1 finely chopped beefsteak tomato
1 finely chopped red chilli (seeds removed)
salt
·

For each omelette:
½ tablespoon olive oil
2 small eggs, beaten with: ½ tablespoon milk
½ teaspoon finely chopped coriander leaf
salt
·

toasted sesame seeds

• Separately cook the rice and lentils in approximately 20 minutes.
• Heat the oil. Soften the vegetables on low heat. Combine with drained rice, lentils, tomato and pepper. Keep warm.
• In a small non-stick frying pan heat the oil. Pour in the eggs, let the uncooked part run under the cooked part and shake the pan regularly.

• Divide one quarter of the filling over each ome-lette and fold over.
• Sprinkle with toasted sesa-me seeds.

☞ The omelette is inspired by the Indian cuisine, which during these years gains in popularity.

Philosopher from Schiedam /
Schiedammer filosoof

With all the worries about food and environment people are getting nostalgic. The past is best, old is in. We colour our interiors brown, hang sackcloth on the walls, and books are published with titles such as *(H)eerlijke gerechten* ('Honest/Delicious dishes'; Wina Born, 1972), bound in sackcloth with pre-made old stains and remarks written with a 'dip pen'. Another title is Uit *Grootmoeders Keuken* ('From grandmother's kitchen'; Ria Holleman, 1972). In her introduction she writes: 'In this book you will find a lot of recipes from the end of the last century and the first decades of this century.' That is no lie! Her recipe for Philosopher, for example, is also to be found in *Het nieuwste Kookboek*, 's-Gravenhage, 1907, in the seventh edition of F. Blom's *Moderne kookkunst*, 's-Gravenhage, 1910, and in the *Menu*-series of the 1970s. Originally made with leftovers, and in its simplest version just potatoes (mashed, diced or sliced), sometimes with a little bacon, meat, onions and vinegar, or even without meat, but with brown beans, apple and gherkins. It could be taken every which way – just like philosophy! In her beautiful book *De aardappel* ('The potato', 1998) Alma Huisken presents us with a recipe from 1926, using curry powder! Ours is a festive version, over which one can philosophize about the relativity of kitchen doctrine.

30 g (1 oz) butter
500 g (1 lb 2 oz) stewing steak, diced
150 g (5½ oz) onion, chopped
salt and pepper
500 ml (2 cups) stock
12 juniper berries, crushed
50 g (1¾ oz) pickled gherkins, sliced
arrowroot or potato starch
2 tablespoons cooked brown beans
2 tablespoon finely chopped parsley
1 glass of young Dutch jenever

·

750 g (1 lb 11 oz) waxy potatoes
breadcrumbs
melted butter

·

500 g (1 lb 2 oz) Brussels sprouts, cleaned
45 g flaked almonds
a little butter
apple compote

• Heat the butter in a casserole. Brown the meat on high heat. Add the chopped onion and brown as well. Sprinkle with salt and pepper. Pour in the stock. Add the juniper berries and slices of gherkin. Simmer on low heat for at least 3 hours (grandmother used her oil cooker!). Thicken the cooking liquid with arrowroot. Add the beans and heat through. Stir in the parsley and jenever.
• In the meantime boil the peeled and sliced potatoes. Place the slices overlapping on the ragout, sprinkle with breadcrumbs, drizzle with melted butter and place the pan (not too close!) under a hot grill to brown the top.
• Serve with quickly boiled Brussels sprouts, garnished with in butter browned shaved almonds and an apple compote.

Breast of duck with leek sauce /
Eendenborst met preisaus

'Le magret de canard à la sauce aux poireaux', according to Gault-Millau, June 1979,
a typical example of Paul Fagel's cooking style: a style overflowing with personality, something of a rarity in the Netherlands, the magazine tells us. Where not? No wonder Michel
Guérard, king of the nouvelle cuisine, left his palace in Eugénie les Bains to try a bite at
Paul's in Wijk bij Duurstede. All this for a member of the Fagel family who in those days
was not the most famous one of the Utrecht's restaurant dynasty. Admittedly, the French
do know how to taste something. Paul reconstructed the dish for us from Het Arsenaal in
Naarden-Vesting, where he resides nowadays. And according to connoisseurs he still fits
Millau's description of 'that little wicked man, who only cooks what he likes'. Luckily his
guests like it too.

Pommes de terre Dauphinoise
A gratin of potatoes that was to replace the until then
inevitable French fries in many restaurants.

.

garlic
butter

.

500 g (1 lb 2 oz) peeled potatoes, very thinly sliced
300 ml (1¼ cup) warm milk
1 egg
salt and pepper, nutmeg
50 g (1 ¾ oz) grated Gruyère cheese

.

50 g (1 ¾ oz) grated Gruyère cheese
25 g (1 oz) butter

Paul Fagel is a heavenly cook, but most people went to Albert's
Corner, where food was a lot cheaper

• Rub a shallow oven-proof dish with garlic and butter it.
Preheat the oven to 175 °C/350 °F/Gas Mark 4.
• In a bowl combine the potato slices with milk, egg, salt, pepper, nutmeg and cheese. Put into the dish and sprinkle with
cheese. Top with a small lumps of butter. Bake for 45 minutes in the preheated oven.

Breast of duck

butter

150 g (5½ oz) white of leeks

150 ml (⅔ cup) reduced veal stock

200 ml (¾ cup) double cream

salt and pepper

(perhaps a little lump of cold butter)

•

2 breasts of duck, each 400 g (14 oz))

salt and pepper

1 tablespoon butter and olive oil

•

(braised leek)

• Thinly slice the white of leek and quickly sauté in the butter. Pour on the reduced stock and cook the leek until soft. Puree in a blender and push through a sieve. Add the cream. Boil the sauce down until it thickens slightly. If wanted, just before serving, from the heat, stir in a small lump of butter.

• Carve the skin of the duck with diamond shapes. Season the meat side with salt and pepper. Heat the butter and olive oil and brown the meat side. Place the breast of duck skin side down in the preheated oven (see previous recipe) for 8-10 minutes, until the meat is rosé. Let stand for 5 minutes, remove from the dish and slice very thinly – important for the taste sensation! Spoon the sauce over to cover half. Nice with Pommes Dauphinoise and perhaps a little braised leek.

Eel in rosé wine / Paling in roséwijn

Already in 1954, Herman van Ham is chef at the Hamert in Wellerlooi, which soon was to become famous for its asparagus specialities (nowadays more than 60.000 kg per year are used). Outside the asparagus season it also is good to spend some time in the dining room on the Meuse, for example to enjoy the *Matelote d'anguille de la Meuse* (early 1970s). When Herman van Ham leaves in 1988 one of the regulars pays him the compliment that he had never lost himself in the fashion of the nouvelle cuisine, with her small portions, ban on butter and cream and preference over presentation instead of the contents of what was cooked. Pieter Smits – the present patron – also honours the classical French theory that 'culinary art is not done by fixed formulas, but one should not mess with the fundamental principles'.

Pieter Smits recommends a Tavelrosé, instead of Matteus or Faisca, both of which are extremely popular in this decade.

800 g (2 lbs) thick eel from the Meuse
1 tablespoon parsley leaves
½ teaspoon thyme leaves
1 fresh bay leaf
1 clove of garlic
salt
½ bottle of rosé
100 ml (½ cup) reduced fish stock
200 g (7 oz) shallots
200 g (7 oz) carrots
450 g (1 lb) pre-cooked baby potatoes
80 g (2¾ oz) butter
arrowroot or potato starch
chives

1975 Teach In wins the song contest

• Diagonally slice the eel in pieces of approximately 5 cm (2 in). Put into a wide pan. Sprinkle with finely chopped parsley and thyme. Add the bay leaf and the peeled, whole clove of garlic. Season with salt, pour over the rosé and reduced fish stock. Cook on low heat until tender.

• Peel the shallots, cook with the carrots, drain and braise with the baby potatoes in 30 g (1 oz) of butter.

• Arrange the cooked eel and vegetables on a serving plate.

Thicken the cooking liquid with arrowroot or potato starch. Sieve the sauce, add the remaining butter and spoon this sauce over the fish and vegetables. Just before serving, put the dish shortly in an oven of 175 °C/350 °F/Gas mark 4. Garnish with chives.

🍷 Tavel Rosé, sturdy rosé form the region between the river Rhone and the Provence.

Kiwi mousse / kiwimousse

Midway this century the Chinese gooseberry from New Zealand becomes extremely popular in Europe. Australia, California, Israel and Japan throw themselves into the cultivation of this fruit, that bears the name of a New Zealand bird. The high consumption in our regions can largely be attributed to the kitchen fashion. Indiscriminately, even in France, slices of (unpeeled) kiwi are used for garnish on the modish plate: with fish, with meat, with everything. A good exception is made by Lauswolt, the country estate in the North (opened in 1954 and still renowned). In Beetsterzwaag the kiwi gets the place it deserves: at the dessert table.

Chef Huibert Bavelaar, now patron at Elckerlijc in Leiderdorp, kindly shared his recipe with us:

15 g (½ oz) gelatine

500 ml (2 cups) water
200 g (7 oz) sugar
½ teaspoon lemon juice
500 g (1 lb 2 oz) kiwis, peeled and diced
4 tablespoons Chartreuse
50 ml (¼ cup) double cream

• Rinse a mould with cold water and leave it upside down. Soak the gelatine in plenty of cold water.
• Bring the water, sugar and lemon juice to the boil. Add the diced kiwi and cook for a few minutes. From the heat dissolve the well squeezed gelatine. Mash the mixture with a hand blender or push it through a sieve and cool.
• Whisk the cream until stiff. As soon as the fruit puree starts to set, fold in the liqueur and whipped cream. Combine carefully. Spoon into the mould.
• Let set in the fridge. With a warm spoon, spoon the mousse into glass coupes or on to plates and if wanted decorate with whipped cream and slices of peeled kiwi.

🍷 Gewürztraminer d'Alsace, preferably one from 1997, since this one is slightly sweeter than the other millésimes.

Grand dessert

Already in 1975 in Paul Fagel's restaurant Duurstede it was possible to order a *grand dessert*. Not by that name as he himself explains: 'It happened purely by chance. I myself was in the kitchen, had no serving trolley and had told the staff that the guests were allowed to have a taste of all desserts. To my amazement they ate everything!' Soon after that, the combined dessert of several sweets has come to stay.

Paul Fagels's 'grand dessert avant la lettre':

Fruit sorbet

Quite novel in this period, since 'water ice' was frowned upon. It also became fashionable to serve sorbets like these in the middle of the menu. They say Kaatje bij de Sluis started it, albeit tomato sorbet.

·

100 ml (½ cup) water
100 g (3½ oz) sugar

·

1-2 tablespoons lemon juice
500 g (1 lb 2 oz) soft fruit. such as strawberries, raspberries, blueberries, red currants
icing sugar, optional

Chocolate mousse

Or, as the Dutch say: 'Hemelse modder' ('Heavenly mud').

2 eggs (or the equivalent of pasteurized yolk and white)
2 tablespoons soft white sugar
100 g (3½ oz) bitter chocolate

• Separate the eggs into yolks and whites. Beat the yolks with the sugar. Whisk the egg whites to stiff peaks. Melt the broken chocolate in a small saucepan. Add the beaten egg yolks and warm through. Spoon the whites on top and blend with a large smooth spoon. Divide into 4 bowls.

Kan eenig dorp, in Delflands kring
Op ouderdom van eeuwen boogen,
Op fraaije ligging, en vermogen,
Door ijver van den dorpeling';
'tis MAASLAND, dat elks oogen streelt,
En door't graveerstift dus natuurlijk is verbeeld.

• Bring the water and sugar to the boil and dissolve the sugar while stirring. Cook on low heat for about 2 minutes. Cool and add the lemon juice.
• Clean the fruit, in a blender or with a hand blender mash with the sugar syrup and push through a sieve. The puree must be quite sweet, since it will loose taste during freezing. Thus, if necessary, add more sugar.
• Spoon the fruit puree in a metal bowl but fill it for no more than three quarters. Place the bowl 3-4 hours in the freezer. Frequently whisk well, until the ice has the correct consistency. Or put the puree in an ice maker and follow the instructions.
• Defrost the ice slightly before serving, and whisk with an electric beater until smooth. Put it back in the freezer until serving time.

1977 Van Agt and Wiegel reach a coalition agreement
in Le Bistroquet in The Hague, perhaps under the positive
influence of the grand dessert

Charlotte Russe

A bavarois set in a ring of sponge fingers.

*A mould of 12 cm (4¾ in) diameter. Height 11 cm (4¼ in). Bottom and
sides are lined with parchment paper: a circle for the bottom and a band for
the sides.*

*

20 sponge fingers ('lange vingers')

*

6 sheets of gelatine (12 g)
100 g (3½ oz) sugar
4 egg yolks
100 ml (½ cup) milk
100 ml (½ cup) crème fraîche
1 vanilla pod
300 ml (1¼ cup) double cream
3 tablespoons icing sugar
1 teaspoon vanilla sugar

- Place the sponge fingers upright in the mould, with the
  sugared side out. Cut off at the correct length.
- Soak the gelatine in plenty of cold water.
- Beat the egg yolks and sugar until foamy. Bring to the boil
  the milk and crème fraîche with the lengthwise split vanilla
  pod. From the heat add the sweet egg yolks. Over hot water
  whisk until the sauce thickens. From the heat dissolve the
  well squeezed gelatine. Pour through a fine sieve and cool.
  Stir regularly.
- Whisk the double cream and sugar until stiff. Fold the
  cream into the sauce as soon as it starts to set. Spoon the
  mixture into the lined mould. Flatten the top with a knife.
  Sprinkle with crumbled biscuits and cool the pudding at
  least 2 hours in the fridge.
- Just before serving unmould the pudding on a round
  serving plate.

1980–1989
'No more eel in chocolate sauce!'

Culinary facts

'The worst is over. No more eel in chocolate sauce!'
This was said by agricultural minister Van der Stee during a
luncheon with Stan Huygens from *De Telegraaf* (1987). Not

1980 · April 30th succession: Queen Beatrix
· First inhabitants move to New Town Almere-stad
· 'Neerlands Dis' ('Dutch cuisine') starts March 1st in many restaurants
· Title SVH-master chef introduced
1981 · First Michelin-star for De Swaen in Oisterwijk
· New presentation of essential food groups by Public Information Service for Food. Eat lots of vegetable products, be sparse with fat. National health campaign 'Nederland Oké'.
1982 · wholesaler's ISPC opens 'fresh line' to Rungis
1983 · Start of restaurant-group Relais du Centre
· Van Benthem wins 13th Elfstedentocht (skating marathon)
· November 6th first Dutch astronaut Wubbo Ockels lands at Edwards airbase in California
· World Nature Fund wants a ban on the consumption of frog's legs
1984 · McDonald's opens 24th restaurant in the Netherlands
· The Fine Eastern Restaurant group is founded
· The Netherlands are 'jogging' and follow alternating-bread-diet
1985 · Ven's fresh market opens in Diemen: exit THE TIN!
1986 · Women's lib movement 'Marie wordt wijzer' discontinued
· Willem te Meij sells his book collection for practically nothing to Culinary Museum Mariënhof in Amersfoort 'to save the trade'
· Accident in nuclear power station Chernobyl
1987 · McDonald's opens three drive-in restaurants
· Steering Committee Good Nutrition installed
· Guild of Dutch Master Chefs founded
1988 · Report 'What do the Netherlands eat?' is published: too much, too fat and too much alcohol
1989 · The Chinese Chang brothers build the eye-catching restaurant/catering business Orient Plaza on the outskirts of Nijmegen
· Eurotoques formed: against general dulling of cookery, in favour of regional and national products and against internationalizing of kitchen cultures: back to the source, the regional culinary art
· SKAL quality mark introduced: guarantee of ecologically sound production

quite, it seems, since in the meantime the 'Chaîne des Rôtisseurs' ate red mullet with rhubarb, and in Leiden at Nieuw Minerva back rib with bamboo shoots and Tia Maria sauce was served. It had not completely disappeared, this rage of never-crazy-enough.

Retired chef de cuisine Willem te Meij from Rijswijk puts it this way in an interview in the above mentioned newspaper: 'This culinary nonsense has to stop. The fuss they make nowadays about serving game with a 'nouvelle cuisine dish' of a few half cooked carrots and mange-touts. Ugh! These modern young ones desperately need refresher courses based on the works of the old kitchen masters.' And Hans Auer writes in *Lekker '84*: 'the Netherlands very much need restaurants with good bourgeois kitchens.'

Funnily enough, the cloche is reinstated. This kind of 'upgrading', plus the continuous renovation of the entire interior, force prices up. At the end of the 1980s, Hans Auer complains how a lot of restaurants go under because of their own airs: 25 year old chefs set the tone by messing about: the result of wanting to be seen as all-round professionals.

1983 Wubbo Ockels, the first Dutchman in space

Restaurant business

In the first half of this decade a worldwide recession reigns. Many businesses have to close their doors, no less than 707 restaurants in 1983. Fewer Americans visit Europe because of the fall of the dollar and the Chernobyl disaster. Less is spent on business dinners, and private individuals suffer from high mortgages (9-11 percent), or prefer spending their money on a new car or caravan instead of dining out. The consumption of wine at home, however, is four times higher than in 1965. In an attempt to lower the threshold the first 'brasserie' in Haarlem is opened, without much success. The first 'eat-cafés' fare better. 'The Dutch taste with their billfolds', says Fred de Leeuw, unbeaten butcher and truffle man of Amsterdam, who apparently still knows where to find a few well stuffed billfolds. A food consumption assessment in 1987-1988 shows 23 percent of food is consumed outside the home. By the end of the decade the restaurant branch no longer complains so much. The percentage of 'dinkies' has gone up to 27 percent in 1985, which results in a continuous increase of fast food restaurants. Foreign cuisines from all over the world are starting to compete with the established Chinese restaurants. Neerland's Dis is introduced to counter that.

Eating at home

The start of the 1980s demands an opinion on food. It is the rise of the 'foodies', people who love to talk about food and pride themselves on their culinary knowledge. Cooking at home, where the role of a true family is played out, is reduced to the weekends: multiple-course dinners, just like in the restaurants. Cooking lessons are attended, for example in one of the 40 different classes by Pat van den Wal Bake, at La cuisine française on the Herengracht in Amsterdam.
According to *Lekker 89* the young woman of average income is the most creative. To lend a helping hand *Lekker* offers a menu calendar with this young woman in mind. A Sunday menu for October looks like this: stockfish, potatoes, rice, fried and raw onion, butter sauce. Avocado with crème fraîche. Those who cannot face all the work involved, may go for dinner to one of the restaurants selected by *Lekker*; a detailed write-up about the owner as well as his culinary abilities is offered.
On working days 'chicken in pieces' is eaten or minced meat. Women rush to the shops for yet another recipe by Ria van Eijndhoven (AVRO's Service-salon, a television programme). Men have their own cooking lessons, where they learn to roll

1980 The ISPC starts the first fresh line to France. This results in giving restaurant owners the quality they expect. Shown here the fish counter and the vegetable and fruit section

meatballs, but also the ways of haute cuisine. Pat van den Wal Bake: 'I teach men to pipe orange cream into puffs' – this obviously gives them a kick. Next to the everyday cookery book, books by top chefs are published.

Kitchen design

The machinery grows and grows! Dishwasher, food processor, hand blender, microwave oven, electric deep-frying pan for mother's own French fries counter – all are sold in bulk. Even culinary publicist Johannes van Dam, although very fond of traditional cooking, writes in his *Fijnproevers Leesboek* ('Connoisseurs' recreational reading book') how he changed his mind about food processors and hand blenders: more is to be accomplished with them than with the bare hand. The ice-cream maker, the kitchen robot, the pasta maker, the espresso machine and the turbo grill oven, all ask for yet another class. But we do not need an engineering diploma.

Tepid salad of wild boar's ham with poached pear / Lauwe salade van wildzwijnsham met gepocheerde peer

Special vinegars (especially raspberry vinegar) and tepid salads are the showpiece of this decade. Hilton Amsterdam already presented this dish in 1980 complete with orange vinegar, then highly unusual now commonly sold.

Tepid salads – they were made from anything one could think of, even smoked breast of starling (in Bruges, Belgium). Another chic vinegar sauce? Combine cider vinegar with mango.

Recipe source: menu Hilton, Amsterdam, collection Culinary Museum in Amersfoort

200 ml (¾ cup) red wine
2 tablespoons sugar
1 cinnamon stick
2 not too ripe pears

*

2 tablespoons orange vinegar
2 tablespoons dry white wine
2 tablespoons olive oil
salt and pepper

*

300 g (10½ oz) boiled wild boar's ham
butter
100 g (3½ oz) mixed salad leaves

♟ Pinot Noir d'Alsace, rosé from the Alsace.

• Bring to the boil the wine with the sugar and cinnamon.
  Peel the pears. Poach the pears and leave to cool in the liquid
  to lukewarm. Cut them in halves and remove the core.
• Stir a sauce of the vinegar, wine and olive oil. Season with salt
  and pepper. Divide the salad leaves onto 4 plates and drizzle
  with the sauce.
• Thinly slice the ham. Shortly heat in a little melted butter
  and arrange on the salad. Thinly slice half a pear and arrange
  with the ham. Place the other half on the side.

Fall pâté / Herfstpaté

Yehudi Menuhin

Pâté still is extremely popular, even though mousses are becoming more fashionable as well. Marja Kruik gives us a flowery description in one of her recipe-books: 'Pâté is like true love: simple, touching, testing and always growing: tenderly soft and yet benevolent.'

Top chef Jan Hekkelman has music on his mind in creating the following pâté. He is in charge when a gala dinner is served in the Kurhaus for the benefit of the corporation Live Music Now, with Yehudi Menuhin in attendance. The chef – quite a creditable pianist himself – keeps the menu in tune with the music programme of the evening. In addition, to honour Menuhin the kitchen has prepared 45 life-sized violins out of sugar. Here the recipe of the dinner overture in three parts inspired by the Vivaldi's Four Seasons, namely Fall.

Pâté mould or rectangular cake mould of 2 litre (2 quarts)
(15 servings)

•

450 g (1 lb) lean veal
125 g (4 oz) white bread, crusts removed
2 egg whites
350 ml (3½ cup) double cream

•

150 ml (⅔ cup) white wine
¼ teaspoon crushed caraway seeds

•

1 tablespoon olive oil
1 tablespoon butter
8 finely chopped shallots
800 g (1 lb 12 oz) cleaned mixed mushrooms, equally proportioned
2 tablespoons chopped parsley
250 ml (1 cup) reduced veal stock
8 tablespoons French Cognac
(100 ml (½ cup) jus de truffes)
salt and pepper

•

coulis of fresh tomatoes

• Cut the meat in strips and put these in the freezer for half an hour. Soak the bread in a little water. In a meat mincer twice mince the meat and the squeezed bread. Put in a mixing bowl and place the bowl on crushed ice. Separately whisk the egg whites and cream until stiff. Into the meat mixture gradually fold first the egg white and then the cream.
• In the meantime simmer the crushed caraway seeds in the wine for 15 minutes, on low heat with a lid on the pan.
• Heat the butter and oil in a large frying pan. Sauté the shallots. Add the mushrooms and cook on high heat for 5 minutes. Drain in a sieve and save the liquid. Boil the liquid with the strained 'caraway-wine' and reduced veal stock until reduced to 50 ml (¼ cup). Add mushrooms and parsley.
• Combine the cooled mushrooms with the meat and Cognac (and jus de truffes). Season with salt and pepper.
• Line the mould with plastic foil, fill and fold the foil over. Poach the pâté in hot water of 80 °C/150 °F for 45 minutes. Cool and leave in the fridge for at least one day. Remove the pâté from the mould, peel off the plastic foil and cut into finger thick slices. Serve with a coulis of fresh tomatoes.

☛ Mushrooms suggestion: button mushrooms, trompettes de mort, pieds de mouton chanterelles or oyster mushrooms.

Avocado soup / Avocadosoep

In 1983 the book *Voedsel* ('Food') is published, edited by Gerjan Huis in 't Veld. It is the sequel to *Voedsel in Nederland* ('Food in the Netherlands') from 1974, and its main topic is: what has happened to our food before we drop it into our shopping basket? The book spares no-one, not 'the sugar free comforters' nor the alternative market. Nonetheless there are about 400 wholefood shops at the end of the 1980s, where prices of 15 percent higher than normal are gladly paid. The farmer's market comes
to Amsterdam, where producers of natural foodstuffs sell their wares. A lot of 'semi-veggies' have sprung up: people who do not eat meat, but do eat fish.
Restaurant Zonnemaire in Rotterdam, under the reign of chef Baris (still playing an innovative role in the Rotterdam restaurant world), is a good – and playful – representative of the trend that later is going to be known as 'fusion'-cooking.

Recipe: Robert Baris and Martin van Huijstee, *De nieuwe natuurlijke keuken, Natuurvoeding voor fijnproevers*. Ede: Zomer & Keuning Boeken B.V., 1984

2 shallots
4 tablespoons olive oil
5 tablespoons flour
600 ml (2¼ cup) cold vegetable stock
100 ml (½ cup) milk

2 ripe avocados
salt and white pepper

2 egg yolks
1 lemon

• Peel and finely chop the shallots. Heat the oil and fry the shallots until transparent. Stir in the flour and cook shortly without colouring. While stirring gradually pour in half of the stock. Stir to make a smooth sauce. Remove from the heat.
• Cut the avocados in halves, remove the stones. Peel and dice the avocado. Put in a blender with the remaining stock and milk. Mash. Add the puree to the sauce in the pan. Season the soup with salt and pepper. Heat, but do not boil.
• Beat the egg yolks with the juice of half a lemon and a ladle of warm soup. Stir into the soup, heat for a few minutes, but do not boil.
• Serve garnished with slices of the remaining half lemon.

🖝 Avocados were still extremely rare and only to be found in translations of English cookery books. Martin van Huijstee remembers the following translation: 'If you cannot find an avocado pear, try a regular pear.' It takes guts!

Bami soup / Bamisoep

Apart from cooking classes in haute cuisine and day-to-day cooking, we are given the opportunity to qualify ourselves in the exotic kitchen. AVRO-television shows 'Chinese Chef', with Nico Tiën as star chef, and the firm Conimex in conjunction with Kluwer publishes *Aziatisch koken, zo doe je dat* (1985).
Here is a recipe as noted down by culinary journalist Sylvia Borger during an interview for *De Telegraaf.* In it Nico Tiën tells us how one is always offered a little bite to eat on visiting Chinese people. And how it is expected of the guest to have a few bites, even though he may just have left the table. Unexpected guests most often are served bami soup, which can also be served as a full meal in itself.

8 servings
4 dried mushrooms
4 jumbo Chinese shrimps, raw
200 g (7 oz) tenderloin of pork
250 g (9 oz) Chinese egg noodles

·

2 litre (2 quarts) chicken stock
50 g (1¾ oz) bamboo shoots (tin)
1 thin leek
a few thin slices of fresh ginger
1 tablespoon Japanese soy sauce
2 tablespoons arrowroot of potato starch
2 eggs

• Soak the mushrooms for half an hour, remove the stalks and slice the caps.
• Cut the shrimps in half lengthwise on the back. Remove the black intestinal thread and rinse under cold water. Pat the shrimps dry and slice the halves at an angle into four pieces.
• Thinly slice the tenderloin of pork. Rinse the slices in cold water so as not to cloud the stock.
• Bring a lot of water to the boil and boil the noodles until tender (about 5 minutes). Drain in a colander and rinse under cold water. Leave to drain.
• Heat the stock. Cook the mushrooms, shrimps, slices of meat and chopped bamboo shoots for approximately 10 minutes. Add thinly sliced leek, ginger and soy sauce. Make a thin paste of arrowroot and water, and thicken the soup while stirring. In a bowl beat the eggs. While stirring pour into the soup to create flakes. Finally, add the noodles and heat the soup a few more minutes.

1989 Orient Plaza is build on the outskirts of Nijmegen. Chinese food remains popular in the Netherlands, in spite of the introduction of many different kinds of foreign food

Hot cheese cake / Warme Kernhemmer taart

Because of the recession at the start of this decade a lot of people economize. Dutch frugality shows its face once again. We change from beef to small amounts of pork. We calculate the price of a bare slice of bread to be 10 cents, and only eat steak with peas, fried potatoes and custard pudding on Sundays. That is to say, 'we'? Not everybody lives that way. As shown in Oisterwijk in De Swaen, owned by Cas Spijkers. There a menu has at least seven courses and apparently no-one is shocked by prices (ƒ 75 to ƒ 155). That should not come as a surprise with a chef who says: 'Cook with your soul, jump into the oven with your product. Know what you want!'

Cas, first guild master of the Guild of Master Chefs, will become extremely popular with the masses in the 1990s because of his role in the extensively watched cooking programme 'Cooking with stars'. In 1999 colleagues select him as 'chef of the century', internationally they crown Paul Bocuse, great source of inspiration for Cas Spijkers (*Lekker 1999*).

Recipe source: Cas Spijkers, *Cas Spijkers en zijn Swaen*. Baarn: Tirion Uitgevers B.V., 1984

Cake tin with a diameter of 24 cm (9 in)

(8 servings)

.

butter for buttering the tin
200 g (7 oz) wheat flour
25 g (1 oz) butter
50 ml (¼ cup) tepid milk
15 g (½ oz) yeast
pinch of sugar
pinch of salt
25 g (1 oz) soft butter

.

7 egg yolks
300 ml (1¼ cup) double cream
200 g (7 oz) spring onions
butter
salt and pepper
400 g (14 oz) Kernhemmer cheese

• Put the flour in a bowl, make a hole. Crumble the yeast into it, pour over the milk and dissolve the yeast. Sprinkle with a little sugar. Place the butter in lumps on the flour, sprinkle with salt. In about 15 minutes knead to an elastic dough that does not stick to the hands. Perhaps a little extra flour is needed. Let rest at a warm place, covered with a damp cloth, for 15 minutes. Roll out the dough and line the buttered tin.

• Preheat the oven to 150 °C/300 °F/Gas Mark 2.

• Beat the egg yolks until fluffy. Whip the double cream. Finely chop the spring onions and partly cook in water with a little butter. Pat the onions dry. Remove the crust from the Kernhemmer cheese, dice the cheese and melt, while stirring, in a small saucepan on very low heat. Combine the egg yolks with the slightly cooled cheese and fold in the whipped cream. Add the onion and season with salt and pepper. Spoon this filling into the lined cake tin and bake for 45 minutes in the preheated oven. Serve hot, with a nicely dressed salad.

Salmon with vanilla / Zalm met vanille

New dishes are flooding the entire country. Do we call that industrial espionage, or mimicking? No, that is called 'creating a school'. John Halvemaan, then chef of the Amstelhotel in Amsterdam, gets the idea to present lobster in a sauce with a very vague, nearly untraceable aroma of vanilla. The chefs of De Pettelaar in Den Bosch, wanting to be on their best behaviour, offer '*Pour se mettre en train: La mignonne de saumon à la vanille*' as part of a dinner on September 30th 1983. The mouthful of French is no problem, since this is a reunion of participants of wine trips, organized by *De Telegraaf* and lead by no other than Thomas Lepeltak, alias the highly valued Stan Huygens.

Recipe source: a menu from the collection of the Culinary Museum Mariënhof, Amersfoort

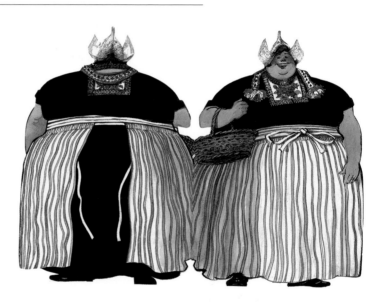

100 ml (½ cup) fish stock
200 ml (¾ cup) double cream
¼ vanilla pod (3 cm / 1¼ in)
50 g (1¾ oz) cold butter
salt

*

500 ml (2 cups) fish stock
4x 200 g (7 oz) fillets of salmon

*

600 g (1 lb 5 oz) vegetables
(such as oyster mushrooms,
bean sprouts,
leek,
courgette)

- Bring 100 ml (½ cup) of fish stock to the boil with the lengthwise split vanilla pod. Add the cream and boil to reduce by half. Remove the vanilla pod and from the heat stir in the diced cold butter. If wanted, season with (a little) salt.
- Bring 500 ml (2 cups) of fish stock to the boil and poach the fillets of salmon in approximately 5 minutes. Remove the salmon from the pan, drain well on kitchen paper and divide onto 4 warm plates.
- Spoon the sauce around it and serve with potato pancakes and steamed vegetables.

Saddle of hare with green pepper / Hazenrug met groene peper

According to Wina Born modernization arrived from the south. And she was right, witness green pepper berries – where were they to be found long before the supermarket started selling them? At Maartje and Kees Boudeling of Inter Scaldes in Kruiningen. The name alone is proof of the erudition: Latin for 'between the rivers Scheldt'. And there is more. Maartje was to become the first woman in the Alliance. In those days the concept of 'top lady chef' did not exist in the Netherlands. What is so beautiful about their establishment in Zeeland is the fact that it still breathes the atmosphere of local well-to-do families. And then the unequalled meal in the cane chairs of the conservatory, with the view of the well-kept Zeeland garden annex little herb paradise. Zeeland at its best. Here is the recipe for a dish that Maartje is supposed to have eaten for Christmas, impossible, of course, since during the Holidays she is far too busy to be able to cook something for herself.

Recipe source: *Lekker 1984*, with permission of Mrs Boudeling

4 fillets of hare (475 g / 1 lb)
salt
50 g (1¾ oz) butter
1 tablespoon green pepper berries

⚬

3 chopped shallots
1 tablespoon Cognac
300 ml (1 ¼ cup) dry white wine
100 ml (½ cup) Noilly Prat, sec
300 ml (1¼ cup) crème fraîche

• Season the hare with salt, and cook on high heat until rosé (that is, not done). Remove from the pan and keep warm.
• Cook the shallots in the fat and pour on the Cognac and white wine. Add the Noilly Prat and the crème fraîche. Cook down to a pleasantly thickened sauce. Sieve the sauce and season with green pepper berries and salt.
• Thinly slice the hare. Place the slices on warm plates and spoon over a little sauce. Serve with a gratin of mashed potatoes.

🍷 Tokay Pinot Gris d'Alsace. A strong spicy white wine, that works well in combination with not too heavy game dishes.

Medallions of turkey with three pepper sauces / Medaillons van kalkoen met drie paprikasauzen

The dish of everyday chicken-in-pieces has lost its appeal for the Dutch restaurants. The customer is not familiar yet with small portions of boned turkey. Terrifying words like 'turkey tenderloin' become en vogue. The competition with the French nouvelle cuisine still continues, where Michel Guérard creates a dish of chicken breasts with two pepper sauces. Chef Johan Neppelenbroek ups this in Beetsterzwaag, where Lauswolt is established. 'The guest becomes a seigneur here. Outside, on the shaven grass, people play golf. If so desired, the menu counts nine holes,' Philip Mechanicus writes in the book published in honour of the 20th anniversary of the Alliance Gastronomique Néerlandaise.

Recipe source: Philip Mechanicus, *Kookkunst in Nederland. Unieke recepten met Nederlandse produkten*, Ede: Zomer & Keuning Boeken B.V., 1987

12 turkey steaks, each 40 g (1½ oz)
salt and pepper
30 g (1 oz) butter
12 large endive leaves
2 red, 2 green and 2 yellow peppers
200 ml (¾ cup) turkey broth
200 ml (¾ cup) double cream
1 red, 1 green and 1 yellow pepper
90 g (3¼ oz) butter
50 ml (¼ cup) stock
4 hearts of lettuce
chervil

• Season the turkey steaks with salt and pepper. In a frying pan heat the butter and brown the steaks on both sides. Cool. Plunge the endive leaves 5 seconds in boiling water and transfer immediately to ice water. Drain on a clean dishtowel. Fold the steaks into the leaves.

• Cut the first 6 peppers in half, remove the seeds. Blanch the halves. Peel off the skin (important for the taste!) and dice the peppers. Mash the differently coloured peppers separately to a fine puree in a food processor.

• Cook down the 200 ml (¾ cup) turkey stock and cream to a lightly thickened sauce. Divide the sauce in three and combine every third with one of the pepper purees. Season with salt and pepper.

• Halve the other peppers, remove the seeds and cut in strips. Stew in a little butter until soft. Heat the turkey steaks for a few minutes in the hot stock.

• On each of four warm plates arrange 3 turkey steaks. Spoon a spoonful of the three different sauces around the three steaks. Arrange a few strips of pepper around them and garnish every plate with a heart of lettuce and a little fresh chervil.

Pear with sabayon / Peer met sabayon

The Netherlands become enchanted with a new dessert: the sabayon, often prepared at the table. At first only to be had in the 'better establishments', such as Prinses Juliana in Valkenburg, Krasnapolsky in Amsterdam (with chef Hans Clemens) and the group of 'Romantic Restaurants'. The dish is not new, by the way: Escoffier already gives the recipe in his most simple book *Ma cuisine* (first edition 1934), which he dedicates to caring mothers. The Dutch translation of this book in 1988 (translated by Jil Elegeer, Utrecht: HES publishers) probably attributed a lot to the growing popularity of this frothy custard.

'Sabayon' is French for the Italian *zabaglione* or *zabaione*, a sweet dish from Piemonte and Val d'Aosta, where it is served for breakfast in the country, preferably made with Marsala.

Recipe of Luuk Koldenhof, master chef since 1984, in those days chef at Prinses Juliana in Valkenburg, nowadays working for the SVH Education Centre in Zoetermeer.

100 g (3 ½ oz) sugar
50 ml (¼ cup) white wine

·

4 egg yolks
2 tablespoons lemon juice
50 ml (¼ cup) pear liqueur
25 ml (5 teaspoons) dry white wine

·

poached pears

1980 Princess Juliana with the new queen, Beatrix

- In a saucepan bring the sugar and water to the boil without stirring. Cool to 25 °C/80 °F.
- Fill a large pan for ¾ with water. Heat to a temperature of 90 °C/200 °F.
- In a mixing bowl whisk the egg yolks, sugar water, lemon juice and liqueur. Place the bowl on the hot water and continuously whisk to make a frothy sauce with a temperature of 50-55 °C/125 °F.
- Serve the sabayon on a warm plate with warm poached pears.

☞ While standing the sauce loses its froth. Therefore, prepare the sabayon no sooner than 10 minutes before serving.

Ice cream with flambéd cherries /
IJs met geflambeerde kersen

Most probably this is an idea of top chef Charles Elmé Francatelli, who lived in London from 1805–1873, and who created this dish for one of the many jubilee dinners that were supposed to cheer up the English Queen Victoria. Since Francatelli had learned the trade from none other than Carême, he also made a name for himself in France, and we see the special occurrence of an English recipe accepted into the classical French cuisine (Cérises Jubilées), which is how it came to be famous in the Netherlands as well. Especially in the 1950s, when it seemed impossible to banish 'cooking at the table'. That certainly held for this dessert, which was used right into the 1980s in order to immensely surprise mother and child – according to menus of family restaurants from this period – with this flaming spectacle.

500 ml (2 cups) vanilla ice cream

·

250 g (9 oz) cherries, without pips, from a jar
100 ml (½ cup) fresh orange juice
1 tablespoon lemon juice
4 tablespoons red currant jelly
1 shot glass Kirschwasser
icing sugar

• Divide the ice cream over coupes. Put these in the freezer to get really ice cold.
• At the table in a flambé pan bring the drained cherries with the juice and jelly to the boil. Pour the Kirsch over the cherries. Put a lid on the pan. Make sure there is not too much light on the table, so that everybody can enjoy the flames. Ignite the Kirsch, sprinkle sugar in the flame and spoon the burning cherries over the ice cream.

♀ Gewürztraminer Vendange Tardive. Exceptional wine, made from grapes of the 'late harvest' and therefore sweeter.

de Kersentuin

1990–1999
Truly culinary

1990 · 'Recognized' cafeteria's soon may be called 'qualitaria'
· The Argentinean chain Los Gauchos has grown to 15 restaurants
· Nelson Mandela released
· Michael Gorbachov, president of the Soviet Union, receives Nobel Prize for Peace
· Gulf War
· Germany reunited
1991 · Alliance Gastronomique awards Wim Meij (journalist Algemeen Dagblad) 'Le cornichon aigre' ('pickled gherkin') because of his sour pieces on the restaurant business. Public Information Service for Food 50 year in existence
· Treaty of Maastricht basis for European integration
1992 · Founding of Patrons-cuisiniers
· Bill Clinton president of the United States of America
· Merger Horecaf and Horeca Nederland (union of hotels, restaurants and cafés). New name: Koninklijk Horeca Nederland
· National restaurant campaign l'Europe à Table
· Bijlmer disaster: plane crashes into flat building
1993 · Jeunes Restaurateurs d'Europe – Nederland is founded. Age: 23-45 years. The aim is a higher level of the profession, a good price-quality balance and minimal use of semi-manufactured products
· Mandela and De Klerk receive the Nobel Prize for Peace
· With a handshake Yitzhak Rabin seals the peace agreement with Yasser Arafat
1994 · Jomanda, medium in blue, causes parking problems in Tiel
1995 · Start of 'Tafelen in Nederland' ('Dining in the Netherlands'): rehabilitation of the regional Dutch cuisine
· SVH organizes master-test
· World Jamboree Dronten huge success
· Sail 1995 has one million visitors
1996 · Café owner must have certificate Restaurant entrepreneur skills
· Second campaign 'Tafelen in Nederland'
· Richard Krajicek wins Wimbledon
· Mad cow disease (BSE) in British cattle
· World Food Summit closed in Rome: there are over 800 million undernourished people. This number must be reduced by half by 2015.
1997 · Fine Eastern Restaurants merge with The Asian Restaurants
· Brussels sprouts grower Henk Angenent wins 15th Elfstedentocht (skating marathon)
· Swine fever hits the Netherlands
· Sheep Dolly cloned
1998 · Amsterdam Historical Museum: exhibition Beroep Huisvrouw ('Profession housewife'), 1898–1998, 100 years of housewives' lives in the big city
1999 · Restaurant campaign 'Een Eeuw tafelen' ('A Century of Dining') in the Netherlands

The upgrading of culinary art

This is the beginning of a serious interest in the history of Dutch culinary art . The Royal Library organizes an exhibition: 'Cookery books throughout the ages'. Museum Boymans van Beuningen opens an exhibition on tableware. Sociologist Anneke van Otterloo takes a Ph D on *Eten en Eetlust in Nederland* ('Food and Appetite in the Netherlands'). Jozien Jobse-van Putten puts her research on food of the ordinary people in the 20th and earlier centuries into a hefty book titled: *Eenvoudig maar voedzaam* ('Simple but nutritious'). In commemoration of the anniversary of the Public Information Service for Food Ileen Montijn writes a book called *Aan tafel* ('To the table'), about food and drink in the past 50 years.

The publishing company De Kan (Heske Cannegieter) reintroduces the first Dutch cookery book *Een Notabel Boeckxken van Cokerijen* ('A remarkable little book on cookery') on the Dutch market. And most beautiful of all: the appearance of Joop Witteveen's magnum opus: *Bibliotheca Gastronomica*, an overview of everything culinary ever published in the Netherlands up to the 1960s. A milestone in the history of Dutch culinary art.

At the same time and completely in line with the above, a new approach to the culinary column arises. The bantering pieces by Ileen Montijn in *NRC Handelsblad*, together with the extremely well documented columns of Johannes van Dam in *Intermagazine*, *Elsevier* and *Het Parool*, create a new outlook on cooking. By the way, Van Dam – he is turning into a national culinary guru – was precursor, with his first collection of columns (*Alles warm*; 'Everything hot') published already in 1988. Later Joep Habets (NRC) and Patrick Faas (*Volkskrant*) swell the ranks. And then there are the restaurant reviews: friendly ones by Wina Born in *Avenue*, biting ones by Wim Meij (*Algemeen Dagblad*), acid ones by De Boer and De Cocq (*Volkskrant*), stern ones by van Dam (*Het Parool*) and sweet ones by Ton de Zeeuw (*De Telegraaf*). In short, we truly have become concerned about all that comes to the table.

Culinary aspects

On the one hand there is 'fusion': East meets West in the kitchen. A movement of the 1980s, launched in California by Ken Hom and Jeremiah Tower. On the other hand, we see more emphasis on the own regional cuisine, stimulated by the European Union. All in all, the Mediterranean tastes continue to be number one. However, there still are top restaurants that adhere to the classical French cuisine, such as Prinses Juliana in Valkenburg, the only restaurant in the Netherlands that has had a Michelin-star for 40 years in a row. 'How would I characterize the 1990s?' Patron Paul Stevens has no problem answering this question: 'Nothing happens, everything just continues in its quiet way. People travel great distances and cease to be easily surprised. Chefs who no longer are familiar with the classical cuisine flee into "fusion". Not every change is good. However, what remains is good cooking! And that is what happens at our restaurant, we even had Robert Kranenborg and Cas Spijkers as apprentices behind the stove.' Maybe slightly exaggerated by an old hand of the profession, but also the young cooking talent is looking for simplicity again, now that the daring and exotic have become commonplace.

Jozien Jobse observes a wave movement, an analogy between the beginning of the 20th and the 19th century, when Carême and Escoffier had the same goal: '*toujours faites simple!*'

Restaurant business

Final words of Johannes van Dam in Alles moet op ('Empty the plates'; 1992): 'The restaurant business is like the still growing popularity of the oyster mushroom: you do not get the tasty chanterelle for which you have sent the kids into the woods, but cultivated tasteless, grey rags that do nothing, but usurp the taste of all other ingredients. However, they can be obtained everywhere.'

Eating out is greatly on the rise especially at the workplace. In 1990 Eurest had a turnover of 140 million guilders and in 1991 a quarter of a million Dutch people ate at Van Hecke Catering. In 1999 controllers of the feared tire company Michelin do not rank our restaurant business too badly, leaving 55 stars. Additionally, there is the opening of an unheard of amount of foreign eateries: about 4000, a lot to the total of 11.038 restaurants in the Netherlands in 1998.

Eating at home

Yes, we are grazing from the fridge. It seems that for many families the shared meal is history. Each member heats in the microwave oven whatever they want, at any given time. Any embarrassment about buying ready-made food is almost gone. Lots of mothers have stopped slaving over stoves. They like watching it done, though... on television. By Ria van Eijndhoven (for a long period daily!), Cas Spijkers en Joop Braakhekke, who turns it into a comedy and whose 'Kookschriften van een Kookgek' ('Cookery notebooks by a culinary cook-mad') sell like hot cakes. There are also at least fifty well-attended cooking schools for people who like to try on their own.

And again we should be made more aware. In 1994, Novib and the Consumentenbond publish De Wereldgids voor Consumenten ('World guide for Consumers'). In it we can read that it would be better not to consume too much meat: it badly affects the environment. Meat has ceased to be a status symbol. According to Jobse the lesser educated, the higher the consumption of meat. And if meat is eaten at all, and enough money is available, we eat veal and lamb.

We continue to love 'something else'. But within reason. Goat's cheese becomes a trend, but may not have a hint of manure. That is why we also have Brussels sprouts without the sprout taste and chicory without a bitter taste. The aim is for the happy medium.

In conclusion

To indicate trends in the recent past is always somewhat tricky. Thanks to better schooling and international contacts there are a lot of very good chefs. Since people travel extensively and many foreigners immigrate into our country, our kitchen becomes more international. Fresh ingredients are flown in from all over the world. Fast food and diets (Montignac!) boom. All in all, cooking is done with a lot of imagination, not only in the restaurants, some times at home, but also in organizations. The democratization, that started with the end of 'lower-class cookery', in the 1920s has been completed.

Provençal vegetable terrine / Provençaalse groenteterrine

Robert Kranenborg, chef de cuisine of the chic Amstelhotel since 1992, is seen by his colleagues as one of the best chefs of the Netherlands.

In his youth he spent a lot of time behind the stove in the south of France, and he likes to be inspired by the simple dishes of this region. To this day, his cooking style breathes the region's glowing atmosphere. Here is the recipe for a vegetarian dish, made the traditional way, that is to say without 'post-modern haste'. With it Robert set an indelible trend: nowadays anyone who does not eat meat – for whatever reason – does not have to go wanting gastronomically either. A fortunate development.

A mould of circa 22 cm (8½ in) long, 8 cm (3¼ in) high, 6 cm (2½ in) wide
(preferably a press mould)
(serves 8)

*

about 1 litre (4 cups) olive oil
2 kg (4½ lb) pomodori or plum tomatoes
1 clove of garlic
thyme
salt and pepper

*

3 red peppers
3 fennel bulbs
a few drops of Pastis
4 medium courgettes
3 medium aubergines

*

12 sheets of gelatine (24 g)

for the vegetable sauce:
1 artichoke
1 carrot (60 g / 3 oz)
1 onion (70 g / 2½ oz)
1 clove of garlic
2 large white mushrooms
15 g (½ oz) mustard
100 ml (½ cup) white wine
olive oil
pinch of coarse sea salt

*

a fresh goat's cheese
chives
sourdough bread

Robert Kranenborg

• Peel the tomatoes, remove the seeds and cut the tomatoes in half. Place side by side on a baking tray. Scatter with thinly sliced garlic, thyme, salt and pepper. Pour over lots of olive oil. Roast for 2 hours in an oven at 80 °C/175 °F/Gas Mark 1. Keep an eye on them, though, since not every oven has the correct temperature. Preferably do this a day ahead.
• Remove the seeds from the peppers. Cut them in pieces. Pour on enough olive oil to cover. Simmer for 45 minutes on low heat (80 °C/175 °F). Peel off the skin after cooling. Remove the

Rosé de Provence,
always right with
Provençal dishes.

skirts of the fennel, cut them to be flat. Also simmer for 45 minutes in olive oil. Lengthwise slice the courgettes and aubergines with a little of the white flesh on it. Simmer in olive oil for 30 minutes. Do not colour.

• In the meantime, for the mild vegetable sauce, finely chop the heart of the artichoke. Do the same with the carrot, the garlic (twice blanched in milk) and the mushrooms. Simmer the chopped vegetables for 10 minutes in a little olive oil. Add the mustard and a little sea salt and, finally, the wine. Cover with parchment paper and simmer for 15 minutes. Mash the vegetables and season the puree.

• Soak the gelatine in plenty of cold water. Cut the tomatoes in half. Drain all vegetables on paper towels.

• Line the mould with plastic foil. Build the terrine. First a layer of aubergine, skin under, then a layer of tomato with a well rinsed, well squeezed sheet of gelatine on top. Repeat as follows: courgette/tomato, fennel/tomato, pepper/tomato, fennel/tomato, courgette/tomato, aubergine with skin up. Close the mould and heat for 20 minutes in a hot water bath in an oven of 175 °C/350 °F/Gas Mark 4.

• Serve the terrine cold, sliced, with the vegetable sauce, and fresh goat's cheese sprinkled with chives on a slice of sourdough bread.

☞ Convinced vegetarians use agar-agar instead of gelatine. Take half the amount as described for gelatine. Cut the agar-agar in pieces, cook them in a little water on low heat for 15 minutes, strain and spoon over the tomatoes.

Creole lobster tail / Creoolse kreeftenstaart

In 1997 the young chef de cuisine Mandy de Jong, who 'cooked the Mariënhof in Amersfoort to a Michelin-star', became *'Lady chef of the year'*. This is an honorary title, introduced by the magazine *Ambiance* as the counterbalance to the hero role male chefs have played for so many years.

For us she created a lovely marriage between the tastes of Southern Europe and the sweet potato of South-America. So very special in colour that it will not surprise anyone to hear this chef first wanted to become a visual artist.

Women in the professional kitchen – the Netherlands have 59 in 1999 – are pioneers, who really need to have strong feelings for the profession considering the prejudices and 'anti-social' working hours. It is like a female Nobel Prize winner once said: 'To reach the same as a man we have to be twice as good, I'm glad to say that is not difficult.'

1 sweet potato
dash of vinegar
drop of nut oil
salt and pepper

•

200 ml (¾ cup) crème fraîche
1 heaped tablespoon mayonnaise
¼ teaspoon fresh horse radish
pepper, sea salt
50 g (1¾ oz) black olives, diced

•

1 small fennel bulb
2-4 lobster tails (clean)
dash of olive oil
pinch of cardamom

• Bring water to the boil. Peel the sweet potato and thinly slice it. Cook for a minute. Rinse under cold water. Pat dry. Coat with a sauce of vinegar, nut oil, salt and pepper. Arrange as a round rosette on a serving plate.
• Stir the crème fraîche with mayonnaise and horse radish to a smooth sauce. Season with salt and pepper. Add the olives.
• Cut the fennel in very thin strips and spoon in a little creamed horse radish sauce.

• In a little olive oil cook the lobster tails on low heat for about 3 minutes and sprinkle with cardamom. Place on the fennel salad and spoon the remaining sauce around it.

☛ According to Mandy very good with jumbo shrimp too.

Mandy de Jong

Turmeric soup / Kurkumasoep

When Frans Gerrits, master chef since 1986, switched to the hospital kitchen of the Catharina Ziekenhuis in Eindhoven after a sparkling career in haute cuisine, he has heard people say a great many times: 'Now you'll be a porridge cook!' That is how people felt in the 1980s.

Nothing less is true, however. Frans can play his expensive tricks during frequently held medical conferences – at his place, of course! What he appreciates most, though, are the warm thank-you notes from patients: 'As if I stayed in a hotel!'

How sick people do not have to go without special food either, is shown in his recipe for this soup. The taste of turmeric (curcuma) is a little like ginger and is used in the Indian, Indonesian, Chinese and Arab kitchens.

2 shallots
1 small courgette
1 small clove of garlic
1 tablespoon olive oil
4 g (little less than 1 teaspoon) turmeric
200 dl (¾ cup) dry white wine
1 litre (4 cups) chicken stock, fish stock or vegetable stock
500 ml (2 cups) double cream
salt and pepper

• Finely chop the shallots, courgettes and garlic. Cook in the olive oil. Add turmeric and slowly fry the turmeric on low heat, or it may become bitter). Pour on the wine.
• Add the stock, bring to the boil. Simmer the soup for 15 minutes. Add the cream. Puree in a blender and push through a fine sieve. Season with salt and pepper.

☛ Advice from the chef: preparation of the soup a day ahead will improve the development of taste. Do not hesitate to make more: the soup can easily been frozen.

☛ Garnish

For vegetarians: diced apple, pumpkin, cucumber, chives.

With fish: scampi, half a lobster, fillet of sole, salmon, monkfish cheeks, diced smoked eel.

With meat: chicken or turkey breast from the wok, braised breast of quail with leg.

1920 The preparation of 'soup' in rest home De Amstelhof, Amsterdam

Cockler's soup / Soep van de Mosselman

The Dutch Bureau for Fish, which continues to playfully remind us about everything good in the water, starts a yearly contest for the title of National Cockler in 1994. The finals are held at spectacular locations, such as a dry sandbar or a marine ship. That alone is quite a happening. More beautiful still is the way young chefs are thus challenged to come up with something different than the traditional preparation of mussels.

Every year special dishes continue to be the result, since once the taste bug has bitten, one continues to experiment. As is the case with Albert Tielemans, an advocate of Dutch cuisine, as proven in the way he applies himself to the campaign 'Tafelen in Nederland' ('Dining in the Netherlands'). No wonder he became both first and second National Cockler. A soup recipe created by him.

300 ml (1¼ cup) dry white wine
500 ml (2 cups) fish stock
1 small chopped onion
2 finely chopped sprigs of celery leaf
1 clove of garlic
a few crumbled threads of saffron
1 bay leaf
1 kg (2 lb 3 oz) fresh, cleaned mussels
½ teaspoon arrowroot or potato starch
100 ml (½ cup) double cream
1 egg yolk
2 tablespoons Cognac
salt
1 tablespoon finely chopped tarragon

1994 Albert Tielemans is National Cockler

• Bring to the boil wine, stock, onion, celery leaf, garlic, saffron and bay leaf. Add the mussels and cook until all mussels have opened. Regularly shake the pan. With a slotted spoon take the mussels out of the liquid and remove the shells.
• Strain the cooking liquid through a cloth and return to the heat. Make a paste of the arrowroot and half of the cream. Stir into the strained stock.
• Boil shortly. Add the mussels and remove the pan from the heat.
• Combine the egg yolk, Cognac and remaining cream. Stir into the soup. Season with salt and sprinkle with tarragon.

☛ Do not let the soup boil after adding the egg.

Marrowfat peas of The Red Lion / Raasdonders van De Roode Leeuw

Ruud Stein

In Amsterdam it is possible to taste the whole world, but hardly anybody offers a real Dutch meal.

And what is more Dutch than marrowfat peas? That is a dumb question for Het Raasdonder Genootschap ('The Marrowfat Pea Fellowship'), ten years in the process of formation and in 1998 'discontinued'. Every year they celebrated the Fresh Marrowfat Pea Meal (with champagne) in restaurant De Roode Leeuw on the Damrak, reigned over by organizer Hans de Goede. The company held eminent prospective members, such as Robert Kranenborg, as passionately a devotee of these peas as Fons van Groeningen from Kaatje bij de Sluis (his way: with minced lamb rolled in bacon).

The Dutch name for marrowfat peas, 'kapucijners', is in reference to the brown habit of the Order of Capuchin ('kapucijner' in Dutch), mendicant friars, who often ate not much more than this brown pea named after them. The fresh peas which we buy nowadays are most often green peas in a blue pod, called 'blauwschokkers' ('blueshockers'). The name 'raasdonder' reflects the sound of flatulence they cause.

At De Roode Leeuw they stick to the old-fashioned seaman's way of serving, with 'all the trimmings' (according to the true-blooded Dutch menu): apple compote, boiled potatoes, golden fried onion rings, raw chopped onions with whole and chopped gherkins, fried suckling pork chops, fried rashers of pork belly, 'blinde vinken' (minced veal wrapped in thin slices of veal), fried bacon, pickled onions with Amsterdam onions, mustard, piccalilli, cucumber, gravy... and champagne, if you like. This adds up to a lot of garnishes for this pea. To give you one more, we found the following: created by Ruud Stein for vegetarians. An inventive chef, as Dutch as his kitchen. He started in The American Lunchroom and via De Doelen, the Amstel (every month a royal party), the Americain and the Victoria hotel, he has finally arrived where he belongs: De Roode Leeuw.

1 kg (2 lb 3oz) unshelled marrowfat peas (about 400 g / 14 oz shelled)

·

500 g chestnut mushrooms
lump of butter
4 spring onions
4 tomatoes
salt
lots of summer savory

·

slices of Gouda cheese
black pepper from the mill

• Shell the peas and cook in plenty of water for 15 minutes.
• On high heat brown the sliced mushrooms in a little butter. Add the coarsely chopped onions for 1 minute. Season to taste.
• Add the tomatoes in wedges and the drained peas. Sprinkle with summer savory. Arrange the cheese on top and place under a hot grill until melted. Pass the pepper mill after serving.

Fillet of guinea fowl for Queen Beatrix / Parelhoenfilet voor koningin Beatrix

This is one of the royal dishes of our culinary collection. We have made a conscious effort to find dishes representative for both the lower and higher classes.

For those stepping into the 20th century differences were enormous. At the marriage of Queen Wilhelmina and Prince Hendrik money was collected in order to buy meat, rice, coffee, peas and pulses, so that the bitterly poor of the slums in the big cities, where a quarter of the population lived in one-room dwellings, could 'feast'.

At the end of the century no-one was surprised by the festive dinner that Beatrix had served on January 31st in honour of her sixtieth birthday. Only three courses? Sea food salad, stuffed breast of guinea fowl, coffee mousse with maple syrup. Could it not have been a bit more luxurious? Of course not, simplicity is the hallmark of the veritable, the adage of the House of Orange then and now.

HOTEL ORANJE

★ ★ ★ ★ ★

Menu

25 g dried morels

•

4 breasts of guinea fowl with stick
150 g (5½ oz) chicken breast
3 tablespoons chopped watercress
50 ml (¼ cup) cream
salt and pepper
50 g (1¾ oz) butter

•

50 g (1¾ oz) butter
400 g cultivated mushrooms to taste
salt and pepper
250 g (9 oz) haricots verts
250 g (9 oz) carrots
3 large potatoes
oil for deep-frying

•

100 ml (½ cup) reduced fowl stock
200 ml (¾ cup) cream
50 g (1¾ oz) cold butter

- Soak the morels 1 hour in plenty of water. Rinse several times under cold water.
- Mince the chicken breast with a food processor. Add cream and watercress, and season with salt and pepper. Put the mixture into a piping bag.
- Cut the guinea fowl breast for filling. Divide the morels into the opening. Pipe the filling in and close with a wooden stick. Brown the fowl on all sides in hot butter and heat for 15 minutes in an oven at 180 °C/350 °F/Gas Mark 4. Keep warm for 5 minutes and thinly carve into 6 or 7 slices.
- In the meantime sauté the mushrooms and boil the vegetables. Make *pommes gaufrettes* (potato waffles): on a mandolin shave the potatoes like this: give the potatoes a quarter turn after each shave, so that little waffles arise. Rinse in cold water, pat dry in a tea towel and deep-fry at 180 °C/350 °F. If you do not own a mandolin, plain shaved crisps are nice too.

- For a nice cream sauce, cook the reduced stock with the cream, and thicken with a few lumps of cold butter.
- Serve the fowl on a bed of warm mushrooms, surrounded by cream sauce, potato waffles and vegetables.

☛ At the royal dinner, the morels were stuffed with the farce of chicken and watercress, and then went into the fowl. Since the everyday kitchen has few lackeys walking around, we have chosen a simpler version, but equally tasty.

☛ Neither did we pack the fowl in pork netting, since there are very few butchers left who sell it. However, this is how that works: buy 100 g pork netting. Brush the fowl lightly with egg white. After filling, fold to close, sprinkle with salt and pepper. Divide the netting in four, brush with egg white and use to pack the fowl. Cut away superfluous net. Continue as described above.

Venison with prunes / Hert met pruimedanten

Hein Willemsen, master chef and patron-cuisinier (De Hofstee, Bladel), member of the Culinary Team that represents the Netherlands at world championships, created a modern venison dish especially for us. He is known by his colleagues as an innovator. 'Yes, that is what I try to be, but I keep a link with the classical taste patterns. Even that frightens my guests sometimes. It happened once that a soup, on the basis of fresh ripe tomatoes, was sent back to the kitchen with the remark: this is not tomato soup! We have all been put on the wrong footing by the food industry, and in my own way I combat that.'

So do not think the ingenious preparation is because of the well known urge to be special: the layers of meat and filling are essential for the subtle taste experience.

6 servings

Sauce

4 litre (4 quarts) water
2 kg (4½ lb) venison bones and strips
1 litre (4 cups) red wine
500 g bouquet (carrot, leek, onion, celeriac)
5 tomatoes

.

150 g (5½ oz) cranberries
200 ml (¾ cup) red wine
200 ml (¾ cup) orange juice
75 g (2¾ oz) sugar

.

150 ml (⅔ cup) double cream
75 g (2 ¾ oz) butter
3 steeped prunes, cut in strips

De Hofstee, Bladel

• Prepare a reduced stock of game: for approximately 6 hours simmer the water with bones and strips, wine, bouquet and tomatoes. Strain through a fine sieve and reduce the stock with the strained cranberries (see below) to 300 ml (1¼ cup).
• In a stainless steel saucepan bring to the boil the cranberries, 200 ml red wine, orange juice and sugar. Remove from the heat and cool. Strain the cranberries, save both berries and juice.
• Add the cream to the reduced stock, thicken with lumps of butter and only then add the cranberries together with the strips of prunes.

Stuffed fillet of venison

A loaf mould of 1½ litre (6 cups)

250 g (9 oz) haunch of venison, deboned
1 egg
1 tablespoon Cognac
6 tablespoons crème fraîche
salt and pepper

•

butter
1 chopped shallot
150 g (5½ oz) wild mushrooms (trompettes de mort, cèpes, chanterelles)
1 clove of garlic, crushed
15 g (1 tablespoon) green pistachio nuts
100 g (3½ oz) soaked prunes, stones removed

•

500 g (1 lb 2 oz) fillet of venison

•

75 g (2¾ oz) clarified butter

🍷 Pécharmant, sturdy and aromatic wine from the Bergerac.

• Dice the haunch of venison. In the food processor make them into a farce (puree). Blend in the egg, Cognac and crème fraîche. Season with salt and pepper. Cover and put in the fridge.
• Cook the shallots 1 minute in the butter. Add the well cleaned, diced mushrooms. Cook for a few minutes. Add garlic and pistachio nuts with the halved prunes. Cool and combine with the farce.
• Line the mould with plastic foil and cut the fillet of venison (on the machine) lengthwise. If necessary flatten to fit the mould, the slices should be 1½-2 cm (¾ in) thick. Place a slice on the bottom of the mould and spread with a thick layer of farce. Put another slice of meat on top and continue as with lasagne. Finish with meat. Place the covered mould 2 hours in the freezer.
• Cut the frozen meat in 12 slices. Fry on both sides in clarified butter. In a warm place, let the meat rest for 10 minutes. Diagonally slice the meat to show off the layers. Pour over a little of the sauce (preceding recipe) and serve the remainder separately.

🍃 Garnish: marinated red cabbage, chestnuts conserved in goose fat, potato pancakes, and crisps of cassava and scorzonera.

Marinated red cabbage

• Overnight macerate very finely shred red cabbage in red wine, orange juice, onion, clove, cinnamon, raspberry vinegar and caramelized sugar. Braise in butter before serving.

Potato 'poffertjes' (tiny, spherical pancakes)

• Very small diced potato is blanched and added to 'poffertjes' batter (pancake batter) and fried the usual way.

Crisps of cassava and scorzonera

• With a vegetable peeler shave thin slices and deep-fry in hot oil until crisp.

Pike perch with cucumber chutney /
Snoekbaarsfilet met komkommerchutney

On the initiative of the European Union, a cooking match takes place, 'Coupe d'Europe des saveurs regionales', in 1995 in Poitou Charentes, France. This is a culinary Europe cup in favour of regional tastes and against the increasing sameness of European food. Three Dutch provinces participate. The result: Utrecht receives a gold medal for the fish dish, Limburg wins silver with the dessert, and Flevoland gets an honourable mention.
Here is the gold-winning recipe by master chef André van Doorn of De Hoefslag (Bosch en Duin). A word of reassurance for those who wonder if this truly is a dish from Utrecht. In the parchment *Recept Boeck van Adriana Elizabet Pit Geb. Abeleven, Binnen Utrecht, Den 20 Maart 1761* we find a recipe: 'Curry of cucumbers by Marie'. André lives in a province with a culinary history as adventurous as his own creations.

---

300 g (10½ oz) peeled cucumber, diced
25 ml (scant 2 tablespoons) olive oil, 'extra vierge'
75 g (2¾ oz) onion, chopped
2 strips of lemon peel without pith
2 bay leaves
2 star anise
40 g (1½ oz) honey
¼ teaspoon curry powder
25 ml (scant 2 tablespoons) white wine
salt, Tabasco, saffron
white wine vinegar

·

4 fillets of pike perch, 125 g (4 oz) each (with skin, scaled, no bones)
olive oil for frying

·

300 g scorzonera, washed
oil for deep-frying

·

fleur de sel (unbleached sea salt)
4 tablespoons olive oil, 'extra vierge'
1 tablespoon aceto balsamico

- Heat 25 ml (scant 2 tablespoons) of olive oil and cook the onion until transparent. Stir in the diced cucumber to soften. Add lemon peel, bay leaves, star anise and honey. Remove the pan from the heat, stir in curry powder and white wine. Season with salt, Tabasco, saffron and wine vinegar, and on low heat cook for 20 minutes. Finally, remove lemon peel, bay leaves and star anise.
- In a non-stick frying pan cook the fish on the skin side in a little oil and place the pan for 4 minutes in an oven at 180 °C/350 °F/Gas mark 4. Sprinkle the fish with fleur de sel.
- With a vegetable peeler shave thin strips of the scorzonera and brown and crisp in oil of 150 °C/300 °F. Sprinkle with fine salt.
- Spoon the chutney in the middle of a warm plate. Arrange the fillets of fish on top. Cover the fish with the deep-fried scorzonera strips. Spoon the olive oil and aceto balsamico around them.

'From the pouch of Zuid-Beveland' / Uit de zak van Zuid-Beveland

This dessert is a good example of the youngest culinary movement 'always keep it simple', based on Escoffier's advice. Or, in other words: 'only restriction breeds a master'. Sjaak Jobse is master chef, which shows in his extremely precise measurements and which can be tasted in the result. In addition, he is a member of the National Culinary Team, and very modern with his regional ingredients.

Perhaps that simplicity is to do with the fact that, day in day out, he has to consider what is best for the people entrusted in his special care. It so happens that he rules over the kitchen of a health centre, the Jacob Roggeveenhuis in Middelburg, located on Walcheren, close to the 'pouch of Zuid-Beveland'. It is here that traditionally people have grown blackcurrants, unique for the Netherlands. Ever tasted Crème de Cassis de Zélande? Do not hesitate!

Sjaak Jobse

For 4 'rings' of 6½ x 4 cm (2½ x 1½ in), put on a tray. Both rings and tray slightly oiled with neutral oil and dusted with icing sugar. Instead of bottomless rings: 4 moulds of 150 ml (⅔ cup)

4 g (1/8 oz) gelatine
110 g (4 oz) strained puree of raw blackcurrants
50 g (1¾ oz) sugar
25 g (scant 2 tablespoons) Crème de Cassis de Zélande
35 g couverture (bitter chocolate)
250 g (1 cup) half beaten double cream
50 g Greek yoghurt or full-milk yoghurt

• Soak the gelatine in plenty of cold water. Heat the puree of berries with the sugar and dissolve the gelatine.
• Put the pan on ice water. Melt the chocolate. Stir into the puree of currants. Also stir in the liqueur.
• As soon as the mixture starts to set fold in the yoghurt and cream. Spoon into the moulds and cool to set. Remove the rings or unmould the pudding. Decorate with shapes made from chocolate couverture and with blackcurrants. Serve with a vanilla sauce.

☞ For the puree of currants you need 200 g (7 oz) blackcurrants. Frozen they are available all year round.

Vanilla sauce
• Bring to the boil 200 ml (¾ cup) milk with a little seed from a vanilla pod. Beat 30 ml (2 tablespoons) pasteurized egg yolk (1 egg yolk) with 20 g (4 teaspoons) sugar and add a little hot milk. Thicken over a pan with hot water (au bain-marie).

Frisian spiced gingerbread bavarois / Friese kruidkoekbavaroise met gember

It is fun to go out for dinner. Cake awakens the child in us: starting from our first birthday, cake equals festivities, and more cake means even more fun.

The Netherlands know few true confectioners. Many people never go to a pastry shop, but make do with baked goods from the supermarket. Once more a case of dulling of the taste, since these are nothing but poor substitutes for the work of a true master confectioner. Such a confectioner is Harry Mercuur. First he showed his art in large restaurant kitchens, now he is famous under his own name. With Amersfoort as the centre, his work spreads over the whole country. This can be done since 'shock frozen' cakes are impossible to be distinguished from fresh ones.

A dessert very old-fashioned yet modern in taste, which only goes to show that sweets last for centuries.

A stainless steel ring of 20 cm (8 in) diameter. Enough for 12-14 servings

Frangipane

30 g (1 oz) butter
125 g (4 oz) sweet almond puree
60 g (3 oz) sugar
pinch of salt
¼ teaspoon anise seeds
¼ teaspoon grated lemon zest
2 eggs
25 g (1 oz) sifted flour

• Knead the butter with the almond puree, sugar, salt, anise seeds and lemon peel until smooth. Whisk in the eggs. Stir in the flour. Leave in the fridge for at least 8 hours.

Hard Viennese pastry

100 g (3½ oz) flour
50 g (1¾ oz) sifted soft white sugar
1 tablespoon beaten egg
pinch of salt
75 g (2¾ oz) butter

• Put all ingredients in a mixing bowl, cut the butter through using two knives. Knead to a dough.

Bavarois

500 ml (2 cups) milk
50 g (1¾ oz) sugar
½ vanilla pod
ground ginger

14 g (½ oz) gelatine
150 g (5½ oz) egg yolk (= 5 egg yolks)
500 ml (2 cups) double cream

Harry Mercuur
bakes gingerbread

- In a saucepan with heavy bottom bring to the boil the milk, sugar, split vanilla pod and ground ginger.
- Soak the gelatine in plenty of cold water. Turn the heat low as soon as the milk boils, and whisk in the egg yolks. Quickly sieve the contents of the saucepan and dissolve the squeezed gelatine into the milk.
- Whisk the cream not too stiff.

100 g diced crystallized ginger
approximately 200 g (7 oz) Frisian gingerbread
250 ml (1 cup) neutral jelly

Construction of the gateau

- Line the ring with the Viennese pastry (1 cm / ⅜ in thick, 1 cm / ⅜ in high). Fill the ring with frangipane. Sprinkle with diced crystallized ginger. Bake for 25-30 minutes in an oven at 170 °C/350 °F/Gas Mark 4.
- Combine the tepid bavarois with the whipped cream. Spread a thin layer over the cooled frangipane bottom, and place thin slices of gingerbread on top. Repeat. Place the gateau for 5-6 hours in the fridge.
- Carefully loosen the cake from the sides and glaze with neutral jelly. Sprinkle with diced gingerbread and dust with icing sugar. Nice with raspberry sauce.

2000 - 2009
How sustainable is our food?

A New Awareness

Nobel Prize winner and climate guru Al Gore's *Inconvenient
Truth* fell into fertile earth in the Netherlands. It further
encouraged discussion about a life style based on respect for
environment and mankind which had always been preached
in this bible-imbued country, albeit with varying degrees of
success. Shopping in a responsible way has now found general
acceptance in the Netherlands. Even the cheapest discount
supermarkets now offer fairtrade and sustainable food.
The fact that many species of fish are endangered causes a lot
of concern and supermarkets had to meet the growing
demand for a supply of sustainable fish. Increasingly, people
realize that the transport of food over great distances is
threatening the environment.The worldwide organisation
'Slow Food' has a won a great number of enthusiastic
supporters in the Netherlands, who campaign for 'the right to
enjoy honest food', promoting small-scale organic agriculture,
organizing excursions to local farmers to taste their products,
such as home-made cheese or the meat of free range chickens,
to rediscover the real taste of foodstuffs which is too often
masked by the artificial additives used in the food industry.
This heightened awareness of responsible stewardship has
given new impulses to Dutch cuisine, both at home and in
public places. Reflection on the methods of food production,
consciousness of what our globe can support in the long run
and an ever growing knowledge about what is healthy for us
proves to be a challenge to the inventiveness of cooks.

Restaurants

When eating out people want to be pleasantly surprised. A few
years ago chefs were fascinated by molecular cooking, a trend

increased by four symposia at Wageningen University, where the scientific side of cooking was emphasized and new techniques were developed to make revolutionary structures and shapes possible. For example, warm pea soup served in the shape of pearls which create the sensation of a taste explosion in your mouth. Or unexpected combinations, like oysters in a chocolate cover. Or mashed potatoes rolled out thin as paper, coloured with ink (from squid) or a foam of violets. This inclination for the extravagant has diminished somewhat but it has become an enrichment for today's cooking, according to the chefs. The most interesting innovation was cooking at low temperatures which is a very effective way to cook meat and fish. Many restaurants offer showy menus of at least 7 small dishes, all artistically composed and garnished with a small crunchy tidbit, sometimes even from spicecake.

But Dutch restaurant guests can also choose from the best no less than 69 different countries are offering. Arabic, Asiatic, Latin-American and African restaurants are on the rise and also dishes from Princess Máxima's homeland Argentina are increasingly popular.

Cooking lessons

In the nineties of the last century the Domestic Science Schools were incorporated in other educational institutes and lost a lot of pupils. Even more disturbing is the fact that few children learn how to cook anymore, as most working mothers do not have the time to cook themselves. Neither elementary nor secondary schools thought this education worthwile to dedicate time to it. But there is hope! Yearly a 'week of the taste' is held at elementary schools, where children led by chefs can taste the difference between, for example, selfmade and ready made mayonaise and can experience the influence colour has on taste. Almost every night there is a cooking program on TV. At the end of the 20th century we counted 50 cooking schools in the country, now there are some 400. It seems that half of the people who follow such a workshop are coming just for the fun of it, but the other half does pick up some useful knowledge, such as: when can we expect the new strawberries or new potatoes. For most of them – being fastfood or ready made food addicts – have lost contact with the seasons. After a serious workshop, cooking studio pupils want to bring something special onto the table. They sometimes become demanding amateur cooks. As a result, some supermarkets

now offer turnips which after the introduction of the potato had become one of the 'forgotten vegetables' in the Netherlands. And amateur cook or not, they buy nice kitchen haberdashery, such as cooking rings to make nice little towers of their food, or a *zesteur* for grating citrus peel, or a special potato press for a good purée. In some cases they do this more to earn the admiring looks of friends than for actual use, but from the one can come the other.

Eating at Home

Just as in the nineties of last century, prefab food is still bought by many hardworking people. But the efforts to promote healthier and more interesting dishes have encouraged many couples to cook together in the weekend as a way of recreation, allowing themselves to be inspired by a wealth of cooking magazines, all very posh and with an emphasis on exotic food.

According to a recent inquiry under the authority of the Federation of Dutch Food Industry most Dutch people still like to put traditional Dutch food on the table, with Italian or Asiatic food as runners-up. The people interrogated mentioned as typically Dutch: *stamppot* (mash with vegetables) first, *erwtensoep* (pea soup) second and third *gehaktbal* (meatball). In 2009 a leading Dutch ladies' weekly called *Libelle* warmly recommended the book *Dutch Cooking*, testifying to a growing interest in national culinary traditions.

In Conclusion

We live in an era of transition. Huge problems are facing us with regard to the sustainable production of food for all. On the other hand, never before the possibilities for creative solutions were as great as they are now. Dutch cooks are committed to a persistent quest for keeping the best from the past and for finding new avenues of improvement. Bright ideas are often born out of necessity.

Menu Margo Reuten

Master Chef Margo Reuten's interest in cooking was aroused when she was helping a local butcher prepare cold buffets. After completing the cooking and catering college, she worked with Dutch Master Chefs. In 1993 she opened her own restaurant 'Da Vinci' in Maasbracht, with partner Petro Kools, connoisseur of fine wines and a perfect host. The restaurant was built in the shape of a boat and they decided to keep its name because an old fisherman of the Meuse that flows past their place told them that changing the name of a ship brings disaster. They developed the restaurant in a highly successful way. Margo became 'Lady Chef of the Year' in 1996 and earned her first Michelin star in 1999. In 2003 she and Petro celebrated the 10th anniversary of their restaurant with a marvellous book *Proeven van bekwaamheid* (Proofs of Competence).

In 2008 Margo received a second Michelin star. She creates numerous new dishes but always with reverence for her native region Limburg. We are very grateful that she allowed us to publish her traditional highlights.

Fried Eggs, sunny side up on raw minced steak from 'Pietjesveld' / Uitsmijter met tartaar van Pietjesveld

The very first guest in the new restaurant asked for an '*Uitsmijter*', which is traditional and ordinary Dutch pub food. Generally two fried eggs upon sliced ham or roast beef on bread. Always with a gherkin 'fan' and a slice of tomato. That version Margo refused to serve. But with a wink she presents her own version, made with the meat her father delivers from the cattle in his meadows called 'Pietjesveld'. As for the olive oil, that was already known very early in this region because of the fasting days. Petro advises wines from their own region: there are vineyards in Limburg since the Romans.

🍷 Pinot Gris Apostelhoeve, H. Hulst, Maastricht

250 g (8 ½ oz) very tender prime rib
4 tablespoons chopped chives
4 small sour gherkins, chopped
3 tablespoons mild olive oil
pepper, salt
frisée or rucola leaves
8 small free range eggs
butter

• Freeze the prime rib lightly, then chop it with a sharp knife as fine as possible. Keep it very cold, otherwise the binding force will get lost. Mix with the chives, gherkins, olive oil, pepper and salt to taste. Line the plates with rucola or some frisée leaves.

• Put a small shaping-ring on every plate, fill with meat, press carefully, then take the ring away. Cover with two fried eggs, sprinkle with pepper and salt.

Cream of asparagus with deep-fried lemon sole / Aspergecreme met gefrituurde tongschar

Light soups became fashionable in the Netherlands in the 18th century and were inspired by the French court (stock = bouillon in Dutch). Limburg was the first to accept this in her many castles. And slowly this soup came down the social ladder. Later on a Dutch Sunday meal without soup became unthinkable. In Limburg often made from asparagus, brought to the region by a priest who was looking for a way to earn money for his parisioners from the sandy Limburg soil. Now you find an asparagus museum there because the white asparagus is still an important source of income in Limburg.
Margo combines the cream with lemon sole, a highly original idea.

Cream

60 g (2 ¼ oz) butter
70 g (2 ½ oz) flour
tail ends of asparagus (see below)
1 litre (4 ¼ cups) asparagus liquid*
100 ml (½ cup) poultry stock
250 ml (1 cup) cream
pepper, salt
4 white asparagus, salt, butter

Lemon sole

1 filleted lemon sole
flour
1 egg white
dry bread crumbs
(preferably Japanese: panko)
salt

• Cream: Melt the butter in a pan, sweat the asparagus tails in it. Add the flour. Stir over low heat until cooked. Add the cold liquid slowly, constantly stirring. Then add poultry stock and cream and cook for about 10 minutes. Sieve and season.
• Cook the peeled asparagus until just done in water with a little salt and butter. Cut each of them into six pieces.
• Lemon sole: Cut the fish lengthwise into 2 or 3 strips. Coat with flour, put into whisked egg white, then roll through bread crumbs. Deep-fry for two minutes, drain on kitchen paper, season with salt

---

* Made from asparagus peels plus cooking liquid of peeled asparagus. You will need more than 4 of course.
  Try them the Dutch way: with peeled new potatoes, melted butter, cooked ham and hard boiled eggs.

Rabbit in gingerbread sauce / 'Knien in 't zoer'

The main course dates from the time when a poor Limburger still used to snare a rabbit occasionally, even though the risk was high because the poacher lost an eye if he was caught. It is a very old Limburg dish, a variant of which is found in the cookbook by Carolus Battus (1593): *Eenen seer schoonen ende excellenten gheexperimenteerden nieuwen Coc-boeck die noyt hier te voren in Druck en is gheweest* ('A very beautiful and excellent, well-tested new cookbook, that was never published before'). The sauce itself derives its spicy flavour from gingerbread. In the oldest Dutch cookbook known, the *Notabel Boecxken van Cokerijen*, we find a recipe to bake '*pepercoecke*' (pepper-cake, as gingerbread was called then) for the specific purpose of making 'all kinds of sauces'. This cake became popular when in the 17th century Dutch merchants brought ever more ginger, cinnamon and cloves from the East. It still is today.

300 ml (1 ¼ cup) vinegar (= 'zoer')
200 ml (¾ cup) water
2 bay leaves
2 large onions
4 front legs of rabbit
4 back legs of rabbit
25 g (1 oz) flour
2 tablespoons butter
5 slices gingerbread
5 tablespoons applespread

Garnish:
Deep-fried onion slices, potatoes, parsley

🍷 Pinot Noir Fromberg Ubachsberg

Combine vinegar, water, bay and onion slices. Marinade the rabbit parts for at least 24 hours. Then pat dry. Sprinkle with flour lavishly. Fry in hot butter on high heat. Pat dry the onion slices and fry them too. Deglaze with the marinade liquid and leave to simmer over low heat until the meat almost falls from the bones. Then remove the meat from the pan. Bring the cooking liquid to the boil, add the cubed gingerbread and applespread. Boil until the required thickness is reached. Season the sauce with pepper and salt and present the dish as on the photograph with deep-fried onion on top, and accompanied with the boiled potatoes, sprinkled with parsley.

This recipe can also be used for 750 (1,5 lb) beef in large chunks. Then it is called *Zoervleis* (sour meat).

'French' toast / 'Wentelteefje'

All over Europe we find recipes for left-over slices of bread. Often with mysterious names. Ours dates from the 17th century and is traditionally explained as 'just turn it' (*wentel 't even*). But there is another name: '*Kuische zusterkoek*' (Cake of the chaste sisters), a variant luxuriously made with cream and raisins, a remembrance of the times when this dish was popular in the cloister kitchens of Limburg. This inspired Margo to make something more of it. As a garnish she uses '*Boerenjongens*' (Farmers' lads), raisins soaked in brandy, an old-fashioned treat at marriage parties and other family feasts. Can be bought ready-made in pots, but Margo makes them herself.

Eau de Vie de Limbourg 'Bellet' (apple brandy)

Caramel racks
250 g (9 oz) sugar
130 g (4 ½ oz) glucose syrup

·

Toast
4 slices of dry 'melkwit'*
2 eggs
300 ml (1 ¼ cup) milk
dash of ground cinnamon
1 tablespoon butter
4 tablespoons sugar mixed with cinnamon
100 ml (½ cup) vanilla perfumed whipping cream
4 balls of premium quality vanilla ice-cream
pear, poached in white wine, cinnamon and star anise
boerenjongens (pronunciation: *booren'youngens*)

* White bread baked with milk instead of water.

Caramel racks:
Put a dash of water in a pan, add the sugar and the glucose. Bring to the boil over moderate heat without stirring. Have ready a large basin with cold water to be able to cool the pan immediately. When the sugar mass begins to colour lightly, remove from the heat and cool off the bottom of the pan in the cold water. Make a rotating movement with a spoonful of the mass pouring it slowly on a sheet of baking paper in a thin trickle. Form the racks in the shape you want. You can keep them in a closed container in the freezer.

Toast:
Mix eggs, milk and cinnamon. Cut the bread slices into rounds. Let them soak up the mixture. Turn now and then. Melt the butter in a frying pan, fry the bread golden on both sides. Coat with cinnamon sugar. Top with ice-cream, caramel rack and whipped vanilla cream. Garnish with pieces of poached pear and 'boerenjongens'.

Menu Jonnie Boer

From his birthday in 1965 onwards Jonnie Boer went his own self-willed way through life. After having finished secondary school, his parents – who owned a regional restaurant in the Dutch province of Overijssel – advised him, a gifted illustrator, to become a commercial artist. As he was too late with his registration for the academy, he followed a private cook's course instead. Thereupon he learned a lot in Amsterdam restaurants but kept longing for his roots in Overijssel and so he accepted a job as a chef in Zwolle. Now he owns the restaurant De Librije in that city for more than 20 years and is a member of the Guild of Master chefs. His very original and artistic way of cooking and the perfect service in his beautiful medieval restaurant, supported by his charming wife Thérèse, vinologue, brought the two of them three Michelin stars in 2004. Jonnie: "My cooking is provocative, so our guests will eat food they are not accustomed to. Such as the side-dish we now offer with each menu: bacon, beetroots and Osciëtra caviare." Despite all this success, he never forgets his native background and gets his inspiration from the products and regional recipes of his surroundings, constantly striving after innovation of the well-tried rural cuisine. Owing to this ambassadorship he was hounoured with a royal decoration in 2005, whereas Thérèse received the same because of her educational and inspirational work and her value for Dutch Culinary culture in 2008.

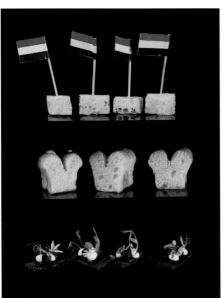

They recorded their ideas in several books (see Selected bibliography), showing the development of their Cuisine. But they stick to their slogan: always remain true to your own pure cooking style. Our chef proposes a light spring menu, full of authentic Dutch elements. Wine suggestions are provided by Thérèse.

Dutch glory (Hollands Glorie)

This starter is an example of the elegant entertainment in De Librije. The 'Herring sandwich' (Broodje haring) looks like a miniature sandwich. But the small slices of 'bread' are made from foam of onion and breadcrumbs, enhancing the herring taste when eaten. It is combined with 'Crunchy beetroots with mayonaise' (Krootjes kroepoek met BBQ mayonaise), garnished with mini gherkins. These two tidbits are inspired by the popular Dutch herring salad, never without beetroot and gherkins. The 'Crunchy Gouda' (Krokante Goudse) is made from microwave dried batter to create an overwhelming Gouda cheese taste.

Cocktails and dreams /
Garnalencocktail en Krabsalade

Just like every artist our chef frequently ponders his work. Fed up with the popular shrimp cocktails, in which the North Sea shrimp (*crangon crangon*) was buried under loads of mayonaise, he dreamt up a totally new taste palette for this small grey miracle. It is surrounded by very young aboveground vegetables. As a counterpart of the well-known, equally over-sauced, crab salad he transforms it into a kind of seabed, planted with small underground vegetables. All tiny delicacies are harvested from the large private herb and vegetable garden of *De Librije*. Inevitably, the recipe below is a simplification for use at home.

Shrimp cocktail
200 g (7 oz) cooked and peeled North Sea shrimps
100 ml (½ cup) home-made mayonaise
1 teaspoon ketchup
1 teaspoon sherry
2 teaspoons tomato seeds
8 mini cucumbers
8 tiny gherkins
4 borage flowers (borago officinalis)
beet leaves and lamb's lettuce

·

Crab salad
2 tablespoons home-made mayonaise
40 g (1½ oz) finely diced blanched fennel, carrot, turnip
pinch of grated lime peel
200 g (7 oz) cooked North Sea crab meat
50 ml (¼ cup) milk
1 pasteurized egg yolk
4 tablespoons toasted whole-wheat bread crumbs
75 g (2½ oz) grated old farmer's Gouda
mini carrots, fennel roots, yellow beetroots, red and white radishes,
4 of each

Shrimp cocktail:

Arrange shrimps on 4 transparent plates. Mix mayonaise with ketchup and sherry. Ladle a tablespoon onto each plate. Make a nice palette with the other ingredients. Put plates onto larger plates.

Crab salad:

Mix mayonaise with diced vegetables and lime peel. Stir into crab meat. Scoop a ring around the small plates. Heat the milk, melt the cheese in it. Add yolk. Do not boil. Leave to cool. Ladle this cream onto the crab. Cover with crumbs and plant the mini vegetables in it.

Riesling, preferably a 2007 Reichsgraf von Kesselstatt Riesling Kabinett feinherb, Scharzhofberger. A typical Mosel Riesling with a fine taste of local minerals and the ideal balance of sweetness and sourness to bring out the fragrance of the delicate vegetables used in this entrée

May Roebuck / Meibok

For most of us the feast of eating game is connected with autumn or winter, but roebuck fills the gap. Shooting time is open from May till September. This Overijssel meat is extremely good when fed with the young leaves of May. In this recipe the delicate fillets are combined with simple vegetables, daily fare in the region. It is the dedicated preparation that brings out the superb taste. For this way of cooking, with respect for local tradition, the convivium Slow Food Zwolle made Jonnie Boer a honorary member. He was kind enough to create this simplified version for the home kitchen.

Beetroot stripe
500 ml (2 cups) beetroot juice
Reduce to sirup. Garnish plates with a
silicon brush as in picture.

·

Crumbs
4 tablespoons toasted wholewheat
breadcrumbs.
Arrange the crumbs on the plates:
beetroots will be placed on it.

·

Beetroots
4 young beetroots
branch of thyme
bay leaf
salt
Cook beetroots for 10 minutes with herbs and salt. Peel, leave the
root on. Keep warm.

·

Celeriac pedestal
200 g celeriac
20 g (¾ oz) boiled smoked bacon (katenspek)
50 ml (1 ½ oz) cream
hunch of garlic and thyme
salt
Boil finely diced celeriac with cream, bacon, herbs en salt until tender. Puree. Keep warm. Make 4 small balls with an ice cream scoop.

Kohlrabi
4 mini kohlrabi with leaves
vegetable stock
butter
Cook until tender in stock with some butter. Arrange warm onto
the celeriac pedestals.

·

Celeriac parcels
200 g (7 oz) celeriac, in 15 cm strips
blanched chives
Blanch celeriac for 3 minutes. Drain. Divide into 4 piles. Tie together with chives.

·

Nettles hotchpotch
200 g (7 oz) peeled potatoes
200 g (7 oz) young nettle leaves
white of 1 spring onion
butter
pepper; salt
Boil potatoes until done. Blanch nettles. Chop finely. Shred spring
onion. Drain potatoes. Mash with some butter. Mix with onion and
nettles. Season. Scoop a small ball onto each plate.

There is no white and green blocked roll in the recipe. This is made from celeriac and parsley paste, which cannot be done at home as in a high ranked professional kitchen very special methods are used. As an alternative the hotchpotch of nettles for which Jonnie Boer is famous. The 'grappa apple', the only extravagance of the dish, is a small green apple, preserved in grappa (Italian import). Here poached in apple juice and glazed

<table>
<tr><td>

Stock

Stock:

250 ml (2 cups) strong veal stock

100 ml (3 oz) red wine

25 g (1 oz) celeriac

50 g (1 ½ oz) onion

2 juniper berries

1 clove of garlic

1 small bay leaf

1 clove

Simmer for ½ hour, sieve and reduce to 150 ml.

</td><td>

Meat

75 g (2 ½ oz) butter

4 roebuck fillets, 120 g (4 ¼ oz) each

pepper; salt

Seal seasoned meat in hot butter. Leave it to rest in aluminium foil.

Add stock to the hot butter. Serve as in picture.

</td></tr>
</table>

☙ Some would prefer the lusty Dutch 'Meibok' beer with this dish, but the more seasoned gourmets among us may prefer an Australian Rosemount Estate Diamond Label Shiraz 2004 with its fresh, inviting nose of dark red fruit, touches of spice and cracked pepper. It is a medium to full bodied wine with generous ripe fruit flavours of blackberry, plum and cassis

Apple pie in two versions / Appeltaart

In the Netherlands every family has its own favourite recipe for apple pie. It is a kind of visiting card. When you are served a whole wheat crust your host is probably vegetarian or leftish, politically spoken. Is it made from puff pastry then you must be the guest of Francophiles. Of course your mother's pie is always best, it has the taste of love. That is why Jonnie Boer allowed himself to model his 'visiting card' after her traditional apple pie. She seasons it with almost the same spices that are already used in the first Dutch cookbook (1514) for *Appeltaerten*. Today a 'Deconstructed apple pie' – note the philosophical touch! – but with the same traditional taste adorns the menu of *De Librije*. It demonstrates the originality of the chef. In spring 2009 he showed this amazing deconstruction in Spain to 200 young chefs and they were flabbergasted: *El Magico*, The Magician, he was called.

Granny's apple pie

For a buttered 20 cm (8 inch) springform tin,
bottom lined with baking parchment

Crust
125 g (4 ½ oz) all-purpose flour
25 g (1 oz) self-raising flour
75 g (2 ½ oz) white caster sugar
125 g (4 ½ oz) butter
2 tablespoons beaten egg
seeds of 1 vanillapod
pinch of salt

Filling
2 tablespoons breadcrumbs
375 g (¾ lb) peeled and diced sour apples (Goudrenet)
60 g (2 oz) drained boerenjongens*
50 g (1¾ oz) sugar
1 tablespoon lemon juice
2 teaspoons cinnamon powder
1 teaspoon anise seeds
¼ teaspoon clove powder

On top
icing sugar

• Mix flours and sugar in a bowl, grate butter above it. Mix with fingertips into small crumbs. Add vanilla, egg and salt. Knead a supple dough quickly. Divide into ¾ and ¼ parts. Coat the tin evenly with the larger part by (floured) hand, up to 4 cm. Sprinkle with bread crumbs. Fill with apple mixed with the other ingredients. Roll out the rest of the dough thinly on a floured surface. Cut strips. Garnish top with a trellis-work of dough strips. Bake 50 minutes on a lower shelf in a preheated oven of 175°C/ 345 °F. Dust with icing sugar. Leave to cool, remove from the tin.

* 'Farmers' lads', raisins soaked in brandy, see also p. 183

Deconstructed apple pie

On the photograph we see all ingredients in their original shape. The cinnamon stick consists of a cream made from cinnamon and mascarpone, piped into a mould and afterwards dusted with cinnamon powder. The vanilla pod - a vanilla jelly - is also piped into a mould. The star anise is moulded from chocolate with a hunch of star anise, the cloves are made in the same way with some clove powder. Moreover the brandy soaked currants. And special crumble.

♈ A sweet wine such as the irresistable (Colette) Jurançon goes well with this brilliant dessert, but if you prefer something truly Dutch Thérèse recommends the Crême de Kaneel of A. van Wees (distillery "De Ooievaar") at Amsterdam.

Selected Bibliography

Pages 9-26

Amelink, Agnes, *Gereformeerden Overzee. Protestans-Christelijke landverhuizers in Noord- Amerika*, Amsterdam: Uitgeverij Bert Bakker, 2006.

Boiten, Lies et al., *Eten om te geven – Leven om te eten. Groningers aan tafel sinds de Middeleeuwen*. Groningen: Culinaire Vakschool en Groninger Museum, 1986.

Burema, L, *De voeding in Nederland van de Middeleeuwen tot de twintigste eeuw*, Assen: Van Gorcum & Comp N.V., 1953.

Cockx-Indestege, Elly ed., *Eenen Nyeuwen Cook Boeck. Kookboek samengesteld door Gheeraert Vorselman en gedrukt te Antwerpen in 1560*, Wiesbaden: Guido Pressler, 1971.

Collen, J.V.A. ed., *'Het "Kock-boeck" van D.Carolum Battum uit de zestiende eeuw, voorafgegaan door het werk van den geneesmeester Carel Baten'*, *Mededelingsblad en Verzamelde opstellen, Academie voor de Streekgebonden Gastronomie*, jg 9, nr 37, Berchem, 1991.

Dam, Johannes van and Joop Witteveen, *Koks en Keukenmeiden. Amsterdamse kookboeken uit de Gastronomische Bibliotheek en de Bibliotheek van de Universiteit van Amsterdam*, Amsterdam: Nijgh & van Ditmar, 2006.

Hermans, Katinka and Johanna Edema, *'Flavourings in Textbooks, Cookbooks and Kitchens'*, in: *Spicing up the Palate. Studies of Flavourings – Ancient and Modern* (Proceedings of the Oxford Symposium on Food and Cookery) 1992, Totnes: Prospect Books, 1993, pp. 81-88.

Jansen-Sieben, Ria and Marleen van der Molen-Willebrands, *Een Notabel Boecxken van Cokeryen. Het eerste gedrukte Nederlandstalige kookboek, circa 1514 uitgegeven te Brussel door Thomas vander Noot*, Amsterdam: De Kan, 1994.

Jobse-van Putten, Jozien, *Eenvoudig maar voedzaam. Cultuurgeschiedenis van de dagelijkse maaltijd in Nederland*, Nijmegen: Sun, 1995.

Kistemaker, Renée and Carry van Lakerveld (eds.), *Brood, Aardappels en Patat. Eeuwen eten in Amsterdam*, Purmerend: Amsterdams Historisch Museum, 1983.

Kruyff, Lizet and Judith Schuyf, *Twintig eeuwen koken en eten. Opzoek naar de eetcultuur van onze voorouders*, Utrecht/Antwerpen: Kosmos-Z&K, 1997.

Landwehr, John, *Het Nederlandse Kookboek 1510 – 1945. Een bibliografisch overzicht*, Houten: HES Uitgevers, 1995.

Laudan, Rachel, *'Birth of the Modern Diet'*, in: *Scientific American*, January 2004, pp. 11-16.

Mak, Geert and Russell Shorto, *The Forgotten History of Hudson, Amsterdam and New York*, Amsterdam/New York: Henry Hudson 400 Foundation, 2009.

Mennell, Stephen, *'Smaken verschillen'*, *De Gids*, jg. 150, 1987, reprinted in: J.van Tol et al., *Kookboeken door de eeuwen heen & Moge het u wel bekomen*, Den Haag: Koninklijke Bibliotheek/ Algemeen Rijksarchief, 1991 pp. 43-51.

Meulen, Hielke van der, *Traditionele streekproducten. Gastronomisch erfgoed van Nederland*, Doetinchem: Elsevier Bedrijfsinformatie, 1998.

Moor, Janny de, *'Dutch Cookery and Calvin'*, in: H. Walker (ed.), *Cooks & Other People* (Proceedings of the Oxford Symposium on Food and Cookery 1995), Totnes: Prospect Books, 1996, pp. 94-105.

Moor, Janny de, *'Dutch Farmhouse Gouda. A Dutch Family Business'*, in: H. Walker (ed.), *Milk: Beyond the Dairy* (Proceedings of the Oxford Symposium on Food and Cookery 1999), Totnes: Prospect Books, 2000, pp. 106-116.

Moor, Janny de, *Dutch Cooking. Traditions, Ingredients, Tastes, Techniques*, London: Aquamarine, 2007.

Natter, Bert, *Het Rijksmuseum Kookboek. Meesterkoks laten zich inspireren door de Gouden Eeuw*, Amsterdam, Rijksmuseum/ Thomas Rap, 2004.

Oostrom, Frits van, *Stemmen op schrift. Geschiedenis van de Nederlandse literatuur vanaf het begin tot 1300*, Amsterdam: Uitgeverij Bert Bakker, 2006.

Otterlo, Anneke van, *Eten en eetlust in Nederland (1840-1990). Een historisch-sociologische studie*, Amsterdam: Uitgeverij Bert Bakker, 1990.

Otterloo, Anneke van and Cathy Salzman, *'The Taste of the Netherlands and the Boundaries of the Nation State'*, in: *Spicing up the Palate. Studies of flavourings – Ancient and Modern* (Proceedings of the Oxford Symposium on Food and Cookery 1992), Totnes: Prospect Books, 1993, pp. 184-188.

Pachrach-Chandra, Gaitri, *Windmills in my Oven: A Book of Dutch Baking*, Totnes: Prospect Books, 2002.

Rose, Peter G., *The Sensible Cook. Dutch Foodways in the Old and the New World*, Syracuse: University Press, 1989.

Rose, Peter G., *Food, Drink and Celebrations of the Hudson Valley Dutch*, Charleston: History Press, 2009.

Schama, Simon, *The Embarrassment of Riches: An Interpretation of Dutch Culture in the Golden Age*, London: Fontana Press, 1987.

Sinke, Suzanna M., *Dutch immigrant women in the United States 1880-1920*, University of Illinois, 2002.

Tol, J. van, et al., *Kookboeken door de eeuwen heen & Moge het u wel bekomen*, Den Haag: Koninklijke Bibiotheek/Algemeen Rijksarchief, 1991.

Vernooij, Aad, *Hard van binnen, rond van fatsoen. Geschiedenis van de Nederlandse kaascultuur*, Wormer: Het Nederlands Zuivelbureau, 1994.

Winter, Johanna Maria van, *Van Soeter Cokene: Recepten uit de Oudheid en de Middeleeuwen*, Bussum: Unieboek, 1976.

Willebrands, Marleen, *De Verstandige Kok. De rijke keuken van de Gouden Eeuw*, Bussum: Pereboom, 2006.

Witteveen, Joop and Bart Cuperus, *Bibliotheca Gastronomica. Eten en drinken in Nederland en België 1474-1960*, 2 vols., Amsterdam: Linnaeus Press, 1998.

Pages 27-189

Cookery books are quoted where the decades are discussed.

Amelink, Agnes, 'Met halfheden komen we niet verder' (article on Abraham Kuyper in America), *Trouw*, 27/28 December 1997.

Amsterdam Culinair 1980: Menukaarten van de goede restaurants, Amsterdam: Teleboek B.V., 1980.

Arnoldussen, Paul and Jolanda Otten, *De borrel is schaarsch en kaal geworden. Amsterdamse Horeca 1940–1945*, Amsterdam: Bas Lubberhuizen, 1994.

Auer, Hans, *Nooit meer eendeborst. Ervaringen van een beroepseter in de toprestaurants van Nederland*, The Hague: BZZTôH, 1993.

Anneli, Beesly and Anne van Blaaderen a.o., *Eating out in Holland*, Amsterdam: KLM, 1984.

Bibeb, *Bij Gast en Gastheer*, with cartoons by Yrrah, Den Haag: Uitgeverij V.A. Kramers, 1960.

Boer, Jonnie, *Puur: Restaurant De Librije Zwolle*, Zwolle: Waanders ²1999.

Boer, Jonnie, *Puurder: Restaurant de Librije Zwolle*, Zwolle: Waanders, 2001.

Boer, Jonnie and Thérèse Boer, *Pure Passie*, Zwolle 2009.

Boer, Thérèse, *Natuurlijk genieten*, Zwolle: Waanders, 2003.

Borger, Sylvia, 'Aan tafel met Picasso', *Telegraaf*, 1-4-1999.

Born, Wina, *25 jaar Nederlandse restaurantgeschiedenis*, z.pl.: Onderwijscentrum Horeca, 1992.

Braakhekke, Joop, *Kookschrift van een kookgek (in collaboration with the AVRO)*, Baarn: Tirion, November 1993 (this one was the first – many were to follow).

Catenius van der Meijden, J.M.J., *Groot nieuw volledig Indisch kookboek*, 4th edition, Semarang- Surabaya-Bandung: G.C.T. van Dorp, 1942.

Daems, Wil, 'De onzin van gezonde voeding', *Eos Magazine*, no. 1, 1989, p. 7 ff.

Dagnelie, P.C., *Gezonde voeding voor lichaam en geest*, Deventer: Uitgeverij Ankh-Hermes, 1990.

Dam, Johannes van, 'Koken in de twintigste eeuw', in: *Quintessens. Wetenswaardigheden over acht eeuwen kookgerei*, Rotterdam: Museum Boymans-van Beuningen, Rotterdam 1992.

Dam, Johannes van, *De dikke Van Dam. Van aardappel tot zwezerik*. Amsterdam: Nijgh & Van Ditmar 2005.

Faas, Patrick, *De inwendige mens*, Utrecht/Antwerpen: Kosmos-Z&K Uitgevers, 1997.

Gastrigt, Ben, *Eten in Rotterdam. Facetten van de Maasstad*, Rotterdam: Publishers Wyt, 1969.

Gault, Henri, 'Nouvelle cuisine', in: *Cooks & Other People* (Proceedings of the Oxford Symposium on Food and Cookery 1995), Blackawton, Totnes: Prospect Books, 1996, pp. 123-127.

Habets, Joep, *Van fazant tot frikadel. Over koken en eten in Nederland*, Amsterdam/Antwerp: Uitgeverij Contact, 1997.

Hartog, A.P. den et al., 'De gestampte pot', in: *Volkscultuur. Tijdschrift over tradities en tijdsverschijnselen*, volume 9, no. 2, 1992.

Hartog, A.P. den et al., 'Voedingsinformatie in reclame. Een analyse van 85 jaar voedingsmiddelenadvertenties', in: *Voeding*, August 1998, volume 50, no. 8, pp. 224 – 230.

Heijer, R.C. den (ed.), *100 Jaar Horecaf. Geschiedenis van het Nederlands Verbond van Werkgevers in Hotel-, Restaurant-, Café- en Aanverwante Bedrijven*, Doetinchem: Misset, 1990.

Hekkens, W.Th.J.M., 'Voedingspatronen in historisch perspectief', in: J.J. van Binsbergen et al. (eds.), *Voedingskroniek 1998*, Houten/Diegem: Bohn Stafleu Van Loghum, 1997.

Huisken, Alma, *De aardappel. Alles over de pieper*, Amsterdam/Antwerp: Contact, 1998.

Huisman, Jaap, *Grands Cafés in Nederland*, 's-Gravenhage: SDU uitgeverij, 1989.

Hupsch, Frans (ed.), *'n Bakkie troost voor het volk: Amsterdam in de jaren '10*, Amsterdam: Amsterdam Publishers, 1998.

Keijner, W.C., *Kookboek voor Hollandse, Chinese en Indonesische gerechten*, Amsterdam: J.F. Duwaer & Zonen, 12th edition (1st edition: Surabaya, 1927), 1955.

Klosse, Jaap, *Een kwart eeuw Alliance Gastronomique Néerlandaise*, Wormer: Inmerc B.V., 1989.

Knecht-van Eekelen, A. de, 'Eten is kiezen. Armenvoedsel en Hollands Welvaren', in: J.J. van Binsbergen et al. (eds.), *Voedingskroniek 1998*, Houten/Diegem: Bohn Stafleu Van Loghum, 1997.

Manden, Mej. A.C., *Recepten van de Haagsche Kookschool*, 13th edition, The Hague: De Gebroeders Van Cleef, 1900.

Matze, Hélène (ed.), *Desserts en patisserie van Harry Mercuur*, Haarlem: De Toorts, 1990.

Montignac, Michel, *Ik ben slank want ik eet, of de geheimen van onze voeding*, Valkenswaard: Artulen, 1996.

Montijn, Ileen, *Aan tafel! Vijftig jaar eten in Nederland*, Utrecht/Antwerp: Kosmos, 1991.

Oldenziel, Ruth and Carolien Bouw (eds.), *Schoon genoeg. Huis-vrouwen en huishoudtechnologie in Nederland*, Nijmegen: Sun, 1998.

Reijnders, Lucas, Rob Sijmons et al., *Voedsel in Nederland. Gezondheid, bedrog en vergif*, Amsterdam: Van Gennep, 1974.

Rijkschroeff, Boudie.R., *Ethnisch ondernemerschap. De Chinese horecasector in Nederland en in de Verenigde Staten van Amerika*, Capelle a/d IJssel: Labyrint Publication, 1998.

Rijkschroeff, Boudie.R., *Oosterse Gastvrijheid. Van stoker tot restaurateur*, Amsterdam: Koninklijk Horeca Nederland, 2008.

Duijzer, Dirk, *Appeltjes van Oranje. LTO Nederland, fruitteelt en de kunst*, Den Haag: LTO Nederland, 2002.

Reuten, Margo en Petro Kools, *Proeven van bekwaamheid*, Maasbracht: Restaurant Da Vinci, 2003.

Salzman, Catherine, 'Margriet's Advice to the Dutch Housewife. Changes in Eating Habits in the Netherlands, 1945–1975', in: Alan Davidson (ed.), *Food in Motion: The Migration of Foodstuffs and Cookery Techniques* (Proceedings Oxford Symposium 1983), London: Prospect Books, 1983, pp. 128-136, .

Scheepmaker, Anne, *Koken op 3 oktober, Leidens ontzet: Hutspot, haring en wittebrood*, The Hague: BZZTôH, 1990.

Scheepmaker, Nico, 'Trijfel', in: *Maak er een feest van*, Utrecht: E.C.I., 1977.

Schellingerhout, Judith (ed.), *De culinaire kruidentuin van het Openluchtmuseum*, Baarn: Tirion, 1994.

Smits, Paulus et al., *50 jaar Hostellerie de Hamert*, Horst, 1990.

Trienekens, G.M.T., *Tussen ons volk en de honger. De voedselvoorziening 1940–1945*, Utrecht: Kosmos, 1985.

Uit eten met De Boer & De Cocq, Amsterdam: Nijgh en Van Ditmar, 1990.

Veen, Hans van de, *Wereldgids voor Consumenten. Wenken voor bewust winkelen*, Den Haag/Amsterdam: Novib/Consumenten-bond, 1994.

Vuyk, Bep, *Groot Indonesisch kookboek*, Utrecht, Kosmos-Z&K Uitgevers, 1973 – 2003.

Winkel, Lydia, *Dat is lekker*, Rotterdam/Amsterdam: De Unie, 1964.

Zeeuw, Ton de, *Smakelijk eten in Nederland*, The Hague: BZZTôH, 1996 and 1998.

Zuiderveld, Ubel, *Snelle hap. De geschiedenis van de Nederlandse cafetaria- en fastfoodsector*, Doetinchem: Misset Uitgeverij B.V., 1995.

Illustration acknowledgements

It has been the publisher's aim to arrange for correct treatments of rights, according to legal regulations. Those who nevertheless are of the opinion that they can exercise specific rights, are requested to address the publisher.

All photographs of dishes: Arnold Meine Jansen, Baarn.
except:

24-26	Fotostudio van Genugten, Veghel
180-183	Paul Evers
184-189	Jan Bartelsman

Menus come from the Army Museum in Delft, the Culinary Museum Mariënhof in Amersfoort, H. Kortman – menu à la carte in Druten, and various private collections

4-12	Courtesy Rijksmuseum, Amsterdam
13	Courtesy Amsterdams Historisch Museum
14	Universiteitsbibliotheek Amsterdam (UvA) Bijzondere Collecties, plaatsnummer OTM O 63-7021
16-23	Courtesy Rijksmuseum, Amsterdam
28-29	Collection Jan Krems
32	Nederlandse Vegetariërsbond, Hilversum
34	Spaarnestad Fotoarchief, Haarlem
36	Foto Ebner, Den Haag
40	W. Berkhoff, Nederlands Bakkerijmuseum, Hattem
42	Nederlandse Vegetariërsbond, Hilversum
44	Wolters Noordhoff B.V., Groningen
44	C.A. Lion Cachet, Koninklijke Nederlandse Jaarbeurs, Utrecht
45	Gemeentearchief Amsterdam
48	Museum voor Noord- en Zuid-Beveland, Goes
52	Gemeentearchief Bloemendaal
53	Grand Hotel Krasnapolsky, Amsterdam
54	Spaarnestad Fotoarchief, Haarlem
56	Gemeentearchief Amsterdam
59	Gemeentearchief Rotterdam, Rie Cramer
63	Kurhaus, Scheveningen
66	Josephine Baker
67	Nederlandse Vegetariërsbond, Hilversum
68	Gemeentearchief Rotterdam, Jos de Rover
70	KLM Fotoarchief, Schiphol
74	KLM Fotoarchief, Schiphol
75	VNU Uitgevers, Hoofddorp
79	Gemeentearchief Bloemendaal
82	Legermuseum, Delft
85	Anefo/Spaarnestad Fotoarchief, Haarlem
88	Zuiderzeemuseum, Enkhuizen
90	SVH Onderwijscentrum
91	Douwe Egberts Nederland
92	Gemeentearchief Amsterdam
94	Spaarnestad Fotoarchief, Haarlem
95	Hotel De Nederlanden, Winschoten
96	De Amstelhof, Amsterdam
100	ABC Press Service, Amsterdam
103	Onno Kleyn, Zaandam
104	Ned. Bureau voor Toerisme
105	Het Voedingscentrum, Den Haag
106	Spaarnestad Fotoarchief, Haarlem
109	KLM Fotoarchief, Schiphol
110	Albert Heijn B.V., Zaandam
110	Albert Heijn B.V./Jeroen Breeuwer, Zaandam
113	Gemeentearchief Rotterdam
116	De Keukenhof, Lisse, G.H. Vetten
118	Grand Hotel Krasnapolsky, Amsterdam
120	Het Stadsblad, Utrecht
122	Collection Jan Krems
125	Kippa B.V., Hilversum
127	Anefo/Spaarnestad Fotoarchief, Haarlem
134-135	Verstegen Specerijen B.V., Rotterdam
137	Kippa B.V., Hilversum
140	Anefo/Spaarnestad Fotoarchief, Haarlem
141	Museum Broeker Veiling, Broek op Langedijk
144	Albert Heijn B.V., Zaandam
146	Kippa B.V., Hilversum
149	Fotobureau Meijer B.V., Den Haag
150	Transworld Features, Fred & Debra Schulke, Miami
151	ISPC, Breda
153	Kippa B.V., Hilversum
155	Oriënt Plaza, Nijmegen
160	ABC Press, Keystone-Sigma
167	De Amstelhof, Amsterdam
172	De Hofstee, Bladel

on the back cover Michiel van der Ham

Acknowledgements

Many persons have contributed to the realization of this new edition. We sincerely thank them all. We highly appreciate Amsterdam Burgomaster Job Cohen's willingness to write the foreword to the book. We express our gratitude to Martijn Pronk of the famous Rijksmuseum Amsterdam for his suggestions and help in choosing the paintings for the first chapter and for his permission to use them as illustrations.

For the special attention they spent to this new edition we are further indebted to Mr. Gajus Scheltema (Consul General of the Netherlands in New York), Professsor Dr. Dries van Agt (former Prime Minister of The Netherlands), Jos Rozenburg (Staff Officer Royal Dutch Navy) and Tilly de Groot (Cultural affairs specialist of the American Embassy in The Hague).

For help at various stages of production thanks are due to Joost van Aalst, Sigrid van As, Babs Baden, Age van Balen, Truus Boone, Karin van Eck, Willem Falter, Caroline Feitel, Peter Garstenveld, Pauline Genee, Ronald van Goor den Oosterlingh, Femke Hoogeveen, Hans Hoogeveen, Gijs de Jong, Anthony van der Klis, Ellis Kloosterman, Hans Krabbendam, Piet Kranenberg, Robert Kranenborg, Jan Krems, Simone Kreutzer, Jan Willem Kuiper, Esther de Lange, Thomas Lepeltak, Mariëtte Lutgerink, Anna Lysenko, Albert Jan Maat, Erik Niehe, Pieter Roelofs, Peter Rose, Annemarie Schravesande, Anouk Susan, Frits Thissen, Conrad van Tiggelen, David van Traa, Hendrik Tuinema, Jack Verhoek, Aad Vernooij, Lodewijk Wagenaar, Willem Wurfbain, Tom Wysmuller and Cor van Zadelhoff.

As to new culinary items in the book and precious information about Dutch food in the United States, we have profited from generous help extended by Agnes Amelink, Thérèse and Jonnie Boer, Renée van Keulen, Petro Kools, Femke Meijer, Ina de Moor, Christa Oudshoorn (secretary of the American Consul General in The Hague), Margo Reuten, Marjolein Schurink and Henry Witte (Honorary Consul, Netherlands Consulate, Grand Rapids).

Last but not least we owe thanks to Fieke van Hulst, on whose shoulders rested the ample, and sometimes frantic, correspondence of the Dutch Culinary Art Foundation which she ran smoothly and with unflagging equanimity. Our design agency VaDéHa Communicatie, in particular Sandra Klercq and Michiel van der Ham, had to redesign the entire book and did so in a highly artistic and dedicated way. All of them have made our teamwork a real pleasure.

The authors

Index of Recipes